The Oxford Anthology of
Indian Wildlife

Volume II
Watching and Conserving

edited by

MAHESH RANGARAJAN

OXFORD
UNIVERSITY PRESS

OXFORD
UNIVERSITY PRESS

YMCA Library Building, Jai Singh Road, New Delhi 110 001

Oxford University Press is a department of the University of Oxford. It furthers the
University's objective of excellence in research, scholarship, and education
by publishing worldwide in

Oxford   New York

Athens   Auckland   Bangkok   Bogota   Buenos Aires   Calcutta
Cape Town   Chennai   Dar es Salaam   Delhi   Florence   Hong Kong   Istanbul
Karachi   Kuala Lumpur   Madrid   Melbourne   Mexico City   Mumbai
Nairobi   Paris   Sao Paulo   Singapore   Taipei   Tokyo   Toronto   Warsaw

with associated companies in Berlin Ibadan

Oxford is a registered trade mark of Oxford University Press
in the UK and in certain other countries

Published in India
By Oxford University Press, New Delhi

First published 1999
Oxford India Paperbacks 2002

ISBN 019 565542 7

Typeset in Garamond by Excellent Typesetters, New Delhi 110034
Printed in India by Pauls Press, New Delhi 110020
Published by Manzar Khan, Oxford University Press
YMCA Library Building, Jai Singh Road, New Delhi 110 001

In memory of
Kailash Sankhala
and
Oona Mansingh

Acknowledgements

Like the tail of Hanuman at the court of Ravana, the list of those who helped me in compiling this set of articles is an ever-growing one. Naming them all would be impossible but all such help is gratefully acknowledged. The sense of *esprit de corps* in the wildlife and ecology fraternity is strong enough to cut across barriers of age, discipline and nationality. Often, an urgent phone call or post card was enough for a friend to flood me with a list of photocopies of articles worthy of inclusion. This collection is only intended to give a glimpse into a genre of writing about nature, not only about the large and spectacular animals of India, but its smaller, equally fascinating furred and feathered inhabitants. In recent years, our own perspectives have widened to include trees and flowering shrubs, reptiles and amphibians, many of which are relatively easy to observe and write about. If a century ago it was the landed gentry, the princes and civil and military officials who recorded their experiences, today it is a mix of professional wildlife biologists, self-taught naturalist-writers or photographers and film-makers and occasional foresters whose works make up the corpus of popular writings. Newspapers such as *The Statesman* and *The Hindu*, the now deceased *Science Today* and *The Illustrated Weekly of India* and smaller, privately published periodicals like *The Newsletter for Bird Watchers* from Bangalore and *The Hamadryad* (Chennai) and *The World Wide Fund for Nature Quarterly* have now joined the ranks with the much older *Journal of the Bombay Natural History Society*. The *Sanctuary Asia* magazine is perhaps unique in being a commercial venture that combines colour pictures and nature writing; *The India Magazine*, with a wider compass also has some excellent accounts of our wildlife.

I would be failing in my duties if I did not thank at least those individuals whose private collections I ransacked and whom I plagued with queries: R. R. Chari, Rom Whitaker, Janaki Lenin, Indraneil Das and S. Theodore Baskaran (in Chennai), D. K. Lahiri

Chaudhury in Calcutta and Valmik Thapar, Divyabhanusinh, Pallava Bagla, Mahendra Vyas, Tariq Aziz and Pradeep Sankhala in Delhi. I am also grateful to Rukun Advani and Anuradha Roy for suggesting I put together this collection and to Rimli Borooah and several others at OUP for all kinds of help. The Director and Fellows of the Nehru Memorial Museum and Library provided an intellectual base and support for which I am grateful. And may those not named here forgive me!

My family has both tolerated my obsessions and encouraged my interests. My mother and my wife Geetha Venkataraman helped in different ways. My daughter Uttara is too young to read the pieces, though she can growl 'like a tiger' when she sees a photo of one. I am especially grateful to them.

It is a matter of deep sadness that two remarkable individuals with whom I shared an interest in wildlife and who played a major role in my formative years are not here today. Both were neighbours in Kaka Nagar, a leafy housing colony in New Delhi but there the similarity ends. Kailash Sankhala was the Director of Project Tiger in 1974 when I first met him. It is typical of him that he treated me (then ten years of age) as an equal once he was convinced we had a shared interest in wildlife. He was never too busy to answer a query, always generous with rare books from his collection and willing to sit and go through drafts of my articles written for newspapers which rarely got published (for no fault of his). When we last met in 1993, he encouraged me, as a historian, to delve into the archives to find out more about the distribution and decline of India's fauna. He died a little more than a year later.

If Kailash Sankhala was a veteran, Oona Mansingh was a peer, scarcely a year older, and like me, an active member of an environmental group, Kalpavriksh. Oona's interests were in the outdoors: she was a member of three varsity teams, shooting, tennis and swimming. After a degree in rural management, she had settled in Kumaon, working to revive community management of forests. Her tragic and sudden death in 1996 due to food poisoning, which also claimed the life of her young daughter, has left a void in the lives of all who knew her. I humbly dedicate this collection to the memory of Kailash Sankhala and Oona Mansingh.

Contents

Introduction:
From Tiger to Flamingo

The eclipse of the Empire in India came in 1947, but many of its old habits lingered. Queen Elizabeth II and the Duke of Edinburgh, later President of the World Wildlife Fund International, visited India in 1961; what led to a row was their tiger shoot in the old hunting reserve of the ruler of Jaipur in the Ranthambore forests. The shoot commenced and the tiger was duly despatched, transformed into a trophy to live on in the hunters' tales of how they had shot dead a master predator. The British tea planter and naturalist E. P. Gee, who had stayed on in India, actually defended the choice of target. He even compared the slaying of a tiger in India to the shooting of a stag in Scotland. Given a sense of restraint, he said, such acts would not harm wild populations; the sport-hunter was a friend of the forest. Keep aside a few choice specimens for his pickings and he would help save the woodland from axe and plough, the deer from the poacher, the tiger from the snare-setter. The logic was not new, but the intensity of the debate pointed to great changes down the road.

The India of the 1960s was not so different from the times of the Raj. It was still mandatory for a Divisional Forest Officer to shoot a tiger before getting charge of his tract of forest. American tourists came out to emulate Corbett's feat of bagging an extra-large male tiger, the famous Bachelor of Powalgarh. Contrast the technologies available to those of a century ago, and the hunter seemed to be inexorably closing in on the hunted. The four-wheel drive, the dry cell battery light, anti-malarial drugs, telephone lines to once remote bungalows, long-ranging rifles: all made it easier to travel faster, shoot more effectively and kill more game than ever before. The decline and retreat of the denizens of the forest accelerated. It provoked not only a revulsion to slaughter but a new sense of love for wildlife.

However, beneath the trigger-happy surface, rumblings of change had been perceptible decades earlier. After the First World War, shocked by the carnage in the trenches of Europe, many British officers turned away from their guns during their subsequent postings to India. There were other early signs of empathy for the wild. One of the finest pieces of Jim Corbett—reproduced in this anthology—is about watching a herd of hangul or Kashmir Stags, spellbound by their beauty. Corbett's gun lay forgotten and he came away empty-handed, but the memory of that encounter lived on. Fred Champion actually gave up hunting and pioneered the photography of large Indian mammals in the wild.

A generation earlier, bag limits had been imposed on how many deer could be shot in state forests, though more as an act of prudent sportsmanship than protection. Others now turned their focus from the mega-fauna of the forest to its smaller, equally colourful inhabitants. Bird-watching had the added charm of being possible even within the confines of big cities or on the outskirts of small towns. A woodland like the Gir, renowned for its lions, could offer more thrills and yield many a secret to one whose trained ear could tell one bird song from another. Early in the twentieth century, came the discovery of the city of flamingos on the salt encrusted flats of the Rann of Kutch. Sálim Ali made the arduous journey to and fro on camel-back, pointing out that watching birds in such hostile and forbidding terrain was as trying as stalking big game on foot.

As the joy of discovery and the shooting of wildlife with the camera gained new adherents, there rose a growing band of critics of the old order. Not all made headway. The English missionary and writer Edward Thompson, who wrote a fine essay on the decline of India's fauna in the 1940s, raised the issue with Mahatma Gandhi. The latter assured him tongue in cheek that even though wildlife was dwindling in the jungles it was increasing in the cities. Others were more receptive. Lodged in the Naini Tal jail, Jawaharlal Nehru busied himself with Sálim Ali's bird book, exchanging notes on identification with fellow inmates and his daughter, Indira. Though he had shot a goral (a goat-antelope) on his honeymoon, the sight of its death had moved him deeply. Similar tales of the penitent butcher turning away from the artefacts of killing were to be played out time and again. The reformed big game hunter, usually one of the local landed gentry, had often begun by shooting as a school boy. It was men like these—Billy Arjan Singh's name comes to mind—who would cross over to conservation in independent India. They are prominent as pioneers in the art of watching animals. A fawn at play, the role of leopards in nature's economy, the behaviour of tigers in the wild: each became first a note in a diary, then the subject of an essay. The pioneers were blazing a new trail. Their writings are a bridge between the *shikari* past and our own Age of Ecology.

For the big game hunter, India was a kaleidoscope of landscapes, each symbolized by a trophy-worthy animal. Assam meant rhinos, Mysore the gaur and so on. The next step was a logical one. The canvas broadened to include trees and wild flowers, common birds and reptiles. As new ways of seeing and asserting the coherence of the world gained ground, the lapwing seemed as engaging as the leopard, the cobra as mysterious as the tiger. Few men have ever played as central a role in changing popular perceptions of nature in this regard as M. Krishnan. If as many as five extracts from his writings figure in this collection, it is a measure of his immense contribution to the broadening of our vision of the wild. He began writing in the 1930s, and was a pioneering publicist of the havoc suffered by India's wildlife as well as part of the new efflorescence of natural history writing, field biology and conservation.

The living landscape would find new men and women to celebrate and record its splendour. Many are names familiar to the average newspaper reader, others are less widely known than they deserve. These new writers form a mixed crew. Kailash Sankhala, writing from the 1950s, was a forester turned conservationist. A generation down the line, A. J. T. Johnsingh set out to do a doctorate on the dhole or Indian wild dog—and demolished a century-old stereotype of an insensate deer-hunting beast. Rom Whitaker, snakeman extraordinary, opened our eyes to the vital role reptiles play in India's economy, ecology and culture. The scientist Raman Sukumar unlocked secrets of the family life of one of India's most beloved creatures, the elephant. The list is long and growing.

Not that the challenges of conserving wildlife have diminished or the threats receded. Park-like enclaves for patches of natural forest or scrub do exist, but these are hemmed in by the growing demands of industry and the modern market. Co-existing with nearly a billion people is not easy for lions, elephants and their neighbours. Yet India's scientific expertise and the sheer perseverances of its conservationists, the deep-seated roles of the wild in its culture, and the growing debate on how best to protect what remains—all of these offer hope for the future. The pressures are mounting, not only in forest or mountain, but also in mangrove and on the coast line. But there is little doubt that a better quality of life for India's people is dependent on these natural treasures. From being an aesthetic luxury or a mere resource reservoir, they are now accepted as the surest sign that the natural cycles of repair and renewal are still intact.

Sometimes particular places symbolize best how far things have truly changed. Ranthambore was a killing field for tigers till as recently as 1961. Perhaps it can also be an emblem, a symbol of the great changes that have since occurred. For decades, tigers were portrayed by hunter-naturalists as creatures with virtually no family bonds. They were killers of the night, untameable and ferocious, fit only to be shot or at least avoided at all costs. It was in this spirit that Col. Kesri Singh organized shoots for the princes with his customary expertise. In 1973, a little over a decade after the Duke's fateful shoot at Ranthambore, the forest became one of India's tiger reserves. What followed was not only a recovery of the fauna and flora, but the amazing and unprecedented phenomenon of wild tigers dropping their nocturnal cloaks. Valmik Thapar's account of the close bonds of a male tiger with his mate and cubs is both remarkable and deeply symbolic. The first because it changed our earlier notions of tiger behaviour: the callous male could even be a doting father. And symbolic, for it showed that even big cats can get over their wariness of people and forge new bonds of trust with people. To keep these ties alive is one of the great challenges of the times we live in.

PART I

Tiger! Tiger!

It is not easy to think of a large animal with as extensive a range and as significant a presence in India's landscapes, ecological and cultural, as the tiger. New evidence indicates tigers even live on the Tibetan plateau, north of the subcontinent, preying on shaggy yaks. But tigers also pad softly down forest paths in Kalakadu-Mundanthurai, in the deep south of Tamil Nadu, sharing living space with hornbills and arboreal giant squirrels. And they live, hunt and breed in lands as diverse as the mangroves of the Sundarbans in the east and the sun-scorched Aravalli hills in the west. If it is today a symbol of diversity, of the fragility of nature, majestic to behold but easy to vandalize, the tiger has also been, across the centuries, an emblem of power, an elusive if powerful adversary to be vanquished or a deity to be propitiated.

Men—and a few women—have long hunted tigers, but match-lock and spear, fall-trap and arrow hardly made a dent on numbers. It was under the flag of the British empire that the tiger began to suffer eclipse. Large 'bags' became the norm for men of status and substance: several officers and princes scored a 'century' or even more. But there was equally a fever for record 'trophies' with each animal shot being measured and recorded. Who shot the largest tiger (ditto panther, bear or wild buffalo) mattered. Some hunters went further, raising questions about the claims, warning against tricksters, and at times sympathizing more with the tiger than those who pursued—or some would say—persecuted it.

Two remarkably gifted naturalists began their forest forays with a gun in hand and shot many animals. One was Jim Corbett, the slayer of many man-eaters; the other, not as famous, was A. A. Dunbar Brander. Their pieces give us a flavour of the days of the hunt, not as a spectacle but as a routine daily activity. A century before Corbett's death, William Rice, also a British military man, had shot tigers the hard way, on foot, but in a very different setting, in the hills of Rajasthan. And lastly, an Indian, Col. Kesri Singh deserves mention. He was an organizer par excellence of tiger beats for the rulers of the princely states of Gwalior and Jaipur. Here the hunt was on a huge scale and only the centre-piece of a large spectacle involving beaters, baits, jeeps and elephants. One of the hunts he describes in Sawai Madhopur was staged in 1961. But the wheel was about to turn, the tiger out-living the hunt. The tiger as a symbol of life was in the process of winning over the glory and the gore of 'the kill'.

A. A. DUNBAR BRANDER

The Largest Tiger?

Dunbar Brander served for over twenty years as a forester in the Central Provinces. He was an excellent observer of wildlife and an accomplished hunter with over fifty tigers against his name. But he had sounded warnings against shooting down all the large tigers in central Indian forests as early as 1908. His concern was not with protection per se: he was worried there would be no good specimens left for future hunters to bag and brag about!

The idiom of sport included weights and measures. Tigers were carefully measured for their length: it was often claimed the results were doctored, the higher the officer the longer the tiger-skin! Dunbar Brander here warns against being taken in by such claims and asks how large an Indian tiger can grow. Such warnings were not misplaced—one prominent Indian prince is even said to have had a special tape with one foot being only 11 inches. His guests always went away pleased with their 'records'.

Within the history of sport, has the 12 ft. tiger existed in India?

Few questions have been more hotly debated, and the matter is by no means settled yet and probably never will be. Advocates of the 12 ft. tiger can quote numerous instances from books on shikar in support of their views, but this does not help much, as everything depends on the accuracy of the writer. That a great many were inaccurate is undeniable. Some of the sportsmen who hunted in the Forties of the last century refer to tigers of even over 12 ft. in the most off-hand way. One gets the impression that anything under 11 ft. is hardly worth talking about. In some cases these men were followed a few years afterwards over identically the same ground by others who record nothing but tigers of 9 and 10 ft., animals no bigger than those killed every year in India to-day. Amongst men of this class I may mention some mighty hunters with the lengths of the biggest tigers they killed.

Shakespeare	one of 10 ft. 8 in.
Simpson	two of 10 ft. 4 in.
Nightingale	one of 10 ft. 2 in.
Sanderson	one of 9 ft. 6 in.
Hamilton	one of 9 ft. 3 in.

What happened to all the big tigers? Did none survive? Did the first sportsman kill them all? Because we must undoubtedly reject many of these records, are therefore all to be similarly treated? That is the difficulty; to discriminate as to whose measurements are reliable.

Most of the authors whose style and records are most convincing give us nothing sensational. Eighty years ago when sportsmen first began to hunt tiger seriously, one must not forget that tigers were much more numerous than now, and often lived in country where no tigers now exist and which may have been specially favourable to their development. Amongst a great number of tigers the chances of an abnormally large animal occurring are increased. Moreover, their comparative immunity from serious hunting up to this time, gave the tigers every opportunity for the fullest development. In those days tigers were measured round the curves. In a normal tiger this adds 3 in. to 4 in. to the length; in a large tiger it may add 5 in., and the larger the tiger the more it tends to increase the length. To measure round the curves gives great opportunities for increasing the length, so much depends on how often the tape is pressed in.

Anyone familiar with the East, knows well how keen the native shikari and the babu are to 'please master,' and we are never told exactly how these large measurements were taken. Even given four or five white men together and getting each in turn to measure round the curves their returns will all vary and some by as much as 3 in. The proper way to measure a tiger is to place it on its back on a flat surface and depress the head, then place two uprights, one touching its nose and the other the tip of the tail—remove the carcass and measure the space between the base of the two uprights. Measurements made in this way will not vary by ¼ in. It is only comparatively recently that sportsmen have commenced to measure in this way. Allowing for the extra 5 in. owing to past methods of measurement, although this will bring the 11 ft. tiger down to within reasonable distance of animals still occasionally killed, it utterly fails to account for the 12 or 12 ft. 4 in. beast.

I know of one authentic case of a tigress measuring 9 ft. 6 in. between uprights, and assuming this animal to mate with a very large tiger, and the cubs to have a prosperous upbringing, and taking the Indian tiger's ancestry into consideration, it is impossible to say that a tiger cannot exceed 11 ft. Nevertheless at the present time the announcement of the shooting of an 11 ft. tiger would be followed by a deluge of questions and since the interest of the whole sporting world has been centred on 11 ft. tigers these have ceased to materialize.

The more improbable the event, the stronger the evidence demanded in order to establish the same. It is significant that Jerdon, in his *Mammals of India,* published in 1874, will not accept even the 11 ft. tiger, and he must have known men who laid claim to having killed animals of over this length. While wishing that fuller details had been furnished as to how and by whom the measurements were made in past days, I think we can accept the occasional tiger of 11 ft. measured round curves, but we certainly cannot extend indulgence beyond this. It is hoped that anyone in future killing a phenomenal tiger will furnish the fullest details regarding the measurements. This is specially required in cases of large animals being killed by important personages, to please whom many are only too ready to stretch a point, and such persons are apt to delegate the work of measuring; at any rate they are always surrounded by a staff to relieve them of personal supervision and they are largely immune from the pertinent enquiries of the sceptic.

The weights given in old records are on the other hand often immoderately small, so much so that when compared with the stated length, and assuming that both are correct, the modern tiger is an entirely different animal. Some of these records have been published in the *Bombay Natural History Society's Journal.* In some cases tigers of the largest size are only made to weigh as much as a fair-sized tigress, and it is impossible that both weight and length are correct. Sir John Hewett probably possesses the most extensive records of any living person, covering as they do 241 animals which he has seen shot, mostly in the Terai. He has been kind enough to favour me with some of his figures. The longest tiger he ever saw shot was 10 ft. 5½ in. and the longest tigress 9 ft. 6 in. The heaviest tiger he weighed was 570 lb. and the heaviest tigress 347 lb. Out of 241 animals nine tigers were 10 ft. or over and ten tigresses were 9 ft. or over 9 ft. One of these was from the Central Provinces.

An exact comparison with animals from the Central Provinces is not possible as the measurements recorded by me were taken between pegs and this reduces the length by 3 in. to 5 in. Another point is that I weighed and measured very few immature animals. The figures I possess refer to forty-two fully mature males and thirty-nine fully mature females, and while I have seen many more mature animals killed than this, I have not got a record of these, and it is probable that in selecting animals for measurement the tendency would be to choose large specimens. Unfortunately some of my diaries were lost or stolen in Bombay. I am unable to say, therefore, exactly how many tigers I have seen shot, but it can be taken as being approximately 200. Out of this number one is of 10 ft. 3 in. and another of 10 ft. 2 in. In addition, there are one of 9 ft. 11 in., one of 9 ft. 10 in., the latter shot by His Royal Highness the Duke of Connaught at Supkar. Another tiger at the same shoot was 9 ft. 9 in. I have another record of a tiger 9 ft. 10½ in. All these six animals, if measured round the curves, would have been 10 ft. or over. The biggest tigress I have seen measured was 9 ft. 1 in. In addition, I have records of two of 8 ft. 11 in., one of 8 ft. 10 in., and one of 8 ft. 9 in., i.e., five animals of 9 ft. or over, if measured round curves. It would seem, therefore, that the occurrence of 10 ft. tigers and 9 ft. tigresses is slightly more common in the Terai and Nepal than in the Central Provinces.

The classification of what is a mature animal has presented some difficulty, and would vary according to the views of the individual. Out of the thirty-nine tigresses selected as mature, the smallest was 7 ft. 10 in. and the largest 9 ft. 1 in. The average is 8 ft. 4 in. and the average weight is 290 lb. The heaviest tigress weighed was 343 lb. The shortest tiger classified as mature was 8 ft. 9 in., and the longest 10 ft. 3 in. The average works out at 9 ft. 3 in. The weights vary between 353 and 515 lb., averaging 420 lb. for a gorged tiger. I weighed one other animal over 500 lb.

The largest animal I actually ever saw, however, only taped 9 ft. 11 in. between uprights. Most unfortunately, I had no weighing machine and could only make a rough estimate of its weight by balancing it against a number of men, and some of these men left before I could weigh them. I firmly believe this tiger was about 600 lb. in weight. This animal had been living on full-grown buffaloes, and was doing an immense amount of damage. It had killed some of the largest animals, including a bull, with apparent ease. The bulk of its neck may be gauged from the fact that while biting its fore paw, after the first shot, I put in what I hoped to be a 'finisher' from a Ross rifle, using the usual copper-nosed bullets. The bullet never even reached the bone, and only stirred the beast up. The line of the backbone was sunk in a depression, and on each side the flesh came out as flat as a table for 8 in. before the curvature of the ribs commenced. In addition, it had what I have never seen on any other tiger. There was a curious wedge, not soft and flabby as one sees in zoo animals, but a hard firm ridge 4 in. to 5 in. deep running all along the belly from the pelvis to the throat. It was so distinct I thought it must be due to some disease, but it turned out to be merely a strip of pure white fat. Some idea of this animal's size can be gathered from the following measurements:

Length of body	7 ft.	3 in.
Length of tail	2 ft.	8 in.
Girth of body		59 in.
Girth of head		39 in.
Girth of forearm		21 in.
Height		43 in.

The biggest tigress, 9 ft. 1 in., already mentioned, was an old beast and was killed in the same jungle as the above-mentioned monster and may have been his mother. In both these animals the tail was short.

Although the size of tigers varies considerably, the shape does not. The greatest difference is found in the tail, which may vary as much as 15 in., and the length is not dependent on the size of the animal; the longest and shortest tails I have measured were 45 in. and 30 in. respectively.

The height of tigers at the shoulder varies from 36 to 44 in. A good average male should measure 39 in. Other average measurements are 37 in. round the head, 32 in. round the neck, and 19 in. round the forearm.

It will be seen from these measurements that there is nothing lanky about the tiger, and that he is a large, powerful, burly animal, differing entirely in a wild state from the impression one gets from looking at specimens in captivity. In fact, I have seen quarters on a tiger that would not have shamed a polo pony. Tigresses are, of course, much smaller than tigers and generally more sinuous.

Excerpted from Wild Animals in Central India *(London: Edward Arnold, 1923).*

JIM CORBETT

The Bachelor of Powalgarh

Jim Corbett is best known for stalking and hunting man-eating tigers and leopards. But Corbett was not merely a scourge of the rare carnivore that attacked people. Very much a man of his times, he was also a sport-hunter, organizing a tiger beat as late as 1946, and continuing to shoot in East Africa where he emigrated after India became independent. His first book, The Man-Eaters of Kumaon, however, includes only two tiger-hunts that are not about man-eating animals. What makes 'The Bachelor' of interest is that it is a celebration of Corbett's success in shooting a particularly large tiger that had long evaded large parties of elephant-borne hunters. Perhaps like many other tigers living in forests where hunting was the norm, this huge male was cautious and wary, and able to get away—until he crossed Corbett's trail.

Three miles from our winter home, and in the heart of the forest, there is an open glade some four hundred yards long and half as wide, grassed with emerald-green and surrounded with big trees interlaced with cane creepers. It was in this glade, which for beauty has no equal, that I first saw the tiger who was known throughout the United Provinces as 'The Bachelor of Powalgarh', who from 1920 to 1930 was the most sought-after big-game trophy in the province.

The sun had just risen one winter's morning when I crested the high ground overlooking the glade. On the far side, a score of red jungle fowl were scratching among the dead leaves bordering a crystal-clear stream, and scattered over the emerald-green grass, now sparkling with dew, fifty or more chital were feeding. Sitting on a tree stump and smoking, I had been looking at this scene for some time when the hind nearest to me raised her head, turned in my direction and called; and a moment later the Bachelor stepped into the open from the thick bushes below me. For a long minute he stood with head held high surveying the scene, and then with slow unhurried steps started to cross the glade. In his rich winter coat, which the newly risen sun was lighting up, he was a magnificent sight as, with head turning now to the right and now to the left, he walked down the wide lane the deer had made for him. At the stream he lay down and quenched his thirst, then sprang across and, as he entered the dense tree jungle beyond, called three times in acknowledgement of the homage the jungle folk had paid him, for from the time he had entered the glade every chital had called, every jungle fowl had cackled, and every one of a troupe of monkeys on the trees had chattered.

The Bachelor was far afield that morning, for his home was in a ravine six miles away. Living in an area in which the majority of tigers are bagged with the aid of elephants, he had chosen his home wisely. The ravine, running into the foot-hills, was half a mile long, with steep hills on either side rising to a height of a thousand feet. At the upper end of the ravine there was a waterfall some twenty feet high, and at the lower end, where the water had cut through red clay, it narrowed to four feet. Any sportsman, therefore, who wished to try conclusions with the Bachelor, while he was at home, would of a necessity have to do so on foot. It was this secure retreat, and the Government rules prohibiting night shooting, that had enabled the Bachelor to retain possession of his much sought-after skin.

In spite of the many and repeated attempts that had been made to bag him with the aid of buffalo bait, the Bachelor had never been fired at, though on two occasions, to my knowledge, he had only escaped death by the skin of his teeth. On the first occasion, after a perfect beat, a guy rope by which the machan was suspended interfered with the movement of Fred Anderson's rifle at the critical moment, and on the second occasion the Bachelor arrived at the machan before the beat started and found Huish Edye filling his pipe. On both these occasions he had been viewed at a range of only a few feet, and while Anderson described him as being as big as a Shetland pony, Edye said he was as big as a donkey.

The winter following these and other unsuccessful attempts, I took Wyndham, our Commissioner, who knows more about tigers than any other man in India, to a fire track skirting the upper end of the ravine in which the Bachelor lived, to show him the fresh pug marks of the tiger which I had found on the fire track that morning. Wyndham was accompanied by two of his most experienced shikaris, and after the three of them had carefully measured and examined the pug marks, Wyndham said that in his opinion the tiger was ten feet between pegs, and while one shikari said he was 10' 5" over curves, the other said he was 10' 6" or a little more. All three agreed that they had never seen the pug marks of a bigger tiger.

In 1930 the Forest Department started extensive fellings in the areas surrounding the Bachelor's home and annoyed at the disturbance he changed his quarters; this I learnt from two sportsmen who had taken out a shooting pass with the object of hunting down the tiger. Shooting passes are only issued for fifteen days of each month, and throughout that winter, shooting party after shooting party failed to make contact with the tiger.

Towards the end of the winter an old dak runner, who passes our gate every morning and evening on his seven-mile run through the forest to a hill village, came to me one evening and reported that on his way out that morning he had seen the biggest pug marks of a tiger that he had seen during the thirty years of his service. The tiger, he said, had come from the west and after proceeding along the road for two hundred yards had gone east, taking a path that started from near an almond tree. This tree was about two miles from our home, and was a well-known landmark. The path the tiger had taken runs through very heavy jungle for half a mile before crossing a wide watercourse, and then joins a cattle track which skirts the foot of the hills before entering a deep and well-wooded valley; a favourite haunt of tigers.

Early next morning, with Robin at my heels, I set out to prospect, my objective being the point where the cattle track entered the valley, for at this point the tracks of all the animals entering or leaving the valley are to be found. From the time we started Robin appeared to know that we had a special job in hand and he paid not the least attention to the jungle fowl we disturbed, the kakar (barking deer) that let us get quite close to it, and the two sambur that stood and belled at us. Where the cattle track entered the valley the ground was hard and stony, and when we reached this spot Robin put down his head and very carefully smelt the stones, and on receiving a signal from me to carry on he turned and started down the track, keeping a yard ahead of me; I could tell from his behaviour that he was on the scent of a tiger, and that the scent was hot. A hundred yards further down, where the track flattens out and runs along the foot of the hill, the ground is soft; here I saw the pug marks of a tiger, and a glance at them satisfied me we were on the heels of the Bachelor and that he was only a minute or two ahead of us.

Beyond the soft ground the track runs for three hundred yards over stones, before going steeply down onto an open plain. If the tiger kept to the track we should probably see him on this open ground. We had gone another fifty yards when Robin stopped and, after running his nose up and down a blade of grass on the left of the track, turned and entered the grass which was here about two feet high. On the far side of the grass there was a patch of clerodendron, about forty yards wide. This plant grows in dense patches to a height of five feet, and has widely spread leaves and a big head of flowers not unlike horse-chestnut. It is greatly fancied by tiger, sambur and pig because of the shade it gives. When Robin reached the clerodendron he stopped and backed towards me, thus telling me that he could not see into the bushes ahead and wished to be carried. Lifting him up, I put his hind legs into my left-hand pocket, and when he had hooked his forefeet over my left arm, he was safe and secure, and I had both hands free for the rifle. On these occasions Robin was always in deadly earnest, and no matter what he saw, or how our quarry behaved before or after fired at, he never moved and spoilt my shot, or impeded my view. Proceeding very slowly, we had gone half-way through the clerodendron when I saw the bushes directly in front of us swaying. Waiting until the tiger had cleared the bushes, I went forward expecting to see him in the more or less open jungle, but he was nowhere in sight, and when I put Robin down he turned to the left and indicated that the tiger had gone into a deep and narrow ravine nearby. This ravine ran to the foot of an isolated hill on which there were caves frequented by tigers, and as I was not armed to deal with a tiger at close quarters, and further, as it was time for breakfast, Robin and I turned and made for home.

After breakfast I returned alone, armed with a heavy .450 rifle, and as I approached the hill, which in the days of the long ago had been used by the local inhabitants as a rallying point against the Gurkha invaders, I heard the boom of a big buffalo bell, and a man shouting. These sounds were coming from the top of the hill, which is flat, and about half an acre in extent, so I climbed up and saw a man on a tree, striking a dead branch with the head of his axe and shouting, while at the foot of the tree a number of buffaloes were collected. When he saw me the man called out, saying I had just arrived in time to save him and his buffaloes from a *shaitan* (devil) of a tiger, the size of a camel, that had been threatening them for hours. From his story I gathered that he had arrived on the hill shortly after Robin and I had left for home, and that as he started to cut bamboo leaves for his buffaloes he saw a tiger coming towards him. He shouted to drive the tiger away, as he had done on many previous occasions with other tigers, but instead of going away this one had started to growl. He took to his heels, followed by his buffaloes, and climbed up the nearest tree. The tiger, paying no heed to his shouts, had then set to pacing round and round, while the buffaloes kept their heads towards it. Probably the tiger had heard me coming, for it had left only a moment before I had arrived. The man was an old friend, who before his quarrel with the Headman of his village had done a considerable amount of poaching in these jungles with the Headman's gun. He now begged me to conduct both himself and his cattle safely out of the jungle; so telling him to lead on, I followed behind to see that there were no stragglers. At first the buffaloes were disinclined to break up their close formation, but after a little persuasion we got them to start, and we had gone half-way across the open plain I have alluded to when the tiger called in the jungle to our right. The man quickened his pace, and I urged on the buffaloes, for a mile of very thick jungle lay between us and the wide, open water-course beyond which lay my friend's village and safety for his buffaloes.

I have earned the reputation of being keener on photographing animals than on killing them, and before I left my friend he begged me to put aside photography for this once, and kill the tiger, which he said was big enough to eat a buffalo a day, and ruin him in twenty-five days. I promised to do my best and turned to retrace my steps to the open plain, to meet with an experience every detail of which has burnt itself deep into my memory.

On reaching the plain I sat down to wait for the tiger to disclose his whereabouts, or for the jungle folk to tell me where he was. It was then about 3 p.m., and as the sun was warm and comforting, I put my head down on my drawn up knees and had been dozing a few minutes when I was awakened by the tiger calling; thereafter he continued to call at short intervals.

Between the plain and the hills there is a belt, some half-mile wide, of the densest scrub jungle for a hundred miles round, and I located the tiger as being on the hills on the far side of the scrub—about three-quarters of a mile from me—and from the way he was calling it was evident he was in search of a mate.

Starting from the upper left-hand corner of the plain, and close to where I was sitting, an old cart track, used some years previously for extracting timber, ran in an almost direct line to where the tiger was calling. This track would take me in the direction of the calling animal, but on the hills was high grass, and without Robin to help me there would be little chance of my seeing him. So instead of my going to look for the tiger, I decided he should come and look for me. I was too far away for him to hear me, so I sprinted up the cart track for a few hundred yards, laid down my rifle, climbed to the top of a high tree and called three times. I was immediately answered by the tiger. After climbing down, I ran back calling as I went, and arrived on the plain without having found a suitable place in which to sit and await the tiger. Something would have to be done and done in a hurry, for the tiger was rapidly coming nearer, so, after rejecting a little hollow which I found to be full of black stinking water, I lay down flat in the open, twenty yards from where the track entered the scrub. From this point I had a clear view up the track for fifty yards, to where a bush, leaning over it, impeded my further view. If the tiger came down the track, as I expected him to, I decided to fire at him as he cleared the obstruction.

After opening the rifle to make quite sure it was loaded, I threw off the safety-catch, and with elbows comfortably resting on the soft ground waited for the tiger to appear. I had not called since I came out on the plain, so to give him direction I now gave a low call, which he immediately answered from a distance of a hundred yards. If he came on at his usual pace, I judged he would clear the obstruction in thirty seconds. I counted this number very slowly, and went on counting up to eighty, when out of the corner of my eye I saw a movement to my right front, where the bushes approached to within ten yards of me. Turning my eyes in that direction I saw a great head projecting above the bushes, which here were four feet high. The tiger was only a foot or two inside the bushes, but all I could see of him was his head. As I very slowly swung the point of the rifle round and ran my eyes along the sights I noticed that his head was not quite square on to me, and as I was firing up and he was looking down, I aimed an inch below his right eye, pressed the trigger, and for the next half-hour nearly died of fright.

Instead of dropping dead as I expected him to, the tiger went straight up into the air above the bushes for his full length, falling backwards onto a tree a foot thick which had been blown down in a storm and was still green. With unbelievable fury he attacked this tree and tore it to bits, emitting as he did so roar upon roar, and what was even worse, a dreadful blood-curdling sound as though he was savaging his worst enemy. The branches of the tree tossed about as though struck by a tornado, while the bushes on my side shook and bulged out, and every movement I expected to have him on top of me, for he had been looking at me when I fired, and knew where I was.

Too frightened even to recharge the rifle for fear the slight movement and sound should attract the attention of the tiger, I lay and sweated for half an hour with my finger on the left trigger. At last the branches of the tree and the bushes ceases waving about, and the roaring became less frequent, and eventually, to my great relief, ceased. For another half-hour I lay perfectly still, with arms cramped by the weight of the heavy rifle, and then started to pull myself backwards with my toes. After progressing for thirty yards in this manner I got to my feet, and, crouching low, made for the welcome shelter of the nearest tree. Here I remained for some minutes, and as all was now silent I turned and made for home.

Next morning I returned accompanied by one of my men, an expert tree-climber. I had noticed the previous evening that there was a tree growing on the edge of the open ground, and about forty yards from where the tiger had fallen. We approached this tree very cautiously, and I stood behind it while the man climbed to the top. After a long and a careful scrutiny he looked down and shook his head and when he rejoined me on the ground he told me that the bushes over a big area had been flattened down, but that the tiger was not in sight.

I sent him back to his perch on the tree with instructions to keep a sharp lookout and warn me if he saw any movement in the bushes, and went forward to have a look at the spot where the tiger had raged. He had raged to some purpose, for, in addition to tearing branches and great strips of wood off the tree, he had torn up several bushes by the roots, and bitten down others. Blood in profusion was sprinkled everywhere, and on the ground were two congealed pools, near one of which was lying a bit of bone two inches square, which I found on examination to be part of the tiger's skull.

No blood trail led away from this spot and this, combined with the two pools of blood, was proof that the tiger was still here when I left and that the precautions I had taken the previous evening had been very necessary, for when I started on my 'get-away' I was only ten yards from the most dangerous animal in the world—a freshly wounded tiger. On circling round the spot I found a small smear of blood here and there on leaves that had brushed against his face. Noting that these indications of the tiger's passage led in a direct line to a giant semul tree[1] two hundred yards away, I went back and climbed the tree my man was on in order to get a bird's-eye view of the ground I should have to go over, for I had a very uneasy feeling that I should find him alive: a tiger shot in the head can live for days and can even recover from the wound. True, this tiger had a bit of his skull missing, and as I had never dealt with an animal in his condition before I did not know whether he was likely to live for a few hours or days, or live on to die of old age. For this reason I decided to treat him as an ordinary wounded tiger, and not to take any avoidable risks when following him up.

From my elevated position on the tree I saw that, a little to the left of the line to the semul tree, there were two trees, the nearer one thirty yards from where the blood was, and the other fifty yards further on. Leaving my man on the tree, I climbed down, picked up my rifle and a shot-gun and bag of a hundred cartridges, and very cautiously approached the nearer tree and climbed up it to a height of thirty feet, pulling the rifle and gun, which I had tied to one end of a strong cord, up after me. After fixing the rifle in a fork of the tree where it would be handy if needed, I started to spray

---

[1] *Bombax malabaricum*, the silk cotton tree.

the bushes with small shot, yard by yard up to the foot of the second tree. I did this with the object of locating the tiger, assuming he was alive and in that area, for a wounded tiger, on hearing a shot fired close to him, or on being struck by a pellet, will either growl or charge. Receiving no indication of the tiger's presence I went to the second tree, and sprayed the bushes to within a few yards of the semul tree, firing the last shot at the tree itself. After this last shot I thought I heard a low growl, but it was not repeated and I put it down to my imagination. My bag of cartridges was now empty, so after recovering my man I called it a day, and went home.

When I returned next morning I found my friend the buffalo man feeding his buffaloes on the plain. He appeared to be very much relieved to see me, and the reason for this I learnt later. The grass was still wet with dew, but we found a dry spot and there sat down to have a smoke and relate our experiences. My friend, as I have already told you, had done a lot of poaching, and having spent all his life in tiger-infested jungles tending his buffaloes, or shooting, his jungle knowledge was considerable.

After I had left him that day at the wide, open water course, he had crossed to the far side and had sat down to listen for sounds coming from the direction in which I had gone. He had heard two tigers calling; he had heard my shot followed by the continuous roaring of a tiger, and very naturally concluded I had wounded one of the tigers and that it had killed me. On his return next morning to the same spot, he had been greatly mystified by hearing a hundred shots fired, and this morning, not being able to contain his curiosity any longer, he had come to see what had happened. Attracted by the smell of blood, his buffaloes had shown him where the tiger had fallen, and he had seen the patches of dry blood and had found the bit of bone. No animal in his opinion could possibly live for more than a few hours after having a bit of its skull blown away, and so sure was he that the tiger was dead that he offered to take his buffaloes into the jungle and find it for me. I had heard of this method of recovering tigers with the help of buffaloes but had never tried it myself, and after my friend had agreed to accepting compensation for any damage to his cattle I accepted his offer.

Rounding up the buffaloes, twenty-five in number, and keeping to the line I had sprinkled with shot the previous day, we made for the semul tree, followed by the buffaloes. Our progress was slow, for not only had we to move the chin-high bushes with our hands to see where to put our feet, but we also had frequently to check a very natural tendency on the part of the buffaloes to stray. As we approached the semul tree, where the bushes were lighter, I saw a little hollow filled with dead leaves that had been pressed flat and on which were several patches of blood, some dry, others in process of congealing, and one quite fresh; and when I put my hand to the ground I found it was warm. Incredible as it may appear, the tiger had lain in this hollow the previous day while I had expended a hundred cartridges, and had only moved off when he saw us and the buffaloes approaching. The buffaloes had now found the blood and were pawing up the ground and snorting, and as the prospect of being caught between a charging tiger and angry buffaloes did not appeal to me, I took hold of my friend's arm, turned him round and made for the open plain, followed by the buffaloes. When we were back on safe ground I told the man to go home, and said I would return next day and deal with the tiger alone.

The path through the jungles that I had taken each day when coming from and going home ran for some distance over soft ground, and on this soft ground, on this fourth day, I saw the pug marks of a big male tiger. By following these pug marks I found the tiger had entered the dense brushwood a hundred yards to the right of the semul tree. Here was an unexpected complication, for if I now saw a tiger in this jungle I should not know—unless I got a very close look at it—whether it was the wounded or the unwounded one. However, this contingency would have to be dealt with when met, and in the meantime worrying would not help, so I entered the bushes and made for the hollow at the foot of the semul tree.

There was no blood trail to follow so I zigzagged through the bushes, into which it was impossible to see further than a few inches, for an hour or more, until I came to a ten-foot wide dry watercourse. Before stepping down into this water course I looked up it, and saw the left hind leg and tail of a tiger. The tiger was standing perfectly still with its body and head hidden by a tree, and only this one leg visible. I raised the rifle to my shoulder, and then lowered it. To have broken the leg would have been easy, for the tiger was only ten yards away, and it would have been the right thing to do if its owner was the wounded animal; but there were two tigers in this area, and to have broken the leg of the wrong one would have doubled my difficulties, which were already considerable. Presently the leg was withdrawn and I heard the tiger moving away, and going to the spot where he had been standing I found a few drops of blood—too late now to regret not having broken that leg.

A quarter of a mile further on there was a little stream, and it was possible that the tiger, now recovering from his wound, was making for this stream. With the object of intercepting him or failing that, waiting for him at the water, I took a game path which I knew went to the stream and had proceeded along it for some distance when a sambur belled to my left, and went dashing off though the jungle. It was evident now that I was abreast of the tiger, and I had only taken a few more steps when I heard the loud crack of a dry stick breaking as though some heavy animal had fallen on it; the sound had come from a distance of fifty yards and from the exact spot where the sambur had belled. The sambur had in unmistakable tones warned the jungle folk of the presence of a tiger, and the stick therefore could only have been broken by the same animal; so getting down on my hands and knees I started to crawl in the direction from which the sound had come.

The bushes here were from six to eight feet high, with dense foliage on the upper branches and very few leaves on the stems, so that I could see through them for a distance of ten to fifteen feet. I had covered thirty yards, hoping fervently that if the tiger charged he would come from in front (for in no other direction could I have fired), when I caught sight of something red on which the sun, drifting through the upper leaves, was shining; it might only be a bunch of dead leaves; on the other hand, it might be the tiger. I could get a better view of this object from two yards to the right, so lowering my head until my chin touched the ground, I crawled this distance with belly to ground, and on raising my head saw the tiger in front of me. He was crouching down looking at me, with the sun shining on his left shoulder, and on receiving my two bullets he rolled over on his side without making a sound.

As I stood over him and ran my eyes over his magnificent proportions it was not necessary to examine the pads of his feet to know that before me lay the Bachelor of Powalgarh.

The entry of the bullet fired four days previously was hidden by a wrinkle of skin, and at the back of his head was a big hole which, surprisingly, was perfectly clean and healthy.

The report of my rifle was, I knew, being listened for; so I hurried home to relieve anxiety, and while I related the last chapter of the hunt and drank a pot of tea, my men were collecting.

Accompanied by my sister and Robin and a carrying party of twenty men, I returned to where the tiger was lying, and before he was roped to a pole my sister and I measured him from nose to tip of tail, and from tip of tail to nose. At home we again measured him to make quite sure we had made no mistake the first time. These measurements are valueless, for there were no independent witness present to certify them; they are however interesting as showing the accuracy with which experienced woodsmen can judge the length of a tiger from his pug marks. Wyndham, you will remember, said the tiger was ten feet between pegs, which would give roughly 10' 6" over curves; and while one shikari said he was 10' 5.09 over curves, the other said he was 10' 6" or a little more. Shot seven years after these estimates were made, my sister and I measured the tiger as being 10' 7" over curves.

I have told the story at some length, as I feel sure that those who hunted the tiger between 1920 and 1930 will be interested to know how the Bachelor of Powalgarh met his end.

Excerpted from Man-Eaters of Kumaon *(Delhi: Oxford University Press, 1944).*

WILLIAM RICE

Tigers on Foot

There are now, even by official estimates, not more than around sixty-five tigers in Rajasthan, a state which includes some of the animal's finest habitats. But in just four years ending in 1854, a British officer and friends, shooting during vacations managed to kill or wound as many as ninety-eight tigers. William Rice's account does more than tell us how he bagged his tigers. It is equally valuable for the account of nature's wealth at a time when human pressures on the forest were much less intense.

Shooting tigers on foot was not easy. The great cats would evade hunters: it was only with the help of Bhil tribals that Rice got so many tigers. Sometimes, inhabitants of the villages were unwilling to wage war against the tiger. Some clans claimed 'he' was an ancestor, some rajas reserved exclusive rights to shoot the big cat. But, with luck, Rice did find some who helped in his sport. The hilly country he shot in was only accessible in summer, when the forest was relatively open. Here, tame elephants were of no use: to get at a tiger, sportsmen waited in machans or raised platforms often built on trees, or they got out on foot. A pug-mark on a forest trail could set off a train of events, launching a party on a tiger's trail.

We commenced our third expedition in March, 1851, having obtained leave of absence from the 14th day of that month to the 14th June, 1851, for the express purpose of shooting large game. Having sent on our small tent and servants to 'Panghur,' twenty miles north of Camp Neemuch, we rode out there on the evening of 14th March. We had not long to wait for action. Early next morning news was brought to us of a tiger having been seen close at hand by some men we had sent out before daylight to look out on the surrounding hills.

It was some time before we were ready to start, having to arrange our 'battery,' and separate the ammunition for our respective guns and rifles, which were of many different bores. This is often a serious nuisance to the hunter, who, in the haste of quickly reloading, is obliged to be very careful not to ram the wrong bullets down the wrong gun. However, we got away by nine o'clock A.M., and, having stationed ourselves at the side of a ravine, in which the game was said to be lying, sent the beaters round to the other end of the cover, first placing a man up a tree to keep guard over a likely place by which the tiger might possibly attempt to leave the cover before passing our position. It was this man's duty on observing the tiger attempt to approach the path over which he was so safely placed, to 'head' back the game, which is easily effected, either by a slight cough, or tapping two stones together. In fact any slight unusual noise will instantly cause a tiger to retire as he comes slowly creeping along, keeping the brightest possible lookout for the least suspicious looking object in his path ahead, for his sole desire on being roused by the beaters is to make his escape unseen, well knowing that so unusual and great a noise in his otherwise seldom disturbed retreats bodes him no good. For this purpose, to as much as possible avoid being observed, we took good care to have our dress of a brown colour, so as to make it very difficult, even at a very short distance, to distinguish us from the rocks and jungle around. At this hot time of the year, all vegetation being dried up, the country presents, for the most part, a general brown tint, but, of course, of many different shades. Owing to this precaution, as well as by invariably preserving the strictest silence, and by remaining perfectly still, we were very rarely indeed detected in the positions we had chosen, or where we attempted to hide ourselves, by any wild beasts we hoped to kill, though they frequently approached us extremely close before we deemed it time to let them know of our vicinity. This regard to one's dress is absolutely necessary; for tigers, and nearly all large wild animals, are extremely cautious, especially if they have been shot at before; when they would, to a certainty, prefer the risk of breaking back past the beaters, in spite of the dreadful din they were making, to facing any strange object they may have discerned, but cannot clearly make out, in their path ahead. This was our sole reason for always directing the beaters to keep well together. Better let any amount of game escape back than have one accident from the men straggling about singly when there are so many chances of the tiger meeting and knocking over, in his flight, individuals whom he would carefully have avoided, provided they kept in a compact body, and allowed him room to pass. To prevent this risk as much as possible, we made it a rule never to fire until he had quite passed our position, when the beast, if not killed, was sure to bolt forward.

In this instance, the beating having commenced, we soon received notice of the tiger having broken cover by his voice as he passed immediately in rear and above the bank on which we were lying hid. We could not see him, but well knew he was much enraged by the continued growls he kept up as he passed. He finds it, of course, very provoking to be suddenly awoke from sleep, and to have to run barefoot for perhaps a mile over rocks and stones almost red hot; for the tiger, from only seeking its prey at night, or in the cool of the day, feels the excessive heat severely, and often refuses to leave his stronghold in spite of all the hunter's means— fireworks, guns, stones, noise—if there is no other retreat near, and he has to attempt his escape across an open, burning, rocky plain. The fact was, the man in the tree had failed to keep a good lookout, and so allowed the tiger to creep past his post unobserved. This we afterwards discovered to be the case by retracing the animal's prints, wishing to find out how we had been outmanœuvred so easily by the tiger. We followed up the prints, and twice again started the tiger. This we knew to be the case by his loud roars close in front of us; but we could neither get a shot, on account of the thick jungle.

Returned to our tent, vexed at losing this tiger, by evening. Hunted next day in another direction, but without success; returning homewards, we again put up yesterday's tiger in the same cover, but could not see him, only heard his voice. Moved our tent to 'Dowlutpoora,' six miles, and set out early to beat the 'Bahara' ravine there, fresh prints of a tiger having been found in that beautiful cover. Soon a fine tiger bounded out for a few yards, but quickly returned to the dense thicket. Being too far off, we did not then attempt to fire at him, in the hope that he would come nearer the rocky ledge on which we were posted. Our men tried hard to dislodge this tiger, but were unable to do so; nor would the cover burn, being too green to take fire. At length a Bheel, named 'Chutra' (the same man that last year told me of two tigers in this very place), being angry at having his bullocks killed lately by these beasts, vowed he would turn out this tiger, so left the rest of the beaters, who, according to our strict orders, had remained on the outside of the cover, and rushed down into the dense bushes sword in hand. The poor fellow was almost immediately seized by the tiger, and mauled severely, being much bitten about the shoulder and arms, and clawed on the legs. On hearing this happen, the other men in a body rushed to the rescue at once, drove off the tiger, and brought the wounded man outside with them.

All this time we had no idea of what had occurred, being at some distance watching for the tiger's appearance. We hastened to the spot on hearing of the accident, and, having sent some of the men to carry home the wounded Bheel to his hut, tried hard to persuade the rest to accompany us into the cover, but they refused, although a body of men could easily have forced their way through the dense bushes, yet for two only to have attempted doing so would have been mere rashness. So we were obliged to let this tiger alone for a time. We next went to see how the Bheel was getting on, and left a good sum for his maintenance with his relations, who promised to take every care of him. He was quite sensible, but much shaken. The other men tried at the time to dissuade him from entering the cover, but he would not listen to their advice. This was the first accident any of our men had met with while hunting with us, but it could not be helped, for the man wilfully disregarded all orders.

We now rode on twelve miles to 'Rajghur,' where the kit had been sent. For the next two days no game could be found in this neighbourhood, or prints even, except those of a panther; but this brute was nowhere visible. On the third morning a Bheel brought us news that three tigers had been lately seen in a patch of jungle, about two miles distant; so off we started for the place with about thirty men. The cover being very wide we took up separate positions, from which we could overlook the best part of it, which consisted of clusters of thick thorn bushes scattered about in some high grass on level stony ground. At first, rather to our surprise, it was drawn blank. Five of the beaters now positively declared that they had caught a glimpse of the three tigers, but this fact the others seemed to doubt, so we went to look for prints on the spot they pointed out; but could see none, the ground being too rocky. While we were discussing what was next to be done, a most unmistakeable roar was heard about thirty yards from where we were all standing together. On quickly sending a man up a tree close by to look out, he saw several men running off in the opposite direction. Presently we were joined by a woodcutter, who seemed in a great state of alarm; he said that while walking a little before his companions, who had come to cut down trees in this jungle, he met a tiger, and only escaped by throwing himself flat on his face as it rushed by him.

We hereupon hastened to our old positions, while the men went round to again beat the cover. Soon two large tigers and one half grown passed by my post, but as I could not get a clear shot, on account of the dense brushwood, I allowed them to pass on to Little's position without firing. I soon after heard him fire two shots. It appeared he had only seen one tiger come by alone, which quickly bounded out of sight in the high grass, on his firing, before he could get another shot at her. The other tigers must have turned away from his position, for he saw but one go by. Having so lately had a man wounded, and the jungle being so dense, we used extra precautions in following up this tiger; so observing the way the slight wind was blowing, we set fire to the grass, and advanced in a body behind it, in the hope of either getting more shots if the tiger started before us, or, if dead, of being able to save the skin before the flames should reach it; but in this last hope we were deceived, for after going about a few hundred yards, which took half an hour's time, we came upon the dead tiger, over which the fire had just passed, singeing off its hair, and so spoiling completely the skin. The smoke from the burning grass had prevented our seeing the body in time to save the skin. We cut off the beast's head and claws, besides taking out the 'collar bones.'

These are two small bones about four inches long, bent like a bow; embedded in a mass of muscle in the tiger's forearm, they are quite disconnected from any other bone, and are only to be found in the panther, tiger, or lion. The natives superstitiously regard them as 'charms' against evil, and have the same notion of the tiger's claws, a pair of which are worn by their children round the neck for protection against all harm. The Bheels call these bones 'goojbul,' and say their use is to give more force to the tiger's blow, when with his paw he strikes down his prey.

To-day, while looking for this wounded tiger, we found a most curious land tortoise, beautifully variegated, of a description that neither we nor any of the Bheels had ever before seen; so it must be of a very rare species indeed, for their whole lives being spent in the woods, they must have observed others, if at all of a common sort.

The next day we hunted over three large covers about a mile apart for the remaining two tigers, but could nowhere find them, although we saw their fresh prints. The rocky nature of the ground prevented their being 'pugged up.'

At night we were kept awake by the continued roaring of a tiger near our encampment. It is rather singular that tigers should indulge in making this seemingly unnecessary noise at night, for any one would imagine that such a row was enough to scare every sort of deer, on which they chiefly subsist, out of the country. The Bheels thus account for such extraordinary conduct, which version I firmly believe to be correct. Tigers for the most part confine themselves to one particular district of perhaps a few square miles in extent, with every inch of which ground they are of course thoroughly acquainted. As night draws on, the tiger will be heard to roar at several different points, separated at a good distance from each other; this is done with the view of disturbing the deer that might be lying in the neighbourhood, and driving them for safety to some more distant part of the jungle, to which the tiger next, silently enough, betakes himself. The deer being thus congregated in one quarter, for they also frequent only particular districts, the tiger, by either lying in ambush over some piece of water at which they will most likely soon come down to drink, or by sallying forth among them, has of course a double chance of securing some victim, with not half the trouble of hunting him up over a large tract of country. This seems far more likely to be the case than that, as some suppose, Providence has purposely caused the tiger to give this timely warning of his presence to the deer and smaller animals to enable them to make their escape, which otherwise would be in a fair way of being speedily exterminated by such a cunning, silent, savage enemy.

From 'Rajghur' we marched to 'Jaat,' beating a ravine on the road, near which we heard a bullock had yesterday been killed, but did not find any game worth firing at. The men started a bear, but we did not see it. On arriving at 'Jaat,' we collected as many men as possible over night, intending to have another try for our old enemy the 'man-eater' here, still the terror of the neighbourhood. Our plan was by starting at the first break of day to see if we could not cut off the tigress before it returned from its night foraging wanderings over the adjacent plain to lie up for the remainder of the day in its stronghold among the disused iron pits. The idea and chase seemed highly popular, for many men at once agreed to accompany us; so we betook ourselves to the iron pits, and then directed the men to spread themselves out over a large extent of ground and commence beating towards our position from a long distance. At this cool time of the morning there was no danger in thus separating the beaters, for we knew the tigress, if out in the plain at all, would at once make direct for its den on hearing the slightest noise. Our calculations were well founded, for scarcely had we heard the first faint noise of the drums and pistol-shots, when to our inconceivable joy we saw from a long way off the tigress making direct for our post. We allowed her to come at a long trot close on within about ten yards, when both our rifles simultaneously discharged dropped her. Two other shots made the kill secure. Great was the excitement of the people on hearing of our good luck, men at once ran off with the news, and the whole populace turned out to meet us on our return with the body, which was carried in triumph on small trees, hastily cut down for the purpose, through the town to our tent. Here we were met, as in this part of the country seems usual, by a bevy of females, the youngest and fairest of whom advanced and presented us with bunches of gay flowers, while the rest continued loudly singing some poetry in praise of all tiger-killers, generally recited on these occasions. Altogether a very pretty custom, quite dramatic! We got back to our tent about an hour after sunrise.

Before proceeding to skin this tigress, the people much wished us to await the arrival of a Bheel from some distance, whom they had sent for. It appeared that some time ago this man was cutting grass, in company with his brother, near this town, when the tigress suddenly sprang out upon his brother and carried him off, but not before the poor fellow had given the brute a severe cut with his small sickle over the face. All this was distinctly seen by the surviving brother, who, on his arrival, at once pointed out a deep scar or seam, now healed up, across the tiger's forehead. This at once removed all doubt as to this very brute being the noted 'man-eater,' which was afterwards confirmed by the fact that on our again visiting this place for three successive years, we heard of no other person being killed in the interim; although the people assured us that it had murdered in the preceding two years upwards of forty persons of this town alone. Thus ended the reign of terror so long established and well enforced of this rapacious pest. Appearances proved that she had left a hopeful family dependent on her well-known system of foraging. The evening before her death she had killed two bullocks, besides lying in wait for, and much terrifying a horseman, who was travelling towards 'Jaat.' This man narrowly escaped the beauty and her two young ones that accompanied her. It was from hearing his account of her being out in the plain that we planned the successful manœuvre which ended in the death of this tigress. She measured ten feet and a few inches; her tusks were, from some cause or accident, quite worn down, although she seemed in full vigour and very fat. Crowds of people from all the neighbouring villages came to look at it during the day; so we held quite a 'levee.' All agreed that no other method would probably have succeeded in destroying this cunning plague, for she had baffled many attempts.

We now determined to make another attempt to kill the tiger that wounded our beater on 18th March; and knowing the hopelessness of expecting any of the 'Dowlutpoora' men to assist us after the accident that had happened to their fellow villager, we started with forty-seven Bheels of this place to storm the cover where we were told this tiger still held possession. We reached the place, six miles off, by 9 A.M.; and having agreed to beat the ravine in a different direction, took up our position. It was by no means an enviable one, for we were on a bank or ledge of rock not four feet high, which was commanded from above, had the tiger appeared in our rear, and was merely sloping, in parts nearly level, below. However there was no better hiding place about. Almost directly the beating commenced, our enemy appeared most unexpectedly close. We instantly greeted her with the contents of our double rifles, which rolled her over, while another volley quite settled the business. This was a fine tigress, with a beautiful bright skin. Having thus had our revenge, we next went to see how the wounded Bheel was getting on, but finding him still in a bad way, he was at once started on a cot, carried by four men, for Camp, in charge of one of our servants, to have the benefit of the scientific attainments of our talented friend Dr M—e, 25th N.I. This man soon recovered, and often afterwards pluckily assisted us to kill other tigers.

We rode back to 'Jaat' in the evening. On the 26th March, while looking about, the fresh prints of a large tiger were discovered leading into a deep ravine. We mustered all our men, and started to beat the place. We had taken up our position on a very steep bank, and were anxiously waiting for the tiger's appearance, when, just as the noise of the beaters commenced, we were surprised by a stone falling from above and a little to the right of where we were posted. On looking up, we saw a splendid panther coming straight towards us. This compelled us to fire; had he been merely passing, as we were after nobler game, we should have let him alone for the time. We struck him with four bullets, on which he bounded down a small branch of the big ravine and was lost to sight, but only for a few moments; for, thinking he was bolting off, we each seized a spare gun and were running after him to get a parting shot, when, to my astonishment, I saw the panther in the act of charging down from a high rock directly over head. Instantly stopping short, I blazed both barrels into the beast, and then sprang off the rocky ledge on which we were standing into a small tree below.

Little, seeing me fire, immediately got ready, and as the panther was in the act of leaping after me, by an admirable shot in the head, actually rolled him over in the air while making his spring in a most determined charge. The panther came tumbling down head over heels, completely doubled up, through the boughs of the tree into which I had jumped, and fell dead at the foot of it. Little was only about three or four yards off at the time he made this wonderfully lucky shot, which no doubt saved me from a good 'mauling,' if not even worse.

We silently and quickly reloaded the empty guns, making signs to the men who came running up on hearing our shots, in the full conviction that we had killed the large tiger, to go back and continue the beating by rolling down the steep sides of the ravine large stones and rocks, which they directly recommenced doing, for we much feared that the tiger, having heard our shots in his front, would break either back or sideways out of the cover, instead of coming on, which, however, he fortunately did, for in a few minutes afterwards we saw a splendid fellow bounding up the steep sides of the ravine immediately opposite our first position, to which we had now returned. In another moment or so he was roaring and biting at everything near him, having received four rifle-balls in his body, one of which luckily broke his back. The rest of our 'battery' soon finished him. The distance was at least ninety yards where he fell. Without double flush-sighted rifles we could not have made such good practice at the pace he was going. This was the finest tiger we had as yet killed; he measured eleven feet eleven inches, counting from the end of his nose, between the ears, to the tip of his tail, and his head was enormous. Both the beasts, after they had been disembowelled to reduce the weight, were carried on tree-stumps with a good deal of trouble, the ground being very stony and broken, to our tent, where we skinned and pegged them down, afterwards rubbing in the arsenical soap to preserve the skins, before sunset. Altogether our good day's sport seemed to rather astonish the natives of these parts.

Excerpted from Tiger Shooting in India; Being an Account of Hunting Experiences on Foot in Rajpootana, During the Hot Seasons, From 1850 to 1854 *(London: Smith, Elder and Co., 1857).*

KESRI SINGH

Shikar Camps

Colonel Kesri Singh claimed to have been present at the killing of over a thousand tigers. For over four decades, starting in 1920, he organized shikar camps, first for the Maharaja of Gwalior, then for Jaipur's ruler, Man Singh. Kesri Singh, however, was a great votary for the tiger as a symbol of strength. He even claimed, though with little evidence, that tigers had wiped out lions in many of India's forests. He also oversaw a plan to restock Gwalior's Sheopur forests with lions brought in from Sudan: they bred, but had to be shot as some turned on people and cattle.

But Kesri Singh's books like Hints on Tiger Shooting *are mostly about the* bagh *or tiger, not the* simha *or lion. As late as the 1960s, he was organizing tiger drives for Jaipur's guests in the picturesque lake-side forests of Sawai Madhopur. It is perhaps ironical that this account was published in 1969. Even as he was recounting past exploits, such hunts were coming to an end. India was beginning at last to cherish and protect the tiger.*

The reserve where these hunts took place became a refuge for the tiger and its fellow inhabitants of the forest. Ranthambore, as it is now known, is one of the best places to watch tigers in the wild. But not so long ago the lake side echoed with rifle shots and huge parties came in for six to eight weeks a year pursuing the big cat. And Kesri Singh was the man in charge.

Shikar Camps at Sawai Madhopur

The Maharaja of Jaipur is a great sportsman and also has a remarkable taste in decorating and designing his various buildings and palaces. Evidence of this is a romantic Shooting Lodge in the beautiful jungles of Sawai Madhopur. The lodge is a small building, neat and comfortable, having a couple of bed-rooms on the first floor. There is a spacious lawn adjoining the house, big enough for croquet and badminton, providing an interesting interlude while the guests are waiting for tiger news.

In order to accommodate a large number of guests a camp is laid out consisting of several double and single pole tents, having baths and dressing rooms attached to each. A big shamiana (canvas pavilion) is pitched in the centre where all assemble before and after the shoot. This area is enclosed with a six-foot canvas screen to keep away trespassers. Recently six huts have been constructed to lodge the guests and this has done away with the necessity of putting up tents.

Inside this enclosure, there is plenty of room for the guests to take their morning exercise on camels. A camel ride before breakfast is a good specific for shaking the liver after a previous hang-over. When time permits, I often take some guests out on my camel and give them short rides round the camp. Some of the guests coming from foreign countries consider this not only beneficial but most entertaining as well.

About half a dozen elephants and camels are sent from headquarters to camp and they are stabled half a mile away from the main camp. In the space between the camp and the stables a temporary market crops up for the convenience of the camp followers.

Sawai Madhopur is a large tract of forest about a hundred miles south of Jaipur and the shooting area extends from the confluence of the river Banas with the Chambal in the midst of many ridges of the Aravali hills, and here stands the fortress of Ranthambhor cradled in its forgotten glory. It was through this valley that the power-drunk Sultan Allauddin Khilji of Delhi attacked Rana Hamir Deo, and a few centuries later Akbar, the greatest of the Moghuls, conquered the last of the major defences of this Rajput stronghold.

The Shooting Lodge is situated at the foot of the outer ranges of Ranthambhor and here we come annually to participate in the grand old game of shikar.

Thirty winters have found us there lock, stock and barrel, and one can look back on these hectic years of tumbling crowns and changing personalities at the people who have trodden these forests with us. We had among us His Majesty King George of Greece, the Duke of Gloucester, the Count and Countess Szechenyi, (the count being the best shot seen in these jungles), the Lady Alice Scott, daughter of the seventh Duke of Buccleuch, who is now the Duchess of Gloucester, with her brother who was serving the Royal Dragoons at Lucknow, Sir Harold Werner and his wife, the Princess Zia who was the daughter of the ill-starred Tsar Nicholas the second, the Georgian Prince Alec Mdvani and his Princess, the fabulous Woolworth millionairess, Barbara Hutton, Lord and Lady Jersey, the polo quartette from America, Laddie Sanford, Michael Phipps, Winston Guest (who is nephew of Sir Winston Churchill), and Earl Hopping and another famous polo-prince, H. H. Nawab Hamidullah of Bhopal, then at the peak of his form with a world-class handicap of nine as well as an assortment of British Residents and Agents to the Governor-General and Prime Ministers of Jaipur State, Sir Robert Throckmorton, Sir George Ogilvie, Sir Beauchamp St John and Sir Bertan Glancy; and the inevitable brilliance of Lord Louis Mountbatten and his delighted family.

Knit into this pattern of personalities were those of the Maharajas who used to form our house-parties, the most venerated of whom were the late Maharaja Sir Umaid Singhji of Jodhpur, who received the rank of Air Marshal in the Royal Air Force and whom we all hailed as 'Monarch', the striking figure of the Jam Sahib, and the great sporting-princes of Kotah, Cooch-Behar; Panna, Baria, Kishangarh, and others. To top the whole list Her Imperial Majesty Queen Elizabeth II of England visited these forests two years ago with her Royal consort the Duke of Edinburgh.

To give an idea of a full day's programme at the Camp I would like to give some extracts from my diary of some successful days which will adequately illustrate our life in this forest.

In the year 1944 we were camping here to provide some sport to Lord Louis Mountbatten, Lady Edwina, and their charming daughter Lady Pamela. Lord Louis was then the Supreme Commander of the South East Asia Command and was on his way to Australia from London, when he broke his journey to be with his friend, the Maharaja of Jaipur, who insisted that he should shoot a few tigers. He was much engrossed in problems of his Command and so he himself refused to shoot but allowed his daughter to take part in it.

To commemorate his visit I had specially prepared a new tiger-beat in the jungle and called it after his name, 'Mountbatten Drive'.

He was surprised to find his name stuck out in tiger territory and it also proved very lucky. In the shoot arranged for his daughter the guns were posted on two separate machans and the beat started at 12.30 P.M. A tiger was driven out successfully up to the Hon'ble Lady Pamela who shot it. The shoot was over by 1.30 P.M. and all the guests assembled in a small patch of green forest close to the scene of action for the usual picnic-lunch. Matters relating to the beat and the appearance of the animal were all discussed over lunch. Some of the guests who had unwittingly gone out for a camel ride were regretting the effects which had made them rather too stiff for the small hill-climb. It was amusing to hear them groaning and complaining and after lunch they stretched themselves out for a little nap.

On another occasion a tiger shoot was arranged at Kali Doongri in which three tigers were bagged by Sir Robert Throckmorton and his two friends.

After tea the guests used to go for drives on the Shikar roads to shoot whatever might come their way. Once I arranged a kill for a panther, and Princess Prem Kumari, the daughter of the Maharaja of Jaipur, whom we affectionately call Mickey, was to shoot the animal.

By half past seven all the guests returned to the Shooting Lodge bringing home a good mixed bag of bear, sambar, chital, pig and partridge. Princess Mickey came back with the panther she had shot over the kill.

After a quick wash-up we all gathered round the camp-fire. A cooking party had been arranged in which everybody lent a hand and a recipe. As I sat by the barbecue with my hunter's pot giving out pagan vapours, our witty hostess the Maharani of Jaipur came over to see what exactly I was cooking this time. She and the Maharaj Kumar Bhawani Singh (Bubbles) pulled my leg over it. 'Bubbles,' the eldest son of the Maharaja, is now serving in the President's Body Guard at Delhi and is a very endearing young man with a sweet temper and winning smile which blend well with his bearing of a sportsman, soldier, and son and heir of the Maharaja. It was ten o'clock before our food was ready and the cooking competition was won by Raja Amarnath Atal.

The next day we had two tiger beats, one before and the other after lunch. It was at Patwa Baori that Lord Jersey got his first tiger and in the second beat a Bodel Prince Alec Mdvani got another tiger. On the third day we had an early beat at Seldhar in which

Mr Woodward (Jr.) shot a tiger before lunch. We had a general shoot in the afternoon in which one bear, a few heads of sambar, spotted deer, chinkara and a wild boar were shot. On another occasion the Maharaja of Baria wounded a ten-foot tiger at Kali Doongri. This gave us a little excitement because he went back towards the beat after being wounded. The Maharaja of Jaipur as usual went to finish it from the back of an elephant. The forest in this area had a growth of small trees whose branches met at about the height of the howdah making it very difficult for him to see anything. As he could not see properly from the howdah, he got down and finished the tiger by meeting him face to face on the ground.

The year 1945 saw another memorable Shikar Camp at Sawai Madhopur. I had a few accidents which could have proved fatal if luck wasn't running my way. It generally takes a long time before all the 'khabar' (tiger news) reaches the headquarters from the various places. To avoid this I go out personally to some of these places very early in the morning to collect the information.

The day after of our arrival at the camp I went out at crack of dawn and as I was nearing the Patwa Baori jungle I ran over a snake and before I had gone a little further I saw a few vultures sitting in the middle of the road. My closed V-8 was going at a speed of about forty and I thought that they would get out of the way. In this I was mistaken as the birds were very heavy and clumsy. The result was that some of them got away but the others crashed on to the windscreen and one broke through the triplex glass and landed on the lap of my Shikari who was sitting in the front seat. Had it been ordinary glass the velocity with which the dead bird hit the Shikari's chest may have proved fatal. I write this for the benefit of sportsmen and also the speedster as a warning against these birds.

I pulled up the car and while we were cleaning it and throwing out the bird I found the snake which I had run over crawling under the mattress. How it was tossed in the air by the fast moving wheel and managed to creep inside the car is still a mystery to me. I was told of a similar accident happening to Mr Bell, the chauffeur of the late Maharaja Pratap Singhji of Kashmir, but I hardly believed him until it happened to me today.

In spite of the above two accidents I was rewarded with good news from three places. I returned to the camp and despatched the

elephants, beaters, flags and machans to those places, and at
12.30 P.M. started a beat in the Sone Kutch area.

On this occasion I had promised a tiger to Sir Beauchamp St.
John, and, therefore, I gave him the better of the two machans. On
the second machan I had put Rao Raja Hanut Singh. Hanut is one
of Jaipur's polo wizards who took all England by storm some 25
years ago when polo in Jaipur had touched the peak that could not
be challenged. In the beat there was only one tiger and he defeated
all my efforts to drive him up to the first machan. The result was
that he appeared at the second and was shot by Hanut.

In the evening another beat was organized at Bodel. The tiger
here was a very cunning animal and refused to be driven in the usual
way. Wherever he found a cluster of thick bushes he would lie low
and would not come out until the beaters were almost on top of
him. When he did come out he made a dash for another thicket
and remained there until the beat closed on him again.

It is my usual habit to go with the beaters just to see that the
tiger was properly driven towards the guns. On this occasion I was
bringing up the left flank when I found that this tiger had been
driven before and fired at. He, therefore, was reluctant to cross the
firing line. However, I rallied a few strong beaters and Shikaries and
took them up to the last thicket in which he had taken up a strong
position. The animal started growling as if he was about to attack.
The firing line was not far away. To discourage him from attacking
us I told the beaters to let off a few blank shots and I covered him
with my loaded rifle.

The scheme worked out successfully and the tiger rushed out of
the bush with a loud roar and went galloping and passed the firing
line. He was going across at such high speed that if it had been an
ordinary gun he would probably have missed but fortunately I had
Count Szechenyi sitting on the machan and he being a good shot
brought him down with a bullet in the neck.

After the shoot was over we collected under a shady banyan tree
and had a picnic tea. It was here that we discussed our evening
programme and most of the guests decided to go out for the usual
drive on the Shikar roads for a miscellaneous shoot.

There was a complaint of a cattle-lifter from Sherpur who had
recently killed a few men who had tried to protect their herds. I
wanted to have this animal destroyed but, finding the place rather
difficult for a beat, I had arranged that he should be shot over a

kill at night. I, therefore, suggested to the Maharaja that while the guests go out for their shooting drive, he should shoot this tiger and save the public from this menace. He agreed to my suggestion and asked two American ladies, who had just arrived, if they would like to accompany him. The ladies, being quite happy with the new surroundings, declined the offer saying that they would rather rest and join the next day's shoot. However, the Maharaja with M. K. Pushpendra Singh of Panna, who is generally called 'Push,' and myself entered the machan early in the evening.

Half an hour after the sun had gone down, we heard a stone rolling on our right from where the tiger was approaching the buffalo. The buffalo got alarmed and we stared in the direction trying to locate the animal. At this critical moment we heard soft steps approaching our machan from the other direction. At first I thought the tiger had changed his position and was now approaching from the other side. Fortunately, there was a full moon and what I saw were the two American ladies whom the Maharaja had asked to join the party but who had refused to do so, coming straight to the machan all by themselves.

The situation was very serious as the animal for which we were waiting had a bad reputation for killing human beings and the women had arrived at a critical time when he was prowling round to catch his victim. There was complete silence from the side of the tiger and it was possible that he had seen the ladies and was stalking them. All this flashed through my mind quickly, and to prevent any accident happening I started talking loudly to the ladies so as to divert the tiger's attention. I quickly came down the machan and joined them also. The Maharaja was also alarmed with the situation and came down himself so that no accident might happen. It was useless to wait for this tiger any more because we had given away our position to the tiger; so we walked back to our car taking the ladies with us.

The ladies were questioned as to why they had decided to commit suicide by walking towards the man-eater. They never realized the seriousness of the situation but merely kept saying that they just wanted to see the fun. Every time when we wanted to bring home to them the perilous situation they had put themselves in, all they said was 'O.K.' and refused to believe that any step of their crazy jaunt could have been fatal to them. Their reply revived my faith in the old, old saying that 'ignorance is bliss.'

The next morning I started early as usual to have news of the tiger. When I reached Nagdigudah, a small forest village, I ran in to a tribesman belonging to the Bawria clan who lived and hunted in these forests long before Ranthambhor was built. Nathu was his name and he looked fairly old when I met him two years ago. He had helped me in locating a nasty tiger and we became friends. When I met him this morning he introduced himself as Nathu Bawria. He looked so young and different that I hardly believed my eyes until he told me a most remarkable story of how he got rejuvenated. He said that while hunting for food he saw a bird of the size of a hawk which he shot and ate. This, he claims, did the trick. He could not identify the bird and said it was the first and the last of the kind he had ever seen. Since then I always think of Nathu whenever I see a strange bird of that size.

It is, however, true that some of these unusual varieties of meat are superb tonics and are well suited for certain diseases. On Nathu's recommendation I have been eating one jackal every winter and that relieves me of rheumatic pains that have come with old age. He also told me that eating the queen of white ants is a wonderful general tonic. The most precious meat of all the animals is that of a pangolin. It is supposed to make one feel ten years younger. I have described in another chapter tiger products, but I have not mentioned whether people eat tiger meat or not. Nathu Bawria was telling me that one can eat it in moderation.

Talking about snakes he told me that if one comes across an albino cobra snake it is the luckiest thing one could desire. The head and tail is cut off and the rest is cooked as a broth and eaten. The belief is that a man who eats such a snake can become air-borne at will.

After I had heard a few folklore tales from Nathu, my Shikaries came around with good tiger news. I went straight back to the camp to make the usual arrangements. The place where we had the first beat was at Moredungri forest where Col. Philips of the Royal Guards shot the tiger while it was bolting fast across the firing line.

Since there was another tiger at Patwa Baori, we had a hurried lunch amidst the forest surroundings and by 3.30 P.M. we reached the place.

This beat produced two tigers out of which one was shot by Sir Arthur Lothian while the other went high up on the hill and made good his escape by breaking through the flankers. A bear also came out in the beat when the Maharaja of Sirmoor took a shot. The bear was wounded and went back towards the beat. A search was made for him and one of my Shikaries, Suraj Bhan, thinking it was dead, approached it. The animal quickly got up and caught him. There were a few other Shikaries on the spot and they speared the bear before he could cause much injury.

The next day I did not get any news from the neighbouring jungles but good news was brought from another jungle 60 miles away where no camp arrangement had been made. It generally requires one week's notice to have a camp laid out for shooting excursions and finding that we had no time at our disposal we gave up the idea of going there.

I remember I had the same difficulty once in Gwalior when conflicting news was received from five different places, situated in different directions, that we could not decide where to arrange the camp. That arrangement was being made for General Rawlinson, Commander-in-Chief of India, in 1923. He being a seasoned soldier, I knew he would not mind living in a caravan car. I, therefore, suggested to the Maharaja of Gwalior that no camping arrangement should be made as the place could not be fixed. When His Excellency came, he should be taken out in the caravan cars, of which we had about half a dozen. My suggestion was approved and we actually did this on that occasion and I am glad to say that we enjoyed the trip better than if we had been under canvas. Finding ourselves in the same situation. I suggested to my boss that he should also have a few caravan cars made for use on such occasions. A caravan car under a shady tree gives one more comfort than a tent.

The next day was the last day of the camp. I went out as usual in the morning to ascertain the tiger news. The Raja Sahib of Kathari and his son Ram Singh accompanied me. Not receiving any good news we decided to return. It was about 11.30 A.M. and as we were approaching Kushli Dara I saw a sort of dirty bundle lying in the middle of the road. We were travelling fairly fast and when I approached that bundle within 50 yards, it came to life and stood in the middle of the road. It was a big panther who probably was lying there to catch a victim not realizing that somebody might turn up who may be looking for him. Being a big animal he did not like to run away but just left the road with an angry snarl on his face. The Raja had loaded his rifle and just as we passed him at close range he fired and dropped him stone-dead.

In the evening all guests went out for drives on the Shikar roads. The Maharaja and Maharani of Jaipur desired to shoot a bear. It is rather difficult to produce a bear to order in this jungle because they were not very plentiful here. However, I took them to Jhumar Baori forest, hoping for the best. As we were going, we first came across a big wild boar crossing the road. The Maharaja being fond of pork lost no time in potting it. We had hardly gone a little further when, as good luck would have it, we saw a bear on our right, digging at an ant-hole and sucking the termites. The car was pulled up and a quick shot was taken which missed the vital part and the animal ran across the road to our left and disappeared. There was only one rifle and a gun with us and finding the bear wounded and disappearing we left the car and followed it. We went round in circle without seeing the bear and the bear had not seen us either. The animal in the meantime crossed the road again passing closely to the car where the Maharani was standing without any weapon in her hand, but fortunately she was not seen by the bear. The Maharani now gave us the signal on which we quickly came and bagged the animal. It was quite an exciting incident in which the wounded bear just missed the Maharani and it was a topic much talked over in the evening when we had assembled for drinks.

The next day we broke the camp after lunch, but before doing so we had a tiger beat at Chinali where the Maharaja of Baria shot one of a normal size.

I have tried to give a brief picture of our activities during our annual Shikar camps at Sawai Madhopur. There had been a very large number of guests every year who had joined us in our shooting camp and if I attempted to describe the bag of everyone it would make it rather monotonous. I therefore close the chapter here.

Cooch-behar Shooting Camp in Assam

I have mentioned before in the chapter on 'Tiger Shooting from Howdah Elephants' that Nepal and Assam are two ideal places where tigers can be shot from howdah elephants with considerable ease.

There are a few other places in the Tarrai, with long elephant grass, where tigers are shot from howdah elephants but they are not organized on a big scale. I had once occasion to join such a shoot organized by His Highness the Nawab Sahib of Rampur when half a dozen elephants were employed to beat the tigers out which were all shot from howdah elephants.

Nepal, certainly, is the most famous place in the world for the kind of sport where several hundred elephants are used to form a ring round or drive the game towards the guns. Any animal within the ring has to face the guns. A very successful shoot of this kind was organized for His Imperial Majesty King George V of England when he visited Nepal. Several tigers and other big game including rhino and wild buffaloes were shot in the shoot.

In India Cooch-Behar used to be the only place where such shoots used to take place. The father and grandfather of the present Maharaja were well-known sportsmen. After the formation of the Indian Union, game in Cooch-Behar has become scarce, therefore the Maharaja now has to go to Assam for his excursions.

I had a few chances of joining these expeditions when many tigers were shot. And I would like to give a description of two or three shots which will give a good idea as how tigers are shot in grassy jungles. The method used there is slightly different from that used in thickly wooded forests.

Baits are put out every evening in such areas as are the natural retreat of tigers. Such arrangements are made not only in one but in various places likely to contain tigers. Very early in the morning scouts are sent out to see the baits and bring in report of a kill. On receiving news of the kill, Capt. Narayan, who was in charge of the elephants, went out with all the animals, leaving a few howdah elephants for the shooters to follow.

On reaching the spot, after a cursory inspection, it is soon discovered in which direction the tiger had gone after the kill. The howdah elephants with the shooters are posted after clearing a firing line in front of them so that they can see the animal coming towards them.

Having fixed up all this, the rest of the elephants form a line, with the flankers on right and left of the line taking up advanced positions. The whole beat moves forward with the two flanks always moving in advance. A beat of this kind was organized on New Year's Day near the Rawta forest range office when Mr Wes. Dixon, Jr, and Mr Tample Buell were mounted in howdahs and posted in their places.

It was a grand sight to see a line of 26 elephants beating the long grass. They advanced silently in a line, each forcing his way straight ahead only deviating from his course when some large tree or branch impeded his progress. The silence was occasionally broken by the crash of a tree knocked down by the elephants, or by the angry trumpet of an enraged animal as he was forced through a thorny thicket or by the abuse heaped upon a lazy or restive elephant by the mahout.

I was in a howdah with Mr Dixon, and Capt. Narayan was with Mr Buell. We constantly directed their attention to anything that moved in the grass. A little stir in the grass and much commotion was caused when some animals were roused. Rifles were raised as the moving grass showed the direction in which the animal was going but on the appearance of a deer they were lowered again.

A little later another rush accompanied by an angry grunt of pigs headed by an old boar who became ill-tempered on being roused from his noon-day slumber, charged back through the beating line and after inflicting a cut on the leg of the nearest elephant broke through.

The line advanced further when an old tusker raised his trunk, then struck it angrily on the ground showing plainly that he was aware of the presence of something that displeased him intensely. His uneasiness was pretty certain proof of a tiger being near. The cover was not very wide here, and after the alarm given by the tusker the rest of the elephants closed up and advanced in compact form preventing any animals from breaking through.

Presently we saw a movement in the grass directly in front of our elephant and I cautioned my friend Dixon to get ready. It was a tiger who having seen our elephant standing in his way first roared and then tried to pass the line on our right flank. My friend fired and was very lucky in killing him with a clean shot on the shoulder.

About the same time as the tiger passed our right flank the tigress, which was also in the beat, came out with a growl and rushed along the left flank of Mr Buell who also secured his trophy in good style.

On another occasion we were shooting on the left bank of Dhanseri River. Capt. Narayan was with Mr Werner, and Capt. Roy with Mr Hermaun, while I was in another howdah with their wives. The Maharaja of Cooch-Behar was on an elephant all by himself.

The country over which we were shooting that morning was a long stretch of narsal grass and low lying ravines where it touched the river. The three howdah elephants with the two shooters and their wives were posted at spots which were supposed to be the tiger's natural retreat. Before posting the guns it was necessary to clean the ground in front of the guns so as to give a view of the animal approaching them. On a signal, the elephants got busy in trampling the long grass and breaking down small trees with their legs, heads and trunks. In a very short time the long grass and the undergrowth were crushed down and trees uprooted or broken all over the required area.

The beat soon started and the line moved in good style. There was much excitement in the line when one of the elephants trumpeted giving warning to all that a tiger had been spotted. It was not a long beat and the tiger, taking advantage of a thick growth of grass on the right flank, dashed out across the line to the right of Mr Werner's elephant who fired at the fleeting tiger and hit him. The tiger gave a roar when hit but soon disappeared from our view into the thick undergrowth behind our line. It was certain that the animal was hit but where he had gone we did not know.

The beat was stopped at once and new plans were made. We put the shooting elephants in the middle and forming a line on both their flanks we advanced slowly towards the direction taken by the wounded tiger. We had not gone very far when the tiger growled and roared. The roars of the tiger mingled with the trumpeting of the elephants and the yelling of the men on the pad elephants who set up a ceaseless and deafening noise created great excitement. It was really a most exciting business to tackle a wounded tiger in thick grass where he could lie unseen within a few feet of the elephant. It is always the elephant which gives the alarm when he smells a tiger.

The tiger after giving a warning signal moved forward. The line was also rearranged and followed in his wake. After advancing a short distance suddenly pandemonium broke out on the left flank, the elephants trumpeting, fidgeting and curling up their trunks with the usual shouts and yells, clearly indicating that the tiger was in that direction. He broke cover again and charged at the howdah elephants when the Maharaja whose elephant was not far from us turned round and with quick aim put a shot into the beast and knocked him over much to our relief.

We broke up the shoot for the morning, giving time to the elephants and their attendants to eat, drink and rest while we also had beer and lunch on the bank of the river. At 4 P.M. we started

another beat two miles down the river where Mr Hermaun shot
another big tiger.

I would like to give a description of one more shoot in Assam
before I close the chapter. This was arranged for Mr and Mrs James
Stewart and Mr and Mrs Kirk Johnson. James Stewart and his wife
Gloria are world-famous American actors.

The previous shoots mentioned above took place in the forest
range of Rawta, while this shoot was arranged in the forest of
Raimona. In this forest the rhino and wild buffalo do not exist, but
herds of wild elephants are found all over the place. Among the
carnivora tiger, panther and wild dogs are found. The deer tribe is
represented by sambar, chital, hog deer, barking deer and occasionally swamp deer. Other animals often seen are bears, pigs and grey
apes (langurs). Among the birds you see the hornbill jungle-fowl,
black partridge and pea-fowl. Wild duck and snipe are found in the
jheels.

One fine morning we left camp after breakfast on our elephants
to a place three miles to the south of our camp. Capt. Narayan was
on the elephant with Mr James Stewart, Capt. Roy and with
Mrs Stewart who was also a shooter, while I was with Mr and
Mrs Johnson. On reaching our destination, we were given good
news of a kill and the people assured us that they had seen the tiger
moving in the direction of the kill a short time before our arrival.

It was a typically suitable jungle for shooting tigers and therefore
we did not take much time in posting the howdah elephants and
starting the beat. The line advanced in perfect order until one of
the elephants in the beat gave the alarm signifying that a tiger was
moving in front of him. We kept on watching the elephant who
gave the warning but the tiger in the meantime had shifted his
position and next time he was detected 50 yards away.

On the beat coming closer we saw the grass moving and the tiger
making his way towards Mr James Stewart. He got ready just in
time before it broke cover and dashed across the firing line at a fast
speed. The world-renowned actor acted quickly and correctly by
hitting the beast as he went past him. The tiger then entered the
cover behind our line but it was not long before we found him dead
and loaded him on one of the pad elephants.

My companion Mr Johnson was a very kind and generous person
and being well advanced in age the whole party, including his wife,

called him 'Father'. I was very keen that he should get a tiger and God soon fulfilled my wishes. On the next occasion when we went out for our shoot I sat with him.

This was a different place from the one we had been to the previous day. There was the track of motor trucks which had passed through this area and we took advantage of this. We posted the howdah elephants along this track with Mr James Stewart on the left, Gloria (his wife) in the centre and Mr Johnson on the right. The beat started in good time and shortly we were alerted by the trumpeting of the elephants and while we all were looking into the grass in front I saw the tiger moving which I pointed out to my companion Mr Johnson. The tiger proved too quick to notice my movement and so he stopped where he was. The line of elephants was closing in on him from the back and he had seen the danger in front of him, so he moved away nearly 50 yards further to our right and then dashed across the line. As we were all alert we saw him going across and Mr Johnson lost no time in levelling his rifle and firing as the beast was disappearing into the thick grass. The distance was too long and the animal was so quick that I thought it was a clean miss.

We collected all the elephants at the spot where the tiger had entered the thick grass and after forming a line with our elephants in the centre we advanced slowly and carefully. We had not gone more than 20 yards when we saw a blood trail. There was great excitement throughout the advancing line and naturally the progress was slow. The tiger after being wounded did not change his direction but moved fast in a straight line and therefore he was easy to follow and within a short distance he was found stone-dead. What actually happened was that the bullet hit him in the heart and the tiger after going 50 yards dropped dead. This is characteristic when it is shot through the heart.

My friend and myself were very pleased to see a fine 10-foot tiger stretched out in an open space. We soon got down from our elephants, had a few photographs taken and after getting him loaded on another elephant marched back to the camp in triumph.

I was feeling much relieved after providing one tiger each to our two friends but Gloria also wanted to shoot one. During the remaining days in the camp we tried to give her a tiger but one thing or other kept on happening in such a way that she could not succeed. She however shot a panther with me at Jaipur a week later. We call it a good shooting camp in which all the shooters got trophies.

Excerpted from Hints on Tiger Shooting [Tigers by Tiger] *(Mumbai: Jaico Publishing House, 1969).*

PART II

Animal-Watching: The Pioneers

Even at a time when wild India was seen as a vast killing field for sport-hunters or a limitless well from which to draw timber, there were dissenting voices in the woods. Even elite sensibilities were undergoing change. Partly this was because game was scarce in many of its former haunts, prompting concerns about conservation. It seemed a good idea to restrain white hunters and the Indian landed gentry—not to abolish all sport, but to ensure it could continue into the future. Some foresters went beyond this, arguing that even game-killing predators deserved to live. Others began to watch animals, note how they hunted or foraged and what enabled some species to survive human pressures even as others perished. Indians too joined in these pursuits: the occasional prince became a naturalist in addition to playing the hunter; members of the merchant communities too took to watching wildlife. More Indian sport-hunters wrote memoirs, a sign of the change that was coming about by the mid-twentieth century. It was slow in maturing but its seeds were sown earlier on by men and women who can only be called pioneers.

A. A. DUNBAR BRANDER

Tigers in the Wild

*For six years the veteran hunter and forester Dunbar Brander put
away his guns to simply observe how wild animals lived and what
they did. In sharp contrast to most early 'tiger books', his is not
a 'how to' account with tips for hunters out to reduce the great
feline to a trophy or a skin on the wall. It is a pity so little was
recorded about tigers when they were so abundant. But Dunbar
Brander was a top-notch naturalist, an early pioneer among people
who watched tigers. To this day, his province, Madhya Pradesh,
remains a tiger stronghold. Much of his work was in the Banjar
Valley Reserved Forest, now the heart of Kanha National Park.
There is even a sub-species of the swamp deer named after him.
But it was as a tiger-man that he first won renown.*

Tigers breed at all seasons, but there are two well-marked periods
during which the majority of the cubs are born—one period after
the rains in November, and the other in April about the time the
hot weather sets in. At the time of pairing, the tiger and tigress are
found together. Both Blanford and Lydekker state that the tiger is
monogamous: on what grounds I cannot say, as I have often known
a tiger to be in 'tow' with two tigresses at the same time. Moreover,
the number of the sexes is not equal, tigresses being more numerous.
The proportion of the two sexes shot is not a correct criterion of
their relative numbers, as tigresses with young cubs are often
difficult to secure. They frequently return to the cubs during the
day and their cunning is developed by maternity.

When pairing, old male tigers sometimes become dangerous;
possibly irritated by the resistance of the female who appears to

expect a rough courting and often gets it, as the marks on the back of her neck will sometimes show. Another motive prompting aggression. may be the desire to 'show off' before the female—a common motive in animals, including man.

An excellent instance of a tiger attacking a man owing to sexual excitement happened to a retainer of mine. He was going along a wide jungle road not far from my camp at dusk. A tigress trotted out, closely attended by a big tiger, and went down the road in front of and away from the man. The man halted; but the tiger happened to turn round, and seeing him, promptly charged. Trees were scarce, the only possible shelter being a Salai (*Boswellia serrata*) tree about 200 yards off. The man was being rapidly overhauled, but had the sense to drop his turban which the tiger stopped to worry. Not satisfied with this, however, the tiger continued the pursuit, and the man just succeeded in scrambling into the tree. The tiger then stood on his hind legs and clawed at the man, but failed to reach him. Both tigers then went into a neighbouring nala and renewed their courtship, the tiger from time to time returning and demonstrating at the man. Meanwhile, the sun went down and the wretched man had to spend the night perched on a limb of the tree in the bitter cold, without food or drink, and most inadequately clothed. At last the wished-for day arrived, and half frozen, he clambered down only to be promptly charged again, barely escaping with his life. He was kept there until nine o'clock, when a cart happened to pass, and shouting to the cartman who replied, the tigers moved off and the poor wretch was rescued. This tiger was in the same locality for a long time after this episode, and never molested anyone, and as I have known of other cases in which they were dangerous at this period, there is little doubt as to the cause of his behaviour in this instance.

Before the cubs are born, the sexes separate, the tigress preferring to be alone until the cubs have a sense of the fitness of things, and the correct attitude towards their male parent. I have known two instances in which a young male tiger had apparently annoyed his father over the dead buffalo they were eating, and in consequence was killed and partly devoured. I came on another case in which a young tiger had been killed and eaten, in which there was no 'bone of contention.'

The tigress will drop her cubs anywhere in the jungle, but often selects a rough shelter of rocks or a cave. Any number up to six at a time may be born, but two or three is the usual number. Best mentions a case in which as many as seven fœtuses were found in a tigress. Lydekker states that when two cubs are born they are always a male and a female. This is certainly not so, as I have even known cases of not merely two but as many as three being all of the same sex. The period of gestation is only fifteen weeks and the cubs are relatively small when born. A long period of gestation with a large fœtus would make it very difficult for the mother to secure her food, and the danger of accidents and miscarriages would be great. The cubs are moved by the mother if she has been seriously disturbed. At night she will remove one after the other to an entirely different valley, carrying them in her mouth. When about two months old they leave the lair and gradually extend their wander-ings, and by the time they are the size of a spaniel regularly accompany the mother. Tigresses have the maternal instinct less strongly developed than panthers, and although they will sometimes defend their young, fear usually overcomes affection and they will slink off. I have known two cases of a tigress following up and demonstrating at the men who were removing her dead cub, and one case in which a large cub followed up the mother. On this occasion, it was dark before we got out of the jungle, and the experience was most unpleasant.

The cubs often remain with the tigress until they are two years old; they are then between 7 and 8 ft. long. At this stage the tigress is usually about to initiate another family and the cubs are discarded. I have known cases however in which cubs born at two different periods have accompanied the tigress. In such circumstances the first family has consisted of one cub only, and the interval between breeding has been short. Before the old cubs are discarded, family parties are not uncommonly met with, but do not last long, as no doubt the approach of the breeding season and the presence of papa is a strong hint to the youngsters to clear out. The largest party I have ever seen together consisted of six animals—one large male and two fully-grown females, accompanied by three young animals almost as big as the tigresses. I had a good view of them as they crossed an open nala after being hunted off the putrid carcass of a chital stag. Parties of five are not uncommon, and I once saw three full-grown males all together.

Tigers grow until they are five years old, and for many years after this they continue to put on muscle and fill out: as a man does after growth has ceased. The age to which tigers live is not known, but I believe it to be much greater than is generally supposed. I once killed a well-recognized tiger of marked characteristics which had been known to be in the same jungle for fifteen years. He must have been some age, at least five, before attention was drawn to him and thus not less than twenty years old when I shot him. He then appeared to be in his prime, with perfect teeth and without any signs of decadence.

One hardly ever comes on a tiger which has died a natural death, and I have only come across two diseased animals out of some two hundred animals I have seen shot. One of these had a complaint of the liver, and the other had small cysts in the lungs containing small white worm-like parasites. Both were very thin. The oft-repeated tale that a tiger's age can be told by the lobes of the liver is a myth; to give one instance, a tame tiger which was eighteen months old had eleven lobes.

Tigers inhabit any jungle of sufficient size which affords food, water and shade. They are found as permanent residents in every district in the Central Provinces except two, and all the Central districts traversed by the main Satpura Range and its offshoots still contain many tigers. They are also numerous in Raipur, Chanda, Bastar and the Feudatory States and Zemindaris in the east of the Province. Nevertheless, tigers have vanished from the comparatively open nalas in which our ancestors found it so easy to kill them, and even in my time they have disappeared, or at most are only occasional visitors in many of the outlying jungles.

The usual daily round of a tiger is to commence questing for food shortly before sunset and to continue doing so all night. In thus questing, they go at a slow walk often following the beds of nalas and jungle roads, especially so in the cold weather when cover is dense and the grass is wet and cold. Their chief desideratum is any spot along which they can proceed silently and which affords a fair vision. In spite of frequent halts to listen for game they often cover great distances during the night. While questing through the jungle the tiger glides silently along. He seems to flow past one like a phantom. This impression is created by his silent tread, but more so by his action, which seems specially adapted for concealment. Both limbs on the same side move together or almost so, and it is this which produces the gliding effect. The only motion which draws attention is the flick of the ear when tickled by grass or a fly.

The ears are full of wax which probably attracts flies; at any rate the tiger is very intolerant of any touch on the ear.

I have seen a tiger half asleep in a cave keeping up a constant twitching of his ears to keep off the flies, and they are probably so accustomed to this motion they cannot avoid giving effect to it on the slightest touch. The highly developed series of hair combs specially adapted to exclude flies and which is so commonly found in antelopes are absent from the tiger's ear. They retire shortly after sunrise to some shady spot where they sleep. In doing this they will adopt any position, either lying on their sides or at full length on their stomachs with their heads between their paws, but a common position when gorged is to lie flat on their backs with all four feet sticking up into the air. Although easily approached when in this position and under the conditions which induced it, to place a bullet in the right position is difficult, and the hunter is advised to arouse the tiger before firing. Another common habit of tigers is to take a dust bath, which they do by rolling in sand or more commonly in the powdered earth of a cart track. They are always infested with ticks. These ticks greedily attack human beings and usually give most virulent bites, the irritation from which disappears but slowly. Ticks harbouring on ungulates are a different species and are tardy to fasten on human beings.

In cold frosty weather they often go up to the hill-tops and sun themselves before lying up for the day. I have often remarked that in Sal Forests tigers are much more liable to be encountered wandering about during the day than in Teak and Mixed Forests. In the hot weather tigers prefer to be near water, and if they can find a shady pool will often lie in the water up to their necks or refresh themselves by a bath from time to time. Although tigers usually drink twice during the twenty-four hours in the hot weather, I have known cases in which they have preferred not to drink at all, and to remain near their kill rather than go a long distance to water.

Another habit of tigers, which they occasionally practise, is to sharpen or clean their claws on trees. This habit seems to be more an individual peculiarity constantly practised, rather than a general habit occasionally practised; as where the marks on trees are seen they are usually numerous and made by the same animal, whereas miles of jungle containing tigers may be devoid of all signs of the habit. I knew a particular Mohwa tree in a certain valley in the

Melghat where a tiger regularly scraped his claws every three weeks or so. He evidently stood up on his hind legs and pulled his claws down, making deep incisions in the bark. This practice had been going on for years, but no other tigers for miles round indulged in it.

It is necessary to mention one more habit of tigers. Before passing their dung they scrape a bare patch on the ground. In doing this the tiger appears to be suddenly seized with a form of cramp, and they shovel their two hind feet back and fore touching each other and scraping the ground so as to leave a clear patch about 12 in. long and 6 in. wide. They then move their heels to the end of the bare place and relieve themselves on the patch. Although they will do this on bare ground it seems clear that the habit is a hygienic one. The fæces of tiger is a black tarry viscid substance, which if deposited in grass would often befoul the tiger's hind quarters. Tigers are very cleanly in their habits, and it is rare to shoot one that has not been perfectly groomed. Although indifferent to their state when killing and eating an animal, they set to and clean themselves thoroughly with their tongues immediately after feeding.

If in the course of the night's wanderings they succeed in killing, they proceed to eat, commencing between the buttocks. They often drag out the stomach as if aware that by so doing the meat would remain fresher. In most cases leopards tear out the inside and commence to eat the heart, liver, lungs and flesh on the ribs. The kill of the two animals can be distinguished by this, but I have known very large leopards such as are often found inside forests and away from villages, feed like a tiger. If a large animal has been killed, he eats up to the ribs the first night and finishes the remains the next night. As the sun rises, the tiger's first care is to secrete his kill, especially from vultures. He does this by dragging it under a bush. If the jungle is a long way off, they will often tear up grass with their teeth and so cover the kill. I have watched them in the act and once shot one with a sheaf in his mouth. I have also known a tiger lie down and go to sleep actually on the top of a dead bullock so as to protect it.

The majority of animals after eating go to water, and if the kill is near a suitable place, they return to its vicinity and then lie up for the day, commencing to feed again about dusk. It is astonishing what a hungry tiger can eat, and I have known three-quarters of a fair-sized buffalo to be swallowed at one meal. When thoroughly gorged, tigers take no serious steps to procure another meal for two days. It is probable that on the average they do not kill more than once in four or five days. When returning to their kill they do so cautiously. Their method of eating is to lick off wads of meat with their tongues, which are bristly, and when a fair-sized piece has been semi-detached, it is severed with the incisors. Skin, bones and all are eaten; hair seems to take the place of vegetables and they do not thrive without it. Their food is entirely animal, but I have been shown cow dung part of which had been eaten and which I was assured was the work of a sick tiger. I cannot vouch for this, however.

Besides killing for themselves, tigers will eat any fresh carcass they may happen across, and I have even known them eat animals which were absolutely putrid. I have already mentioned six tigers on a putrid chital stag. This animal was one I had wounded and lost, and it had been lying dead in long grass for a week. I discovered it by the smell. The men sent to fetch the head returned in great excitement, reporting several tigers on the carcass, and when I arrived I found that the body was a mere shell and that these tigers had been scooping out the inside which consisted of smell, maggots, and putrid flesh.

On another occasion I was out stalking in May in the Chanda district. There had been a heavy shower of rain and the fallen leaves being soaked it was possible to move silently. The bamboos had seeded some years previously, and the jungle was a mass of fallen bamboo clumps, making progress difficult and tortuous. I was behind a fallen clump when I became aware of the smell of some dead animal, and also heard crunching. Looking between the dead stems I made out a tiger's head on the other side of the clump about 10 ft. away. Firing between the stems I killed him stone dead with a shot in the forehead. He died with his mouth full of maggots which he was scooping out of a young sambar.

Owing to the position the tiger holds in the jungle, he is brought into contact with every animal it contains. This is not the case with any other animal. The tiger occasionally kills wild buffalo, bison, bear and leopards. Their chief food consists of cattle, sambar, pig, nilgai, barasingha, chital and porcupines. They also occasionally kill goats, barking deer, and four-horned antelope. Their relations with wild-dogs have been described under the chapter on Wild-dogs.

They are sometimes in touch with a jackal who acts as a sort of 'chela.' There is a common story that a jackal utters a peculiar cry called 'pheal' when in the company of a tiger. The only one I ever heard calling in the company of a tiger did make this peculiar noise, but I have often heard them do so when there was no tiger within miles. The call is probably one of alarm or suspicion irrespective of the cause. I once saw three full-grown male tigers walk out abreast in a beat, only a few feet separating them, and a jackal was scampering in and out between the tigers quite obviously 'sure of his ground.' The jackal is a cheeky, intelligent, adaptable and insignificant animal, in no danger from the tiger, but to whom it is quite conceivable that he might be useful. The jackal referred to above and which uttered this peculiar cry did so on becoming aware of my presence of which the tiger was ignorant. The jackal is very much alive to his own interests, and one attached to or adopted by a tiger would have a very easy time, and he is the only animal which has anything in the nature of friendly relations with the tiger. All other animals fear and hate and shun him. His progress through the jungle either by night or in the daytime is advertised by the screams of alarm of peafowl, monkeys and all the deer.

It is not every tiger that will attack a large wild-boar, and natives sometimes give one most circumstantial accounts of the tiger being worsted. This is conceivable, the pig's neck is almost unbreakable and as a large jungle boar may weigh as much as 300 lb. the fight is not so unequal as it might appear. Porcupines, judging by the frequency with which one finds quills sticking in tigers' paws, are probably killed by a blow of the paw. An instance of a tiger having been killed by a porcupine's quills has been recorded.

Tigers, when disturbed on their kills, will usually abandon the same without protest; but if the kill happens to be a pig or a porcupine, they will often defend it, and it is not safe to drive a tiger off one of these animals. Whether this conduct is due to their being inordinately fond of this fare, or whether the difficulty they sometimes experience in killing these creatures enhances their value, I cannot say; but this attitude of the tiger, which I have personally experienced, cannot be due to mere coincidence. Moreover, the tame tiger which I kept was always most reluctant to abandon a piece of pig meat. He, of course, had had no experience of killing pigs, and this would make one inclined to think that tigers were particularly fond of the flesh.

With regard to a tiger's character and intelligence such observations as I have been able to make are based on a wide experience with the wild animal, but I am largely indebted to a tame tiger I once reared. This tiger was caught in the Mandla district when about two months old, and was brought up loose with a pack of dogs I then had. This tiger while I had it, was not tied up except at night and roamed about at will. It used to come for walks with me in the jungle. It was fed very much as a wild tiger is, getting a gorge when meat was plenty, and again sometimes going two or three days without food. I had it under conditions which approached those of nature as nearly as possible, until it was quite a fair size, as big as a St. Bernard dog. Now, the impression I got from this animal, and from the wild tiger as well, is that they are animals of extraordinarily little intelligence. They possess very fixed habits and instincts, and these serve them to get through life and deal with the exigencies thereof. No doubt cubs get a certain amount of instruction, notably in the art of killing, from their mother, but the great mass of their habits and character are inherited and they acquire little beyond this.

The cub, although brought up with dogs, learned no dog habits and he was always a tiger, pure and simple, and acquired nothing except what developed out of his own nature. He would proceed down a nala, take cover and stalk in exactly the same way as a wild tiger, all of which actions, under the circumstances, were meaningless. The first time he killed one of my sheep he did so as to the manner born. Viewing the history of the tiger, all the intelligence he requires is to be able to stalk and kill game. This requires little or no reasoning. His instincts serve the purpose. He is accustomed to conceal himself in stalking game and knows how to apply this art when hunted, but he has no education in 'self-preservation' and has missed all that this means. Circumstances under which he is often hunted and shot preclude his being an animal of much intelligence.

In dealing with his senses, his most important are his powers of hearing. It is on his ears that he chiefly depends, especially in thick cover, for detecting the presence of game. Their powers of hearing are quite remarkable and much beyond anything usually imagined. When out for a walk in the jungle, my tame tiger would often wander into the grass at the side of the path. He had been trained to associate food with a very low whistle, and he could hear this at an incredible distance and return when summoned in this way.

The eyesight of the tiger is also remarkably good, and it is on this sense and hearing that he depends. They nearly always detect the slightest movement, but unless they look directly at one may fail to pick one out from the surroundings provided one remains motionless. Their powers of vision are therefore very much less than the peacock's. They possess great self-control however, and on suddenly catching sight of one need not disclose that they have done so, which deer and most animals invariably do. I have known tigers come slowly out in a beat, and suddenly becoming aware of the sportsman, continue to come slowly on until they reached dead ground and then break back. No deer has this self-possession, and they would always make it evident that the sportsman had been seen.

With regard to the sense of smell, they hardly possess any, and what little they do possess they seldom use. Animals develop this sense either to hunt game, get their food, or for self-protection. None of these causations apply to the tiger. They find their game by their ears and eyes, and having stalked it they rush upon it. They do not run things down like wild dogs. They have been 'top dog' in the country they inhabit for so long, their strength and ferocity have been all the protection they required. If they possessed even reasonable powers of scent it would often be impossible to drive them up to guns under the circumstances commonly in vogue. The tame tiger I had, if his food was removed and hung up on a branch, was unable to locate it. Moreover, if removed and dragged along the grass, he never even attempted to scent up the trail, but hunted round in circles until he came on it. I have seen a wild tiger do the same in cases when his kill had been moved. Any animal accustomed to use its nose or place any reliance in the same would have followed by the scent.

A common experiment with my tame tiger when eating the leg of some animal in long grass close to camp, was to throw a blanket over his head and remove him, at the same time removing his food. He would then be released in long grass 50 yards off. He had a marvellous sense of locality and would return exactly to the spot where his food had been, but never attempted to find it by scent. He circled round until he came on it in its new position. It was curious to note also how his anger or ferocity seemed to be aroused by eating, or possibly the instinct of defending what was his. The Arabs have a proverb, 'The lion gets angry even with his dinner.' This might be said equally well of the tiger. Another curious habit was his addiction to lapping hot water, and he always visited the bathroom at tub time. Other wild animals will do this.

Tigers are still often referred to as having a good sense of smell. He is a very wonderful animal in many ways, and it is probable that on this account he is unthinkingly endowed with powers he does not possess.

From time to time there has been much correspondence on how the tiger kills his prey. One reason for this is that one is apt to forget that a tiger kills a number of different kinds of animals under varying circumstances, and that he varies his methods accordingly. Few observers have been lucky enough to have seen an animal killed more than once or twice, and the circumstances may not have been the same as those witnessed by somebody else. The tiger is a most efficient engine of destruction, and although he has his favourite methods even he has to vary these. I have seen tigers kill deer under natural conditions twice, and bullocks in a herd three times. I have come on numbers of wounded animals, including bison, and of course I have examined innumerable carcasses of most animals. In addition, I have frequently seen tigers kill a bait right under my feet both in broad daylight and in bright moonlight.

With regard to the deer and the loose bullocks, which were of course capable of moving, the tiger sprang up and in three short bounds had seized the neck. The animals had started into motion, but the shock of the tiger's rush immediately rolled them over, and the tiger, hanging on to the neck, twisted the same in the opposite direction to which the body of the animal was revolving. The weight of the revolving body opposed by the twist on the neck in the opposite direction resulted in instant dislocation. This method of breaking the animal's neck will be referred to again when tied-up baits are under discussion. Sometimes a tiger will rush into a herd of cattle and down three or four beasts, far more than he has any use for. This is generally the work of a young tiger proud of his skill and rejoicing in the ease with which he kills.

I have several times shot animals recently mauled by tigers, which had evidently got 'under way' in time, and had thus avoided being seized by the neck. I recall a typical case of a nilgai bull in which the tiger had fastened his left paw into the nilgai's ribs and had seized the buttock in his mouth. The strength of the bull had enabled him to break loose, and he got away with a deep score along his ribs and flank, and about 2 lb. of meat and skin flapping on his hind quarters. The sambar's habit of holding his head up and antlers back, when galloping or startled, often foils the tiger.

We have so far been dealing with animals which the tiger can master and whose neck he can break. He cannot do this to fully-grown bison or wild buffalo, and therefore other means must be adopted. Large heavy animals are helpless if they have lost the use of one leg, and in all cases that I have known, in which it seemed clear that the tiger could not attack the neck with much chance of success, they have first of all hamstrung the beast. I have never seen this actually being done, but such animals have been found hamstrung, and appear to have been bitten on the hock joint. Col. Fenton states that when tigers kill camels they invariably attack the legs.

Various observers, from time to time, have recorded that in Burmah, tiger constantly hamstring animals, even comparatively small beasts like sambar hinds, and one instance has been recorded from the Central Provinces by Caton Jones of a tiger attacking this animal's hind leg. Except under the above circumstances, tigers in the Central Provinces hardly ever attack the hock. I am not aware of the conditions prevailing in Burmah, but I have always been led to understand that the cover there is generally much denser than in the Central Provinces. If so, this would often make it difficult for a tiger to rush in and make a frontal attack. To be sure of success he must see the neck clearly and keep it in view. It is possible, therefore, that in dense cover the tiger finds it easier to creep up to the animal from behind and seize it by the hind leg, and I venture to suggest that this is the reason for the difference in the behaviour of tiger in the two countries.

I have only once known a case of an animal killed by a blow of the paw, and this was done by a large tiger in Mandla which probably despised buffaloes as food. Anyway he walked up to a bait, broke in its skull and then passed on.

With regard to buffaloes which have been tied up as baits, I once saw a young tiger completely disconcerted because the buffalo did not attempt to bolt, and the tiger pulled up and retreated. It would almost seem as if he did not know how to deal with a stationary animal. However, they soon learn. This young tiger returned and commenced leaping back and fore over the buffalo's back. No sooner did it alight on one side than it was back again to the other. I never learned whether it was trying to get the buffalo to run, or merely playing with a helpless animal, as it suddenly saw me. I was in a bush on the other side of the road and of course had to shoot it.

The above circumstances are exceptional. There are two ways in which I have seen buffaloes killed, and these have been repeated so often that it is fair to say that they are the usual or normal ways. Before proceeding to describe these ways, it is necessary to point out that two very common mistakes are made by sportsmen. The first is that they are far too ready to assume that the neck has been broken: this often cannot be ascertained unless a detailed examination is made, and the neck is not broken at all in a great many more cases than is generally supposed. The next most common mistake in the diagnosis of the night's happenings is to presume that the buffalo has been seized by the throat. In a great number of cases this is not so, and the animal has been seized on the top of the neck. The position of the teeth marks will show: when these are on the throat the animal has been seized from above, and when on the neck it has been seized from above, and when on the neck it has been seized from below. Failure to appreciate these facts has led to some confusion, and apparently accounts for the contradictions of Baldwin, Forsyth and Sanderson.

If the bait is fairly large and a tigress or small tiger turns up, the throat attack is preferred. It may be of interest to mention that if tigers come on the bait unexpectedly, they often give a 'whoof' and make a temporary bolt, but soon return. The tiger advances stalking within 20 yards or so of the bait, head on—stands poised for a few second with one foot up, tail out straight, and swaying slightly backwards and forwards to get its balance. Two or three long rapid strides are then taken, and dipping its head like lightning under the buffalo's chin, the throat is seized and immediately pulled down on to the ground. The tiger remains thus pinning the beast's head and neck on to the ground. When in this position, the tiger is down on its elbows but the hind quarters remain up. The buffalo struggles to remain standing but presently falls over and in so doing sometimes breaks its own neck, which of course is pinned firmly to the ground all the time. On the other hand, this very frequently does not happen, and the two animals simply remain as they are until the buffalo is dead from strangulation and suffocation.

Assuming that a large tiger had turned up, a tiger who felt confident of being able to deal with the bait in a masterful manner, he comes in at the gallop, pulls up, rears on his hind legs, seizes the buffalo in his jaws right across the back of the neck and passes one fore paw to the far side of the neck. He then swings his hind quarters and hind legs into the position assumed by animals in breeding and while violently thrusting the buffalo's hind quarters forward with his belly, he at the same time, with equal violence, pulls back its head and neck, which cannot withstand the strain, and breaks. The tiger then dismounts on the opposite side on which the attack was made, still retaining the neck in his jaws. By doing this he gives an additional twist to the neck. I have seen a tiger hang on and continue this twist until the buffalo's head was reversed and looked along its back. This, however, always appeared to be unnecessary, as the terrific purchase the tiger had obtained by being able to press the buffalo's body forward at the same time as the neck was wrenched back, effectually broke it. I once shot one in this position, but the buffalo dropped dead. On another occasion I shot a tiger stone dead which had completed the movement, and although still holding on to the neck, had twisted it so completely as to be facing the buffalo, having turned through 270 degrees. After death, the jaws remained in situ held by the canine teeth embedded in the neck. Unfortunately, it was too late to photograph. Sometimes the above procedure is varied by the tiger giving the buffalo a preliminary shaking, apparently with the object of satisfying himself and settling in his teeth.

Anyone witnessing these attacks is bound to be awed by their ruthlessness, and the savage ferocity of the tiger, and cannot help being struck with the lustful pleasure the tiger evidently takes in killing his prey.

I have never seen a tiger suck the blood from the neck, nor have I ever seen any signs of this having been done. It has always been a matter of some astonishment to me how the story that they indulge in this practice is so commonly repeated even in recent publications such as Best's, who, while admitting that he has never seen a tiger kill its prey, refers to their lapping the blood. It is presumed that sportsmen notice the absence of blood in any quantity on the ground, and without considering the matter, wrongly attribute this to the tiger having disposed of it. So far as I am aware, out of all the authors mentioned in the Preface the only ones who show any doubts on the subject were E. B. Baker in *Sport in Bengal* and Sanderson. A large vein is tough and elastic, not easily served by a blunt instrument like a tiger's tooth, and the jugular is seldom cut. But even if it is, no great amount of external bleeding can take place. The facts are that the tiger retains his hold on the neck long after the animal's heart has ceased to beat and the holes in the neck are thus effectually stopped so long as circulation continues. Such active bleeding as takes place is, therefore, internal; moreover, this must be largely reduced by the vice-like pressure of the tiger's jaws on the part seized.

When the tiger releases his prey only a little of the local blood trickles out by gravity from two of the wounds. If the absence of blood is to be accounted for by the tiger sucking the blood, it is incumbent on him to suck four different holes at the same time. The real facts of the case are as I have stated, and there is little or no blood to dispose of, nor does the tiger suck the wounds.

One other method of hunting, rather than killing, must be touched upon. Two tigers hunting in company will separate, and one will stalk and then try to rush the deer on to the other tiger which lies concealed. How far this plan succeeds and is adopted in thick cover, I cannot say, but probably seldom. I have only known it adopted in the case of a herd of barasingha which persistently refused to leave bare open ground, where no tiger could approach unseen. This ground was a small area surrounded by long concealing grass. The barasingha seemed to be thoroughly aware of the position of the concealed tiger and avoided going near it. They continued to feed, pending the next onslaught. The tiger that did the driving rushed out of the long grass at full gallop, roaring, and then retired to whence he came. The same manœuvre was repeated three times from different sides. On one occasion the tigress also charged. My participation in proceedings only resulted in one of the tigers being wounded, which subsequently escaped.

Sometimes the presence of a tiger seems to have a mesmerizing effect on deer and appears to benumb their faculties.

On one occasion I was out in a Sal forest at daylight. The cries of deer and monkeys advertised the presence of a tiger or a leopard in a neighbouring maidan, so we pushed the elephant along and came on a very large tiger crossing the bare open ground of a deserted field. Two barasingha stags were standing at the edge of the field and within 12 ft. of a wall of grass 10 ft. high. They were close together facing the tiger, but braced back, and stood motionless, braying. The tiger's line would have taken him past the stags, but he gradually swung in and approached the stags which allowed him to come within 20 yards. The tiger then straightened his tail, lifted one huge fore paw, and started the usual preliminary swinging which indicates his intention to charge. The stags seemed rooted to the spot and had by this time ceased to bray. They were certainly in the greatest danger. This seemed to be entirely due to their inability to move, as long before danger arose, they could have disappeared at one bound in the long grass. I was halted at the edge of the forest about 80 yards off. Unfortunately, the play ended before the last act. I was accompanied by a friend who was anxious to shoot the tiger. He was using a heavy rifle and black powder. Everything vanished behind a cloud of smoke and when this cleared the maidan was empty.

Man is so feeble an animal, tigers do not require special methods of attack in order to break his neck, and can kill him easily by biting him either through the body or the neck. I once saw a case in which a man-eating tiger had driven in a man's skull with a blow from his paw delivered on the top of the head. Evidence of how man-eaters behave in killing, or towards a live victim which they can carry off as easily as a dog does a rabbit, is of course scanty. Apropos of their strength I once saw a tigress drag a half-grown buffalo up the bank of the River Tapti without apparent effort. The bank was alluvial soil and so steep, a man could only have climbed it with difficulty without the use of his hands.

I was once stalked and charged by a man-eater which got within a few feet of me before I shot it. I cannot say, therefore, if it would have taken me at the gallop, or pulled up and then bitten, but this is probably what it would have done. Man-eaters usually reject the skull and the palms of the hands and the soles of the feet. The story of Jezebel was evidently recorded by an accurate eye-witness, as animals which eat men seem to dislike these parts.

When a wounded tiger charges, if the man is running away or moving, they will take him at the gallop, but if one stands still they invariably pull up dead and then attack. But for this habit, some sportsmen, including myself, would not be here to-day. In attacks by wounded tiger they usually knock the man down and give him two or three rapid bites, often through the thigh, and then leave him. I have known an unwounded tiger in a beat, however, round on the men, and after mauling one, pick up another and carry him off. In this case, although the tigers had been headed back, the attack was chiefly due to the tiger being with a female at mating time, and after the tragedy he came out on a fireline dancing on his toes, with his tail waving in the air and evidently very proud of his prowess, for which he no doubt expected to be rewarded.

Tigers, when making a galloping charge at man, give vent to a deep short grunting cough repeated two or three times. The volume of sound is so great, it is sometimes difficult to locate its direction accurately. On occasions they will steal in and attack silently, and they nearly always attack animals in silence. A tiger suddenly disturbed and retreating often gives a 'whoof,' and when trying to break a line of beaters they will gallop along the line roaring. This noise is quite different, however, from the cough they make when intending to attack. Tigers growl as a warning when angry. A deep long drawn out 'meow' is another call, and when pleased they make a purring noise by blowing air on to their lips which vibrate, not unlike the action and noise made by horses when they wish to clear their mouths and nostrils. They show emotion by a twitching in the end of the tail. This may be either pleasure or annoyance.

Cubs make complaining squeaks, but on the whole the tiger is a silent animal, and considering their numbers they are seldom heard to give a regular roar. When they do this the sound is awe-inspiring, and the whole valley will sometimes ring with the volume of sound produced. The noise is produced by taking a deep inhalation and then expelling the air violently against the roof of the mouth, the lower jaw being slowly closed at the same time. The result is a long drawn out 'H—o—w—n.' They sometimes repeat the sound three or four times in succession, and commence moderately, but 'work up' and with each repetition increase the sound. When tigers do this they are generally trying to get in touch with a mate.

On one occasion, when camped in the middle of a forest, I heard the roaring of a tiger taken up and answered by another. The two animals gradually approached each other and a terrific fight ensued not far from the camp, the scene of which I was able to visit next day. About six weeks after this, in all probability I shot one of these tigers, judging by the marks on his neck and body. He was an immense beast. Nevertheless, he appeared to have had the worst of it. However, we never saw 'the other fellow,' and this deduction may have been that of 'the casual observer.' For some unknown reason tigers are more given to roaring in some districts than in others, and I have always found them more noisy in Sal forests than elsewhere.

One more noise, which is rarely heard outside Sal forests, has to be described. This is the curious 'pook' they make not unlike the sound produced by a sambar, and about which there has been considerable discussion. This noise can be mistaken for that of a sambar, but it is really softer and not so loud or harsh. No sambar could mistake it for the call of another sambar, and the suggestion that tiger call up sambar in this way can be turned down. Moreover, the noise made resembles the sambar's cry of alarm, and how this could be an inducement for the sambar to approach the spot whence the alarm issues, is not understood. It might be argued that by making the noise the tiger induces a sambar to 'bell,' and thus locates him, but the tiger has other means of doing this. The call is really a mate call and is used by tigers to locate each other. I have nearly always heard it made when there were two tigers going about together. I have had a tiger make it at me, thinking I was his mate or at any rate wishing to find this out.

Two tigers had killed a fairly large buffalo in long grass. The tigress had left the kill, but when I came to it the tiger was on the buffalo. Hearing me coming he picked up the buffalo and took it off with him through the grass which was very high and dense. I followed up, when he dropped the kill, and commenced this noise at me. He repeated it a number of times from different points and retreated making the noise. Of course, I could not give him the reply he wanted, but this came presently from the hill-side, and he went off and joined his mate. These tigers both returned after dark and spotting me in a tree roared lustily for some hours. Seeing it was useless to wait longer, I got down and returned to camp. They then came up to the kill and ate everything except the skull and hoofs.

Tigers seldom attempt to climb trees, but that they can do this to a much greater extent than is generally supposed, I firmly believe. They can certainly get up a branched tree at which they can rush. The number of fatal accidents is evidence of this. I do not think a large heavy tiger could climb a smooth limbless tree, but tigresses and smaller tigers can get up a tree with only a small amount of assistance from side branches. Credible witnesses have told me on different occasions that they have seen tigers treed by wild-dogs, and I have been shown the hair of a tiger on a branch 15 ft. from the ground.

Tigers take to water readily and are strong swimmers. I have known them swim the Nerbudda to escape out of a beat, and on one occasion a wounded tiger that was being hunted did this. They must have swum to get on to the Island of Singapore, and some years ago it was reported that a tiger had actually crossed over on to Hong Kong. They are great wanderers, and at times seem to lose themselves and get into the most extraordinary places. There is a circumstantial account of one being found in a pagoda in Burmah. Three tigers were once found in the Buldana District treking across open country, and miles from any real holding ground.

Again, while I was Divisional Officer of the Melghat, a young tiger left the jungles and took up its abode in some Pan gardens near Ellichpur. It was hunted and actually shot in a Pan garden after an exciting chase in which it displayed the activity of tigers. I was informed that, during the hunt, the tiger leaped the sides of the garden, which were 6 ft. high, like a greyhound. I myself have seen a tigress clear a 19 ft. gully in one stride without effort or gathering herself to leap, and in alighting she gave the impression that she would not have crushed an egg, so easily was her weight carried. Straying into unusual places is the more surprising as the chief characteristic of the tiger is his retiring habits. Their chief endeavour in life seems to be to avoid being seen or having attention drawn to them. On the other hand, there are instances of extraordinarily bold behaviour at night, and they have been known to return to their kills again and again after being fired at. These cases however are exceptions.

For so large an animal, tigers must be considered rapid breeders. At one time in parts of India at the beginning of the last century, they were so numerous it seemed to be a question as to whether man or tiger would survive.

Up till about the beginning of the present century, sportsmen only visited the Central Provinces in moderate numbers, but about this time shooting became a popular pastime amongst army officers, and tigers were much reduced. The war practically put an end to shooting, except by district officers, and during its duration, the tigers rapidly increased. Few tigers are killed by native shikaris. These chiefly shoot deer. It is the European sportsman that thins out the tiger.

Any cause which prevents a tiger getting his natural food, tends to create man-eaters, as tigers fall back on the easiest animal of all to kill and his instinctive dread of man is overcome by hunger. Moreover, this instinctive fear soon goes once he realizes how helpless man is. Tigers may be unable to procure their ordinary food by reason of worn-down teeth, lameness, or some wound. Again, there may not be a sufficiency of natural food to meet their requirements. A man-eating tigress will also bring up her cubs to kill man. Since the war, there has been a very large increase in the number of man-eaters. Hardly a gazette is issued without announcing special rewards for about twenty different animals. The bulk of these animals is in the east of the Province. It is possible that the rapid increase in the number of tigers during the war, with no increase in the food supply, but rather the reverse, has led to the present conditions.

The presence of a confirmed man-eater in a jungle tract is a dreadful scourge. Some people have to pass though jungle almost daily, and no man on leaving his village can be sure of returning. The man-eaters often develop boldness and a fiendish cunning, and their presence is a blight on the whole community. A book could be filled with jungle tragedies.

The knowledge man-eaters acquire of men's habits, as well as their habit of eating up most of the corpse at a meal and not returning, adds to the difficulty in killing them. Moreover, there is a widespread belief that the ghost of the last victim sits on the tiger's head, and that he who gives information regarding the tiger's habits is selected by the ghost for the next victim. There is often much difficulty, therefore, in obtaining the necessary assistance to encompass a man-eater's destruction. If the perusal of this chapter induces even one sportsman to hunt down one of these man-eaters, it will not have been written in vain.

Animals which have become confirmed man-eaters usually decline to kill a buffalo or bullock, but will often kill a pig or a pony, if these are tied up as baits. I have known other tigers, not man-eaters, to have a similar preference, but the disinclination of man-eaters to eat beef indicates that their palate has undergone some definite change.

The great mass of tigers are partly cattle killers and partly game eaters, but some animals living in forests such as are found in Mandla and Balaghat, where game is very abundant, hardly ever kill cattle. On the other hand; many parts of the Province now contain little or no game, and in such places the tiger lives on nothing but cattle, and follows the herds about as these are shifted for water and grazing. In tracts of this nature tigers are particularly liable to develop into man-eaters.

In the Zemindaris of Bilaspur, I found the tigers had definitely changed their habits and did all their hunting by day. It was some time before I found this out, and I was surprised at the difficulty in getting a bait killed, which of course was tied out all night. The facts were that there was absolutely nothing for a tiger to hunt at night, as there was no game, and all the cattle were driven into pens at dusk. Each tiger made a round of about six villages, taking a bullock from each in turn. On the other hand, I have known tigers living in forest containing little game and yet seldom killing cattle, and it has often been a matter of no little speculation when shooting an animal in the pink of condition in jungles of this nature, where the tiger obtained his food.

Although tigers do a great deal of damage, they have their uses in preserving the balance of nature. There is an outlying patch of forest in the Hoshangabad district which always contained a few tigers when I was there in 1906. Some years after this, they were all shot out, and the forest being isolated no others wandered in. I visited this tract again in 1917, and the surrounding villages were simply overrun with pig and nilgai. Many fields had gone out of cultivation. To enlarge a couple of tiger in this forest would be a great boon to the local people. This is not the only instance of the kind, and the extermination of tiger in such places should not be permitted.

Excerpted from Wild Animals in Central India *(London: Edward Arnold, 1923).*

F. W. CHAMPION

What is the Use of Leopards?

It was almost routine for sport-hunters to label the leopard or panther as 'a lawless killer', 'a bounder' or a 'secretive, vicious beast'. Even in the Indian princely states, leopards rarely figured on coats of arms the way lions and tigers did. Often living in close proximity to villages and, being smaller than tigers, leopards were more common and elusive than the former. Perhaps this ability to make itself invisible helped it to survive.

Champion was a forester in the United Provinces, with an intimate knowledge of the Shivalik hills and the wet savannah. He gave up shooting partly due to revulsion with slaughter after the Great War of 1914–18 and out of an interest in photography. An early advocate of wildlife protection, Champion had a keen appreciation of the positive role predators play in the economy of nature. His With a Camera in Tigerland *(1927) is a classic for its pictures of animals in the wild. He pioneered flashlight photography using trip wires; and his are among the first photographic records of free-living tigers and leopards in India. This excerpt is from his next book, a more wide-ranging account of wildlife, published in 1934. Evidently it was not the tiger alone that had found someone to champion its cause.*

> 'Nature hath made nothing so base but can
> Read some instruction to the wisest man.'

ALEYN

A question often put to the naturalist and student of wild life is: 'What is the use of creatures like the leopard, the scorpion, the cobra, or the malarious mosquito: what is their place in the general scheme of life and would not the world be a much better place if they did not exist?' Such a conundrum is not easy to answer, for many complicated factors are involved, including the questioner's religious beliefs as to the respective influences of creation and evolution in the formation of wild life as we see it to-day. In any case, hard though it may be to convince the man who has just been stung by a scorpion, or whose dog was taken yesterday by a leopard, there can be little doubt but that every living creature has some definite place in the general scheme of life on this earth. The inter-relationship between animal and animal, or the 'balance of nature' as it is termed by naturalists, is the guiding principle upon which the whole scheme of life is built up, and it is perhaps the most marvellous organization that it is possible to imagine. The numbers of each kind of animal must be kept within reasonable limits, and Nature does this by limiting the food supply, by providing most animals with others which prey upon them, by variations in the rate of breeding, and by means of epidemic diseases when other methods have failed. I have been ridiculed by reviewers and others for standing up for tigers, but it is possible that the man who cannot see the use of creatures like the great carnivores and scorpions, if he thinks at all, may come to realize that perhaps he is a little short-sighted, and is considering mankind only, forgetting that there are myriads of other creatures which are also fellow-inhabitants of this earth.

Suppose we consider cobras first. Now rats, since they carry plague, which is possibly man's most dreaded disease, as well as destroying enormous quantities of the cereals which provide the chief food of mankind and other creatures, are really far more serious enemies than cobras; and the chief food of cobras is rats. In other words, the cobra's place in the balance of nature is to act as a check on the undue increase of rats, not necessarily so that man alone shall benefit, but because, in the general interest, the number of rats must be kept within bounds. True it is that this terrifying snake sometimes kills man as well, in self-defence, but that is not his normal function and provided one keeps well out of his way it is possible to look upon even the dreaded cobra as a friend of man. The same argument can be applied to the scorpion, which preys upon certain types of insects whose numbers might otherwise become excessive. The venom in his sting is there to enable him to do this effectively, and, however unfortunate it may be that this venom is extremely painful when injected—in self-defence only be it noted—into one's body, it is not quite fair to claim that the scorpion serves no purpose.

The malarious mosquito is a more difficult creature to justify. Some regard it in the light of one of the curses cast upon the world consequent upon the expulsion of Adam and Eve from the Garden of Eden; or another school of thought will hold that the food-supply of mankind is distinctly limited, in the same way as that of other animals, and some check must be put upon an excessive increase in his numbers or there would soon be insufficient food to go round. Actually medical science is making such rapid strides that it is possible even now to imagine the day when the population of the earth may exceed the limits of the food-supply, and one dreads to contemplate what must happen should that terrible calamity ever befall mankind. Those of us who believe in the balance of nature, however, doubt whether the human population of the earth will ever increase to such an extent, for Nature has her own ways of dealing with excessive numbers of any particular species. Giant earthquakes are always a possibility; new epidemic diseases such as the terrible influenza plague of 1919 may spring upon us at any time; the rate of breeding tends to decrease as food and employment become scarcer; and in any case the abolition of war and such Utopian ideas would soon disappear should men's stomachs remain empty.

So much for other creatures: now let us see if we can justify the existence of the leopard, or panther as he is more commonly called in India. Some people—sportsmen these—claim that the leopard was specially created in order to provide the exile with good sport; others state that such a marvellously beautiful creature requires no justification for its existence; another class of thinkers vehemently uphold the idea that the leopard, like the tiger, is an anachronism which should be wiped out at the very earliest opportunity. But the real facts are that the leopard is a very important unit in the general scheme of animal life in India. Deer and wild pigs are extremely prolific and voracious animals which, if allowed to breed and increase without any check, would soon become so numerous that they would consume all the available food inside the forests they at present mainly inhabit. When this food had become exhausted they would scatter in all directions, and would thus become a very serious menace to the vegetable and cereal food supply of man and other creatures. No: Nature knows better than that, so she arranges a balance between the Ungulates and the Carnivora which works in an astonishingly efficient manner. A concrete example will make the position clearer. There is a certain forest division in the foothills of the United Provinces, with which the writer is intimately acquainted. The area of this tract of forest is about three hundred square miles, and there are usually roughly about fifty tigers and fifty leopards permanently in residence. It is a safe estimate to say that each of these leopards and tigers kills at least one deer a week, or fifty in the year. Hence the tigers and leopards check the increase in the deer population in this small forest alone to the extent of five thousand annually! Now, supposing the tigers and leopards were all to be removed, what would happen? Inevitably, in a very short time, the deer would increase beyond the food supply. Many would scatter elsewhere and the remainder, enfeebled by insufficient food, would in all probability be attacked by rinderpest until the numbers were again reduced to normal. In the meantime, other wandering tigers and leopards, finding plenty of food and no rivals, would settle down in comfort and breed rapidly until the normal balance was once more restored.

In India sportsmen are constantly shooting the carnivora, and, considering the extreme efficiency of modern firearms and the great facilities afforded by the advent of the motor car, it is remarkable that they have managed to keep up their numbers; although tigers are undoubtedly less common than they were, say, a century ago. Hence many forest officers are of the opinion that it is high time that the greater carnivora were afforded some measure of protection, if the normal balance of nature is not to be seriously upset.

Now let us take the case of ungulates and carnivora in places where man has not appeared to interfere with the normal working of Nature's rules. At first sight it would appear that the carnivora, having no enemies, must breed so rapidly and increase to such an extent as to eat out their own food supply, and thereby destroy their own means of existence. Yet in actual fact this does not happen, as has been observed many times by explorers penetrating into wild and lonely parts of Africa. These explorers have found places totally uninhabited by man where the relative numbers of lions and ungulates always seem to be correctly adjusted, and it is difficult to explain how this is done. Probably Nature arranges that the lions breed more slowly when they suffer no casualties, and certainly the

larger and more powerful males drive others away from their
hunting grounds as soon as they find that there are too many of
their tribe in the neighbourhood.

Times without number has man interfered with the normal
balance of nature with disastrous results, and the commonest way
that this has been done is by introducing some animal into another
country where its normal check may be absent. The classic example
is of course the introduction of rabbits into Australia, where they
have been an unmitigated nuisance ever since. In one case—in
New Zealand I think it was—an effort was made to get rid of the
rabbits again by introducing stoats and weasels; but unfortunately
these animals themselves increased very rapidly, and instead of
eating the rabbits, turned their attention to defenceless indigenous
birds, such as kiwis and ground-parrots, some of which are now on
the verge of extinction!

India has so far escaped the evil results following upon the
admission of exotic animals, which luckily has never been permitted
upon a large scale, but she is suffering severely from the introduction
of foreign plants, which, having no competitors, have in some cases
increased to an appalling extent. The two best-known examples are
the water-hyacinth in Bengal and the *lantana* shrub in the United
Provinces (Haldwani), both of which were originally introduced by
misguided individuals as ornamental plants. The water-hyacinth in
Bengal has become a provincial problem and has very seriously
interfered with navigation upon the numerous waterways of that
low-lying country, vast sums having to be spent annually in
unsuccessful attempts to check its further spread. The *lantana* also
is rapidly spreading over some of the forests of Upper India and
is totally preventing the regeneration of the valuable tree species
under which it forms such a dense undergrowth.

Enough has been said to show that, so far as we know, every
creature has its definite place in Nature's great balanced scheme of
wild life, and even the leopard, despite his numerous detractors, has
ample justification for his existence. What else can be said in his
favour? He is certainly not a popular inhabitant of the jungle, where
so far as we can judge he is even more feared and disliked than the
larger and more renowned tiger. This is possibly because he is
perhaps even more destructive, for he often kills an animal like a
cheetal, makes one meal, and then abandons the carcass. The tiger,

on the other hand, provided he is not disturbed, generally completely consumes the whole of every animal he kills, and thus is not
quite so distrusted by the jungle population, particularly the
monkeys, who never feel safe from leopards morning, noon, or
night. I remember one occasion, late in the afternoon, when I
followed a leopard down a jungle path for a mile or two. I was
mounted on an elephant and maintained a constant distance of
about one hundred yards, the leopard remaining totally unaware of
my presence. Every fifty yards or so some sambar, or kakar, or
monkey saw the dreaded feline calmly strolling down the path and
the chorus of abuse which followed the leopard's movements vividly
reminded me of the shouts of 'Simon, go back,' which were such
a familiar accompaniment to the progress of the Simon Commission in India. The leopard, like Sir John Simon, realized that the
only thing to do was to maintain a calm demeanour and to continue
his progress unperturbed; but the inhabitants of the jungle were
wiser than the non-co-operators, for once the object of their hate
had passed out of their sight they promptly forgot all about him
and continued their happy life without brooding upon their
supposed wrongs, or longing for a swaraj of the jungle where all
from the cheetal to the leopard, from the kakar to the tiger, should
stand on an equal footing and have equal rights!

No: the leopard is certainly no more popular in the Indian jungle
than is the policeman in the Indian village, but he is there for the
definite reason that, unless deer, pigs and monkeys can be taught
the principles of birth-control, some check must be put upon their
unlimited increase if the jungle is to continue to be able to support
them all. And the leopard, like the Indian policeman, has some very
fine qualities. He is generally courageous to a degree, and his
physical fitness would put the ordinary human athlete to shame.
Further, he can climb trees with the greatest ease; he has marvellous
patience when hunting; he can live for days at a stretch without
water; and he can conceal himself, thanks largely to the extremely
useful spotted coat with which a kindly Nature has endowed him,
in a way which is the constant envy of the human hunter, scout
or soldier. In addition the mother leopardess shows great devotion
to her cubs, for whom she will fight till the last gasp, and the whole
leopard race would take a very high place in a beauty competition
for animals.

To counteract this long list of qualities there must be, obviously, corresponding vices, but at least it can be claimed that the latter list is shorter. Undoubtedly leopards are unnecessarily destructive on occasions, and cases have been known of a leopard entering a goat-pen and killing the whole of the thirty or forty animals which it contained. The leopard is also less scientific in his killing than the tiger, so that he sometimes inflicts more pain in the process than is necessary; although it goes without saying that he does not do this with the object of being deliberately cruel, for it is my firm belief that man alone practises the debased vice of cruelty for cruelty's sake. From man's point of view, also, the leopard has his bad qualities. He is particularly fond of dog-flesh, and many are the loyal and trusted canine friends of man which have ended their career in the stomach of a prowling leopard. Again some leopards, generally of a lazy and debased type, discover that in preference to the comparatively hard work of stalking alert wild animals it is much easier to catch and devour the numerous cattle which are so carelessly left about in the neighbourhood of Indian villages. They undoubtedly do a good deal of harm in this way, although the fault is not entirely theirs but often lies at the door of those cattle-owners who place temptation in the way by carelessly leaving their cattle unattended at night, in places where they know perfectly well there is considerable risk from a wandering leopard. But perhaps the Hindu villager is not always quite so careless with his cattle as he seems to be. Like the farmer throughout the world he would not be happy without his 'grouse', and he really kills two birds with one stone when he leaves his old, worn-out and useless cattle where they are likely to be killed by tigers or leopards. He provides himself with a very comforting source of complaint and at the same time gets rid of the useless beasts which his religion prevents him from destroying with his own hand. It is even whispered that some of the Buddhists of Burma are distinctly fond of meat, but cannot obtain it because the taking of life is forbidden by the teaching of the great Lord Buddha. Suppose an old cow were to stray into a jungle where a leopard might be lurking. The cow is, perhaps, struck down and the indignant owner arrives just too late to save its life, but not too late to prevent the leopard from enjoying the meat. Well, the poor cow is dead, and the owner's conscience is quite free—he hasn't taken life! But why leave good food to be eaten by such sinful creatures as leopards? Why waste what is really his own property? No: those of us who have some glimmering of the inner workings of the Eastern mind do not place very much value upon the statistics of cattle killed by wild animals when used to try to prove that leopards are so terribly destructive that they ought to be wiped off the face of the earth.

Then there are the fatal accidents which frequently occur when men hunt leopards for the sake of sport. Well, few sports appeal to the true sportsman unless they require considerable skill or entail a certain amount of risk, and the hunted leopard cannot be blamed for putting up the best show he can. After all, the hunter is armed with a marvellous rifle with which, provided he has sufficient skill in its use and the necessary knowledge of woodcraft, he can kill the leopard long before the latter can approach sufficiently near to make use of the close-contact weapons of teeth and claws which are all that Nature has given him. If the hunter makes a mess of things and wastes the tremendous advantages he has—well, it is undoubtedly very sad, but the leopard is fighting for his life in an unequal contest, and it is only fair that he should occasionally turn the tables and kill the man, who is trying to kill him often for the sake of pleasure alone.

Lastly, there is the leopard man-eater, who from man's point of view is a terrible foe capable of paralysing a whole countryside, and, moreover, owing to his exceptional cunning, one often extremely difficult to bring to book. Man is not the normal food of leopards, and the man-eating leopard is therefore an abnormality without a word to be said in his favour. Probably not one leopard in ten thousand, however, develops into a man-eater, and the average representative of the race is, as I have attempted to show here, an animal with many good qualities and full of interest to the sportsman and naturalist. May the day be far distant—as it undoubtedly will be—when the name of the leopard will have to be added to the long list of wild animals that have been exterminated by the hand of man.

Excerpted from The Jungle in Sunlight and Shadow *(London: Chatto and Windus, 1934).*

JIM CORBETT

Vigil on a Pine Tree

In all of Jim Corbett's man-eater books, the only full-length narrative of a single hunt is The Man-eating Leopard of Rudraprayag. *But the work reveals another facet of Corbett. Though he stayed mainly in Kumaon, he did range further afield as a hunter and naturalist, in this case into the valley of Kashmir. He had gone to angle and shoot far from tiger country, but coming face to face with the hangul or Kashmir stag, he hesitated, captivated by its sheer beauty. Confined to the valley, this rare animal was much sought after by anyone fortunate enough to be invited by the Maharaja. This makes Corbett's preference to watch, not shoot, all the more remarkable. Of course, this is a late Jim Corbett already well established as an author, and moving towards conservation, away from the gun. He takes us to a mountain setting, high above Kumaon's foot-hills, for an encounter he never quite forgot.*

Ibbotson returned to Pauri next day, and the following morning, when I was visiting the villages on the hill to the east of Rudraprayag, I found the tracks of the man-eater on a path leading out of a village in which the previous night he had tried to break open the door of a house in which there was a child suffering from a bad cough. On following the tracks for a couple of miles they led me to the shoulder of the mountain where, some days previously, Ibbotson and I had sat up over the calling goat which the leopard later had killed.

It was still quite early, and as there was a chance of finding the leopard basking on one of the rocks in this considerable area of broken ground, I lay on a projecting rock that commanded an extensive view. It had rained the previous evening—thus enabling me to track the leopard—and washed the haze out of the atmosphere. Visibility was at its best and the view from the projecting rock was as good as could be seen in any part of the world where mountains rise to a height of twenty-three thousand feet. Immediately below me was the beautiful valley of the Alaknanda, with the river showing as a gleaming silver ribbon winding in and out of it. On the hill beyond the river, villages were dotted about, some with only a single thatched hut, and others with long rows of slate-roofed houses. These rows of buildings are in fact individual homesteads, built one against the other to save expense and to economize space, for the people are poor, and every foot of workable land in Garhwal is needed for agriculture.

Beyond the hills were rugged rock cliffs, down which avalanches roar in winter and early spring, and beyond and above the cliffs were the eternal snows, showing up against the intense blue sky as clear as if cut out of white cardboard. No more beautiful or peaceful scene could be imagined, and yet when the sun, now shining on the back of my head, set on the far side of the snow mountains, terror—terror which it is not possible to imagine until experienced—would grip, as it had done for eight long years, the area I was now overlooking.

I had been lying on the rock for an hour when two men came down the hill, on their way to the bazaar. They were from a village about a mile farther up the hill that I had visited the previous day, and they informed me that a little before sunrise they had heard a leopard calling in this direction. We discussed the possibilities of my getting a shot at the leopard over a goat, and as at that time I had no goats of my own, they offered to bring me one from their village and promised to meet me where we were standing, two hours before sunset.

When the men had gone I looked round for a place where I could sit. The only tree on the whole of this part of the mountain was a solitary pine. It was growing on the ridge close to the path down which the men had come, and from under it a second path took off and ran across the face of the mountain skirting the upper edge of the broken ground, where I had recently been looking for the leopard. The tree commanded an extensive view, but it could be difficult to climb, and would afford little cover. However, as it was the only tree in the area, I had no choice, so decided I would try it.

The men were waiting for me with a goat when I returned at about 4 p.m., and when, in reply to their question where I intended sitting, I pointed to the pine, they started laughing. Without a rope ladder, they said, it would not be possible to climb the tree; and further, if I succeeded in climbing the tree without a ladder, and carried out my intention of remaining out all night, I should have no protection against the man-eater, to whom the tree would offer no obstacle. There were two white men in Garhwal—Ibbotson was one of them—who had collected birds' eggs when boys, and both of whom could climb the tree; and as there is no exact equivalent in Hindustani for 'waiting until you come to a bridge before crossing it', I let the second part of the men's objection go unanswered, contenting myself by pointing to my rifle.

The pine was not easy to climb, for there were no branches for twenty feet, but once having reached the lowest branch, the rest was easy. I had provided myself with a long length of cotton cord, and when the men had tied my rifle to one end to it, I drew it up and climbed to the top of the tree, where the pine-needles afforded most cover.

The men had assured me that the goat was a good caller, and after they tied it to an exposed root of the tree they set off for their village promising to return early next morning. The goat watched the men out of sight, and then started to nibble the short grass at the foot of the tree. The fact that it had not up to then called once did not worry me, for I felt sure that it would presently feel lonely and that it would then do its share of the business of the evening, and if it did it while it was still night, from my elevated position I should be able to kill the leopard long before it got anywhere near the goat.

When I climbed the tree the shadows cast by the snow mountains had reached the Alaknanda. Slowly these shadows crept up the hill and passed me, until only the top of the mountain glowed with red light. As this glow faded, long streamers of light shot up from the snow mountains where the rays of the setting sun were caught and held on a bank of clouds as soft and as light as thistledown. Everyone who has eyes to see a sunset—and the number, as you might have observed, is regrettably few—thinks that the sunsets in his particular part of the world are the best ever. I am no exception, for I too think that there are no sunsets in all the world to compare with ours, and a good second are the sunsets in northern Tanganyika, where some quality in the atmosphere makes snow-capped Kilimanjaro, and the clouds that are invariably above it, glow like molten gold in the rays of the setting sun. Our sunsets in the Himalayas are mostly red, pink, or gold. The one I was looking at that evening from my seat on the pine-tree was rose pink, and the white shafts of light, starting as spear-points from valleys in the cardboard snows, shot though the pink clouds and, broadening, faded out in the sky overhead.

The goat, like many human beings, had no interest in sunsets, and after nibbling the grass within reach, scratched a shallow hole for itself, lay down, curled up, and went to sleep. Here was a dilemma. I had counted on the animal now placidly sleeping below me to call up the leopard, and not once since I had first seen it had it opened its mouth, except to nibble grass, and now, having made itself comfortable, it would probably sleep throughout the night. To have left the tree at that hour in an attempt to return to the bungalow would have added one more to the number who deliberately commit suicide, and as I had to be doing something to kill the man-eater, and as—in the absence of a kill—one place was as good as another, I decided to stay where I was, and try to call up the leopard myself.

If I were asked what had contributed most to my pleasure during all the years that I have spent in Indian jungles, I would unhesitatingly say that I had derived most pleasure from a knowledge of the language, and the habits, of the jungle-folk. There is no universal language in the jungles; each species has its own language, and though the vocabulary of some is limited, as in the case of porcupines and vultures, the language of each species is understood by all the jungle-folk. The vocal chords of human beings are more adaptable than the vocal chords of any of the jungle-folk, with the one exception of the crested wire-tailed drongo, and for this reason it is possible for human beings to hold commune with quite a big range of birds and animals. The ability to speak the language of the jungle-folk, apart from adding an hundredfold to one's pleasure in the jungle, can, if so desired, be put to great use. One example will suffice.

Lionel Fortescue—up till recently a housemaster at Eton—and I were on a photographing and fishing tour in the Himalayas shortly after 1918, and we arrived one evening at a Forest Bungalow at the foot of a great mountain, on the far side of which was our objective, the Vale of Kashmir. We had been marching over hard ground for

many days, and as the men carrying our luggage needed a rest, we
decided to halt for a day at the bungalow. Next day, while Fortescue
wrote up his notes, I set out to explore the mountain and try for
a Kashmir stag. I had been informed by friends who had shot in
Kashmir that it was not possible to shoot one of these stags without
the help of an experienced shikari, and this was confirmed by the
chowkidar in charge of the Forest Bungalow. With the whole day
before me I set out alone, after breakfast, without having the least
idea at what elevation the red deer lived, or the kind of ground on
which they were likely to be found. The mountain, over which there
is a pass into Kashmir, is about twelve thousand feet high, and after
I had climbed to a height of eight thousand a storm came on.

From the colour of the clouds I knew I was in for a hailstorm,
so I selected with care a tree under which to shelter. I have seen
both human beings and animals killed by hail, and by the lightning
that invariably accompanies hailstorms, so rejecting the big fir-trees
with tapering tops I selected a small tree with a rounded top and
dense foliage, and collecting a supply of dead wood and fir-cones,
I built a fire, and for the hour that the thunder roared overhead
and the hail lashed down, I sat at the foot of my tree safe and warm.

The moment the hail stopped the sun came out, and from the
shelter of the tree I stepped into fairyland, for the hail that carpeted
the ground gave off a million points of light to which every
glistening leaf and blade of grass added its quota. Continuing up
for another two or three thousand feet, I came on an outcrop of
rock, at the foot of which was a bed of blue mountain poppies. The
stalks of many of these, the most beautiful of all wild flowers in the
Himalayas, were broken, even so these sky-blue flowers standing in
a bed of spotless white were a never-to-be-forgotten sight.

The rocks were too slippery to climb, and there appeared to be
no object in going to the top of the hill, so keeping to the contours
I went to the left, and after half a mile through a forest of giant
fir-trees I came to a grassy slope which, starting from the top of the
hill, extended several thousand feet down into the forest. As I came
through the trees towards this grassy slope I saw on the far side of
it an animal standing on a little knoll, with its tail towards me. From
illustrations seen in game books I knew the animal was a red
Kashmir deer, and when it raised its head, I saw it was a hind.

On my side of the grassy slope, and about thirty yards from the
edge of the forest, there was a big isolated rock some four feet high;

the distance between this rock and the knoll was about forty yards. Moving only when the deer was cropping the grass, and remaining still each time she raised her head, I crept up to the shelter of the rock. The hind was quite obviously a sentinel, and from the way she looked to her right each time she raised her head, I knew she had companions, and the exact direction in which these companions were. To approach any nearer over the grass without being seen was not possible. To re-enter the forest and work down from above would not have been difficult but would have defeated my purpose, for the wind was blowing down the hill. There remained the alternative of re-entering the forest and skirting round the lower end of the grass slope, but this would take time and entail a stiff climb. I therefore finally decided to remain where I was and see if these deer—which I was seeing for the first time—would react in the same way as chital and sambhur do to the call of a leopard, of which I knew there was at least one on the mountain, for I had seen its scratch-marks earlier in the day. With only one eye showing, I waited until the hind was cropping the grass, and then gave the call of a leopard.

At the first sound of my voice the hind swung round and, facing me, started to strike the ground with her forefeet. This was a warning to her companions to be on the alert, but those companions whom I wanted to see would not move until the hind called, and this she would not do until she saw the leopard. I was wearing a brown tweed coat, and projecting a few inches of my left shoulder beyond the rock I moved it up and down. The movement was immediately detected by the hind, who, taking a few quick steps forward, started to call; the danger she had warned her companions of was in sight, and it was now safe for them to join her. The first to come was a yearling, which, stepping daintily over the hail-covered ground, ranged itself along side the hind; the yearling was followed by three stags, who in turn were followed by an old hind. The entire herd, numbering six in all, were now in full view at a range of thirty-five yards. The hind was still calling, while the others, with ears alternately held rigid or feeling forward and backward for sound and wind direction, were standing perfectly still and gazing into the forest behind me. My seat on the melting hail was uncomfortable and wet, and to remain inactive longer would possibly result in a cold. I had seen a representative herd of the much-famed Kashmir deer, and I had heard a hind call, but there was one thing more that I wanted. That was, to hear a stag call; so I again projected a few inches of my shoulder beyond the rock, and had the satisfaction of hearing the stags, the hinds, and the yearling calling in different pitched keys.

My pass permitted me to shoot one stag, and for all I knew one of the stags might have carried a record head, but though I had set out that morning to look for a stag, and procure meat for the camp, I now realized that I was in no urgent need of a trophy. In any case the stag's meat would probably be tough so, instead of using the rifle, I stood up, and six of the most surprised deer in Kashmir vanished out of sight, and a moment later I heard them crashing through the undergrowth on the far side of the knoll.

It was now time for me to retrace my steps to the bungalow, and I decided to go down the grassy slope and work through the lighter forest at the foot of the mountain. The slope was at an angle that lent itself to an easy lope, provided care was taken to see that every step was correctly placed. I was running in the middle of the hundred-yard open ground and had gone about six hundred yards when I caught sight of a white object, standing on a rock at the edge of the forest on the left-hand side of the slope, and about three hundred yards below me. A hurried glance convinced me that the white object was a goat, that had probably been lost in the forest. We had been without meat for a fortnight and I had promised Fortescue that I would bring something back with me, and here was my opportunity. The goat had seen me, and if I could disarm suspicion would possibly let me pass close enough to catch it by the legs; so as I loped along I edged to the left keeping the animal in sight out of the corner of my eyes. Provided the animal stayed where it was, no better place on all the mountain could have been found on which to catch it, for the flat rock, at the very edge of which it was standing, jutted out into the slope, and was about five feet high. Without looking directly at it, and keeping up a steady pace, I ran past the rock and, as I did so, made a sweep with my left hand for its forelegs. With a sneeze of alarm the animal reared up, avoiding my grasp, and when I pulled up clear of the rock and turned round, I saw to my amazement that the animal I had mistaken for a white goat was an albino musk-deer. With only some ten feet between us the game little animal was standing its ground and sneezing defiance at me. Turning away I walked down the hill for fifty yards, and when I looked back, the deer was still standing on the rock, possibly congratulating itself on having frightened me away. When some weeks later I related the occurrence to the Game Warden of Kashmir he expressed great regret at my not having shot the deer, and was very anxious to know the exact locality in which I had seen it, but as my memory for places, and my description of localities, is regrettably faulty, I do not think that particular albino musk-deer is gracing any museum.

Excerpted from The Man-Eating Leopard of Rudraprayag *(Delhi: Oxford University Press, 1947).*

R. S. DHARMAKUMARSINH

An April Day in the Gir Forest

The Gir Forest is widely known as the only abode of the Asiatic lion. In fact, the sprawling jungle of acacia and teak in the Gir hills is more than just that. It is the only substantial stretch of natural forest that survives intact in the entire peninsula of Saurashtra. Dharmakumarsinh was from the Gohel Rajput family that ruled Bhavnagar, one of the larger states in the region. Though he had shot lions in his youth, he turned to studying the rich and varied bird life of the region. As an ornithologist he was the first to film and ring floricans in the wild and became an expert on the vanishing bird of the plains—the bustard. In Gir itself, he predicted the local extinction of the grey hornbill due to logging of hollow trees in which it nested and the killing of fledglings for use in indigenous medicine. His Birds of Saurashtra *is remarkable not only for studies of particular species but for his essays on bird-watching in forest and on the seashore. Here, he captures the sights and sounds of Gir on an early summer's day.*

Half an hour before sunrise to an hour after it is undoubtedly the best time for bird-watching during the hot weather. It is, therefore, well that we have started our drive through the forest at dawn while the last calls of the Spotted Owlet are still heard and as the King-Crow has begun giving out his alarm calls.

As we drive through the thin forest, we hear the song of Magpie-Robins. They are ubiquitous in the Gir and their song is singularly melodious. The cover on the roadside consists of almost pure teak, the stems standing bare with only a few dead leaves on them and giving one the vivid impression of rows of hat-stands with caps on the pegs. Now and then we pass by some green and red foliage consisting mostly of 'Karamda' bushes and 'Karapti' *(Garuga pinnata)* trees; a solitary Banyan tree or a 'Kadayo' *(Sterculia)* tree is also seen every few hundred yards before we reach a dry ravine where we stop and get out.

The place greets us with tall trees such as the 'Jambuda' *(Eugenia)* the Chanothi *(Abrus)*, the Tamarind and the *Terminalia*. A 'Karanj' *(Pongamia)* in leaf, appearing as if freshly painted with green, is refreshing to the eyes. Under this canopy of trees are thick bushes of 'Karamda', indeed an ideal refuge for bird and animal during the hot hours.

It is now sunrise. A pair of Magpie-Robins is seen seeking food from the lower branches of trees and walking amongst the fallen leaves. Grey Tits in pairs emit their *whichee-whichee* as they fly from tree to tree. Suddenly, we hear the metallic song of the Tickell's Flycatcher and, then, we catch sight of him as he darts into deep shades of the trees and back again to his perch. Then the pleasing and rhythmic song of the White-browed Fantail Flycatcher is heard. Presently, we see him as he flies low in his usual restless manner, turning round and flitting from one branch to another and often descending to the ground to pick up a minute insect. He displays all kinds of tricks such as looping the loop, spreading the tail, etc. He is one of the loveliest of the forest birds. These Flycatchers are usually found in pairs, prancing amongst low branches or chasing each other in a playful manner. What delicacy there is in their flight and movement!

Almost all the birds are seeking food by now and, strangely, it is in the leafless teak and thorny *Acacia* trees that we see most of them, flying from tree to tree almost in relay. We hear the harsh and prolonged call of the Golden-backed Woodpecker. His way of searching food is totally different to that of the Magpie-Robin and the Flycatchers. He alights near a trunk of a tree and works himself up spirally, stopping now and then to tap for wood-borers; occasionally, he is seen alighting on the ground to pick up a large insect. A golden flash and the red crest is all what strikes our eyes as he flies. Amidst slim branches, we catch a glimpse of the Pygmy Woodpecker as he moves up and down looking for food. His call and tapping are less audible and he seems to take a longer refuge among leaves and twigs. Also, some Small Minivets are seen on the *Acacia* trees situated in the open glade and the dry river bed.

As we walk along the river bed, we come to a drying pool of stagnant water which is alive with small fish, rising to the surface for air. Frogs are croaking to their heart's content all around. At the pool, we disturb a Fish-Owl which suddenly but silently flies away to a tree top. A Green Sandpiper in his grey and dark brown dress flies up swiftly and is in a moment out of sight, emitting his call. A pair of Common Kingfishers is fishing at the pool. These brilliantly coloured birds are the flying jewels of the forest.

From amongst the ruffling noise of dry teak leaves, we hear the alarm calls of the Jungle Babblers and in a moment or two, from the direction from where the calls were heard, a long-tailed mongoose appears chased by a troop of chattering Babblers.

Now, it is almost 8.00 a.m. and it is best to wait and watch at this pool. We might see some *chital* coming for a drink or a sounder of wild pigs approaching their favourite wallow close by. Also, the birds are returning to the green and shady trees in the ravine.

A Black-headed Oriole emits his harsh Jackdaw-like call. A group of amusing White-throated Babblers sneaks along the bank and flies in single file amidst bushes. A Pitta scurries into teak coppice and is quickly out of sight. One by one, we see birds coming down for a drink or to bathe, even in the smallest water hole. Central Indian Ioras, Spotted Doves, Magpie-Robins and all the rest mentioned above, except Woodpeckers and Owls, are quenching their thirst. What an unexpected assembly!

The Purple Sunbirds are seen and heard everywhere and the harsh call of the Large Cuckoo-Shrike is heard in the distance. A Black-headed Cuckoo-Shrike alights close by with his bill open and the wings half extended. An Iora makes a drumming sound with his wings as he flies. The variety of sounds one can hear in a jungle makes it a very fascinating place.

With the help of binoculars we look across the pool and spot a Black-capped Blackbird amidst dry dung close to a 'Nes', digging for insects in its Thrush-like style of cocking his head, first to the left and then to the right as if listening. It is rather late for it to stay, which makes one wonder whether it might not breed with us during the Monsoon months.

Sitting in the shade and leaning against a trunk of a tree, and carefully scanning the surroundings, we may catch sight of a slight movement which betrays an animal or bird well-camouflaged in its natural background. There we may discover a pair of rat-snakes

entangled in copulation amidst branches of trees, or a Scops Owl
which may have been watching us all the time. Or we may spot
a Jungle Nightjar resting on an overhanging branch or even a Green
Pigeon with only his tail and vent visible. Moreover, it is possible
that a Bird of Prey which has remained undetected with its back
towards us may betray itself by moving its head or tail. It is amazing
how many different birds and animals slowly begin to 'de-freeze'
and thus reveal themselves as they gain confidence about a man
sitting silently and motionless and blending well with the background.

After waiting for some time by the pool, we leave the place and
drive further on. Every few hundred yards or so we see a covey of
Jungle Bush-Quail on the dusty road bunched together, or come
across a Painted Sandgrouse crossing the road. A four-horned
antelope stands like a statue close to the road but bolts after a
moment or two. We pass small ravines and on the roadside banks
we disturb a White-breasted Kingfisher from his nest-hole who flies
away to a tree. A solitary Green Bee-eater is seen perched on a
slender twig and a pair of Indian Rollers is seated in thin forest close
to habitation.

The next place where we stop is a running stream with its banks
covered with *Eugenia* trees. On the riverside are Large and Little
Egrets, Red-wattled Lapwings, Common Sandpipers, and Ashy
Wren Warblers which emerge from the reed-beds and pour forth
their song with the bill pointing towards the sky and then disappear
as fast as they had come out. White Eyes are everywhere in the
greenery. We may even get a glimpse of a Reed-Warbler as he darts
into the reeds. The water is full of large and small fishes and an
occasional crocodile makes its appearance; turtles lazily rise to the
surface.

As the heat increases and the sun reaches the zenith, Vultures
fill the sky. A Crested Hawk Eagle sails in circles followed by a flock
of Crows. Crested Honey-Buzzards with their long necks and tails
are seen perched close together on leafless trees. If lucky, we may
even come across a solitary Crested Serpent Eagle, emitting his
double whistle or see him seated on a dry branch of a tree. When
this bird soars, its wing-tips curve upwards and it has a distinct
broad white band on its tail and wings. It has a habit of soaring
high, waiting for reptiles to come out and bask.

As we walk upstream amongst the *Eugenia* trees the overhanging branches of which shade the shallow waters, we flush a pair of White-necked Storks and a Fish-Owl. Today, the luck is with us because we spot a Mottled Wood-Owl. Of course, Tickell's Fly-catchers, Magpie-Robins and Fantail Flycatchers are all there; we cannot lose sight of them even if we wish to because they seem to be everywhere in the woods. However, it is noon already and too hot to walk and, therefore, we better go back to the camp for lunch and rest.

At 5.30 p.m., we return to the woods and wait near a slow flowing stream. The bird activity is at its ebb now, and the birds seem to feel the heat and have their mouths open. Later, however we shall perhaps see some birds which we missed in the morning.

Here comes a flock of Green Pigeons which settles on a nearby *Ficus* tree situated in an opening in the forest. What a gathering of birds there is all around us: Mynas, Red-vented Bulbuls, Crimson-breasted Barbets, Doves, Tree-pies, and Drongos! A pair of beautiful Blossom-headed Parakeets flies out emitting their characteristic squeaks which betray them from a distance. A pair of Crested Swifts flies low over the teak spreading their sharply forked tails when they glide. Here, near the road where the ground is firm and the forest thin, a Stone Curlew is sitting on its eggs under a solitary stunted thorny tree. A few yards away, a pair of White-bellied Minivets call at each other from the top of *Acacia* trees and a Yellow-fronted Pied Woodpecker utters his *kickerr*.

At sunset, we get a glimpse of a Paradise Flycatcher who bids us good night with his harsh call. This is the time when the Painted Sandgrouse come either in pairs or in flocks for a drink, uttering their *yek-yek* calls. They are even heard throughout the moonlit night. Presently, the nocturnal birds begin to call: the *pink-pink* of the Scops Owl, the *ghoom-ghoom* of the Fish Owl coming from a tall tree on the riverside, etc. A Painted Partridge is heard calling in the distance. As it becomes darker, the *chuck chuck-chuckerrr* of the Common Nightjar catches our ears, monotonous but pleasant. A Spotted Owlet calls close to the camp but the calls of the Jungle Nightjar which resemble the continuous *chook-chook, chook-chook* of a slowly puffing flour engine come from the thicker forests where the Mottled Wood Owl dwells.

On our way back to the camp, a black-maned lion reluctantly gives way to us as we pass by. After dinner, as we rise to go to bed, we hear a leopard sawing in the distance and a sambar giving his alarm call.

Indeed, we had a most interesting day and must now hasten to our beds to snatch a few hours sleep before we begin another glorious day among the birds and animals of the Gir Forest.

Excerpted from Birds of Saurashtra, India *(Mumbai: Times of India Press, 1951).*

EDWARD THOMPSON

Mainly about Lions

Thompson is best known as a historian for his work The Other Side of the Medal *(1926) which challenged the mainstream British imperial view of the Rebellion of 1857. Having lived and taught in Bengal, he was able to be closely in touch with several Indian leaders. As a votary of Indian freedom, Thompson also broached the issue of saving India's wildlife with Mahatma Gandhi but the latter assured him that it was on the increase in cities though not in the jungles! This essay reflects Thompson's keenness to go beyond cultures of shikar towards an India where wild birds and animals could live in safety.*

'The *Rhinoceros sondaicus* keeps on cropping up, though only on paper. He is a very rare beast indeed, there being only half-a-dozen or so of his species left. He inhabits this province [Burma] and Mr Verney, who is well known as a naturalist and explorer, has arrived and will attempt to shoot a specimen for the British Museum. Mr Verney is a very painstaking naturalist of the new school and spares himself no effort in an endeavour to present his specimens to the public in their correct settings. He came out not many months ago to shoot Tapir.'

The gratifying tidings I have quoted from an Indian weekly are of a recurring kind. 'A popular official' is reported as having bagged eighteen panthers in three days or it may be forty black buck in one day. Some may feel dubious as to whether the surviving party in these meetings is the more ornamental denizen of Indian ways; but it is not often that a panther or a black buck bags a popular official. We must take the world as we find it. The reader will be glad to know that Mr Verney's mission was entirely successful.

Rhinoceros sondaicus, as the paragraphist points out, is a very rare beast indeed. As the train crossed the Indus at Attock it was hard to believe that the first Mogul invader killed it there. All three Indian rhinoceroses must, I suppose, be taken as doomed to extinction. The last traces in the Sanderbans, so a Commissioner of Fisheries, whose work had kept him constantly there, told me in pre-War days, were reported as seen in these marshy flats somewhere about 1887. There used to be, before that, not very convincing rumours of rhinoceroses in the Mahanadi delta, but I never heard that any European ever saw them there. 1885 or so (I write from memory of old conversations with all sorts of wanderers) saw their disappearance from the Sonthal Parganas. *Sondaicus indicus* will (just) survive a while longer in the Nepal Terai (and Kuch Behar?), and *sondaicus* in Assam and Burma, and *sumatrensis* in the Chittagong hinterland and where Burma runs into Malaya. But I should like to know more definitely, from men who have seen these animals.

The beasts that must vanish are those that breed slowly or are hard to hide or exist in isolated spots. The Nilgiri Ibex is being looked after by means of permits, but needs this close supervision. The Kashmir Stag, a magnificent creature, would have gone long since if the Maharaja's private preserves had not kept it; it is to be hoped that these preserves will not be flung open in the present discontents and confusions, as those where the European Bison survived in Poland were flung open during the Great War. The Indian Bison is safe in South India. Indore in Central India still has a tiny herd, which the Prince protects and told me he had every intention of continuing to protect. He had taken note of what happened in the neighbouring State of Gwalior, whose last bison, a herd of thirty, were surrounded and shot down fifteen years ago by 'temporary gentlemen' (I am quoting a seditious Englishman who lives in Gwalior) who had taken the trouble to come over twenty miles in order to achieve this feat. As regards the wild ass, I told His Highness of Bikaner, in London last autumn, that I wished to intercede with him 'on behalf of an oppressed minority resident in his dominions'; the official books allege that Bikaner has 'a herd of about a hundred wild asses'. He told me that the books were wrong, and that he himself had never seen one, but that very occasionally one strayed into his borders from Bhawalpur. They still exist in Cutch, however, or did until yesterday. These, too, are in an isolated area, where they cannot be replenished from outside.

The fauna of India is so interesting because Malayan and African elements mingle, Central India being the actual meeting place. I was told that Princes and others who wanted cheetahs for hunting purposes now got them from Hyderabad. But the officer in charge of the Gwalior shikar department (who knew the whereabouts of everything shootable in his territory and kept a census) said that fifty or sixty survived in the State. They are found in Indore also. The hunting lynx, the caracal, is in both these States.

Everyone knows that the last lion in Central India was shot at Guna, in Gwalior, in 1873 (on Waterloo Day—too good a day for such a deed). Eleven years previously, one officer had shot eight at Guna; and late in the sixties, when the railway was being built, engineers shot two near Allahabad. A few months before the very last of all was killed, in 1873, four were shot in Jodhpur. The late Maharaja of Gwalior's praiseworthy effort to give his dominions lions again, nearly a quarter of a century ago, will be remembered. Unfortunately, tigers have increased in Gwalior, and they drove the lions (which in any case had been made too familiar with human beings before their enlargement) to the outskirts of the villages, whose inhabitants hunted them down. Nevertheless they managed to survive in the Sheopur jungles until two years ago. In 1930 the last isolated members were shot in several widely apart places, the very last of all near Jhansi. People still say they are there, but the Head of the Shikar Department says he knows that they are not. The Maharaja of Indore told me that one lion (whose lioness had been among the 1930 victims) was said to be hiding on the confines where Gwalior and Indore meet. 'I have been thinking of getting another lioness for him. I should like to entice him into my State and protect them.' 'If Your Highness will get him another lioness, that will be the best way of enticing him over.'

The lion seems certain to slip out of existence in Asia. During my Mesopotamian sojourn I kept a watchful mind open for news: a lioness and cubs were seen by an Indian trooper near Ahwaz in 1917 (reported in *The Times*), a lion cub was brought through Arab Village near Sannaiyat in 1916, one was shot in the Wadi marshes a year later, they lingered in the Pushtikuh and perhaps on the Khabur River, in pre-War days one had been shot at Sannaiyat by Commander Cowley (who perished in the Julnar attempt). These were the teasing stories I collected and kept against the background of such experiences as Englishmen had had not a century before (Layard, for example, reports in the most casual way seeing a flock of eight walking about on Tigris banks). Sir Arnold Wilson told me recently that the lion was now definitely extinct in Persia. He will be, or should be, glad to hear that this was undue pessimism. An official of the Bombay Natural History Society told me that they had received proof of lions still in Persia, in those Pushtikuh which we used to watch growing more deeply snowcapt, in the days of 1916; and also elsewhere.

Junagadh in Kathiawar, again as everyone knows, has the last Indian, and will keep the last Asiatic, lions. They once shrunk to about a dozen, and are now believed to be about a hundred. They have established themselves in several parts of adjoining Baroda, and the Diwan Sahib of Baroda assured me that the State intended to protect them. The Junagadh lions are reserved for distinguished executioners, Princes or Governors. It is the ritual for every Viceroy and Commander-in-Chief to shoot some before leaving India. They told me that Lord Reading came to do his duty with no great enthusiasm. A high Muslim official told off to attend him left off his jewelled slippers and climbed into the *machan* respectfully barefooted. Out of the jungle came a lioness and cubs, and the lioness proceeded to show her children, using the dead buffalo as a model, how to kill. Lord Reading proved a bad sportsman; instead of shooting them he looked on fascinated. Presently the cubs, their faces all gory, found the slippers and entered on a happy game, worrying them like kittens, and finally carried them off into the bush. Lord Reading came down from his *machan* and said, 'Drive me at once to the nearest telegraph office,' from which he sent a wire to Lady Reading saying that he had seen the greatest sight of his career, a wild lioness teaching her cubs to play. I shall be very sorry to hear that this story is not true.

Excerpted from A Letter from India *(London: Faber and Faber, 1943).*

SÁLIM ALI

Flamingo City

Sálim Ali was the grand old man of Indian ornithology. His Book
of Indian Birds *published in 1941 was the first of many tomes,
documenting the birds of South Asia, their behaviour, ecology and
distribution. He is best known for his ten-volume work* The
Handbook of the Birds of India and Pakistan, *co-authored with
S. Dillon Ripley and completed only a decade before his death.
But it is* The Fall of a Sparrow *(1985), from which this excerpt
is taken, which gives us a glimpse into the man behind the
genius.*

*Many of the young Sálim Ali's surveys for the Bombay Natural
History Society had to be carried out with private funding. Often,
he turned to the princes who ruled over a third of India. It was
the hospitality of various rulers that enabled him to survey diverse
ecosystems from Cochin and Travancore in the south to Sikkim
in the east and Bahawalpur in the west. The Maharaos of Kutch
who had a longstanding association with the BNHS made it
possible for him to visit the flamingo breeding grounds in the Rann
of Kutch. The 'city of flamingos' had been first reported in the
1890s by Maharao Khengarji but it was Sálim Ali's work that
forms the first major account of this amazing phenomenon. Ever
a shikari-cum-naturalist, in his original report on the Little Rann
of Kutch, he could not resist adding how the wild ass tasted if
cooked with spices! But it was the flamingos that were the
centrepiece of the landscape in the Great Rann and the young
Sálim Ali celebrated the spectacle of their breeding grounds, when
for a few weeks every year, the salt pans became a city of
flamingos.*

Among the Indian princes and princelings whom I had opportunities of knowing a little more intimately than others—chiefly on a naturalist's plane—was Maharao Vijayarajji of Kutch. He was over sixty when he came to the *gaddi,* having been on a patient and seemingly unending probation as Yuvraj for forty years or more, thanks to the robust good health of his father, Maharao Khengarji, who had come to be regarded by two generations of his loyal subjects as an ancient, indestructible monument of Kutch. Both father and son were keen sportsmen and knowledgeable naturalists, the former as a hunter of big game, the latter particularly interested in birds—game as well as in general. Besides being an excellent shot with gun and rifle, Vijayarajji was an accomplished tennis player in his younger days and a 'habitual' entrant in all-India tournaments, which he frequently won since many of the renowned players of the day were only too happy to partner him in the doubles.

I first became acquainted with Maharao Vijayarajji in 1942, soon after he, at long last, ascended the *gaddi.* By then he had lost some of his youthful vigour and assumed a comfortable, portly shape, abetted by lack of exercise forced by an injury to his knee. Though having to cut down on shikar jaunts needing physical exertion and mobility, he still retained an enviable expertise in small-game shooting and a lively interest in watching birds, especially of his own state. Thus it was at his invitation and under his generous sponsorship that I undertook a field survey of the bird life of his fascinating state with a view to producing for him an illustrated book on the birds of Kutch on the lines of my *Book of Indian Birds,* which had caught his fancy. In 1943 World War II was still very much on and petrol was severely rationed in India, bringing private transport virtually to a standstill. As a special sop to the ruling princes, however, an extra quota of petrol was allotted to them which, in the case of Kutch, enabled freer movement for the bird survey and visits to out-of-the-way places otherwise difficult to reach.

In between camps my party usually spent a couple of days in Bhuj for re-fitting, and each time I was in, the Maharao would invite me to accompany him on his evening drives to some scenic point in the environs of the town and 'take the air'. He was usually alone, attended only by a flunkey armed with a thermos, a bottle of 'pegs' and a supply of pistachios and almonds and things of that sort for

His Highness to while away his time pleasantly, while listening to or discussing my report on the progress of the survey. One of the things that struck me as singularly odd at the time—especially coming from a man normally so courteous and considerate—was that never in all these outings did he even once offer me any of the things he was stolidly munching away while the replenishing flunkey stood attentively at his elbow. That it should never have occurred to him to do so seems queer and inconceivable, yet there it was.

I am reminded by a note in my diary of that time of a crude manifestation of the anachronistic feudalism that still persisted in Kutch. I felt outraged, while responding to the Maharao's request to meet him at the palace for some discussion, to discover too late that it was mandatory for 'natives' to alight from their vehicles—whether car or horse carriage—at the main palace gate and cover the fifty yards or so up the drive to the entrance porch on foot. This mandate applied uniformly to all *Indians,* of whatever status, whether residents or visitors, official or non-official. The enormity of the *diktat* was that even the Indian *dewan* (chief minister) of the state visiting His Highness on official business had to 'crawl' in this fashion, while *any* European or Anglo-Indian of howsoever dubious a quality could drive straight up to the porch without let or hindrance, and perhaps even with a welcoming salute from the armed sentry at the gate. The 'reigning' dewan at the time of my survey, a highly respected senior Indian civilian, had to submit to this perverse indignity, while the lowly Anglo-Indian Customs Inspector could drive right up to the porch. I got a shock when ordered to alight at the main entrance, created a scene, and later protested to the Maharao in no uncertain terms about this insulting iniquity. I hope it had some effect, but I never had occasion to visit the palace a second time.

A peculiar oddity that amused me greatly when observing the intra- and interspecific habits and behaviour of that now-extinct genus—the maharaos, maharajas and nawabs—in the course of my bird surveys of the various Indian states, was the comic ostentation with which the rulers addressed each other, back and forth, as 'Your Highness' in tête-à-tête conversation, even though they might be old friends and contemporaries or close relations. When talking to one of 'lesser breed' some of them took good care, when referring to a brother Highness, to slip in inconsequentially—as though in parenthesis—such vital information as 'He is 13 guns, you know, I am 17' and thereafter run on with the discourse.

Kutch is a chronically drought-prone area, and a succession of bad monsoons will often inhibit breeding of the flamingos for two or three years. The birds need an optimum depth of six to eight inches of shallow inundation of their breeding ground to generate their mound-building activities. If the monsoon has failed or been deficient, this depth is never attained on the nest site. In that case the water leaves the site high and dry before September or October, when the normal breeding season should commence. If the monsoon has been heavy, as in 1944, the water on the site is too deep, and may take a long time to dry to the acceptable depth. Hence, unlike most nesting grounds in Asia, and in Europe, Africa and the New World, the season in Kutch is a moveable feast and unpredictable. It may range anywhere between September/October and March/April or be completely suppressed. The 'city' itself lies deserted the rest of the year, since after the birds have finished breeding they disperse far and wide along with the newly fledged young in small flocks or large feeding concentrations, frequenting coastal lagoons and salt pans, as at Point Calimere, and in Saurashtra and Sri Lanka. In the non-breeding season they also frequent brackish lakes such as Sambhar in Rajasthan, Chilka in Orissa, and others.

Knowing my special keenness to study the Kutch flamingo and the disappointments I had had on earlier visits to the breeding grounds, the Maharao had a special lookout kept on flamingo movements in the Great Rann. That is how I received an express telegram from him one day in April 1945 while I was in the midst of hectic preparations in Bombay for the birding 'pilgrimage' to Kailas and Manasarovar the following month. The breeding colony—'Flamingo City'—was then at the peak of its activities and I was urged to come immediately. This long-awaited opportunity, coming even at such an awkward moment, was too good to miss. I arrived in Bhuj by air two days later. Air flights were elementary and erratic in the war years and trains were slow and leisurely, involving connections at Viramgam and elsewhere with metre-gauge lines through various Kathiawar principalities, each of which insisted on maintaining a few measly miles of its own railway system, more as a status symbol than anything else. These operated to uncoordinated timings, no doubt to assert their independent status on neighbouring princelings across the fence. Since the states did not subscribe to the fetish of punctuality you were lucky if you sometimes caught your connections. Then, finally, you had to bivouac for the night on the crowded platform at Navlakhi in Jamnagar—a sort of open air dormitory free for all—to take the motor launch across to Kandla in Kutch next morning, followed by four hours in an exasperatingly sluggish narrow-gauge train before you finally arrived in Bhuj, a total of forty hours or so from Bombay.

In Bhuj I had the pleasure of meeting Sir Peter Clutterbuck, a former Inspector-General of Forests in India who had done a stint as Chief Conservator of Forests in Kashmir State after retirement, and was now in Kutch at Maharao Vijayarajji's invitation to reorganize the Forest Department of the state. Throughout his Indian service, Sir Peter had the reputation of being an exceptionally able forest officer and a dedicated naturalist and conservationist. Though no longer young, he had expressed to the Maharao a keen desire to visit Flamingo City along with me, in spite of the summer heat and physical hardships involved in the journey.

A fairly sybaritic rented camp had been set up by the Kutch durbar for our overnight halt at Nir, which was reached from Bhuj via Khavda, partly by car and partly on camelback (about seventy miles). I recall the acrimonious political key on which my relationship with Sir Peter opened at the tête-à-tête dinner that night—damask tablecloth, silver cutlery, liveried waiters! The years of the World War and the decade or so before, with Mahatma Gandhi and the Satyagraha Movement in operation, had embittered relations between Indians and the British to an unprecedented degree. All the British in India, government servants high and low, as well as the boxwallahs—were scandalized and almost foaming at the mouth over the 'subversive' preachings and mischief of that 'seditionist rat Gandhi', as Meinertzhagen had called him, and his traitorous henchman Nehru—even after the correct education he had received at Harrow and Cambridge. Earlier in the evening Sir Peter had thus gratuitously started unburdening himself on the subject, and now gave me an unprovoked broadside of the pent-up venom of his spleen. As I have confessed before, I have never been famous for the sweetness of my temper, and here was sufficient provocation for jettisoning restraint. I am afraid perhaps I said more nasty things than the occasion called for, but it did help to clear the atmosphere between Sir Peter Clutterbuck and myself for ever after. I made it plain to him that I had no wish or intention to convert him from his firm convictions, nor would it be worth his while to try to change my views—and that was that; we both had a deep common interest in birds and wildlife, so why not confine ourselves to those topics and leave politics to the politicians? After this first unfortunate but decisive confrontation, I found Sir Peter a singularly charming and delightful companion, and the friendship and mutual regard generated on that flamingo trip endured till his death in about 1958 in England, where I was happy to have met him a few months earlier. The catalyst in our bond of friendship was partly also his doting son Brigadier J. E. (Jack) Clutterbuck, R. E., who retired from India in 1948 as Chief Engineer of the then G. I. P. Railway after many years of meritorious service, to start a new life in England—farming in Somerset. Jack was to me a kindred spirit, an altogether lovable and admirable character, mad about the Indian jungles where we had spent many happy days together from time to time camping, shooting, trekking and naturalizing. He was one of my closest and most cherished English friends.

The traditional Flamingo City—the same as used by the birds year after year at least since 1896 when first reported—lies some 10 kilometres north-east of Nir (at the tip of Pachham Island), out in the pancake-flat featureless Rann. To reach the place one has to wade on foot or ride on local ponies or camels which skid and slither alarmingly through the ankle- to thigh-deep water, more or less concentrated brine, of over-soft, slippery slush often overlaid by a deceptive crust or razor-sharp salt crystals like splintered glass. Under the intense desert sun it produces the blinding glare of freshly fallen snow. The fetlocks of the ponies sometimes get badly lacerated as the hoofs sink through the crunchy surface. Thankfully, the April heat felt less oppressive than the 45°C+ shown by the thermometer, because a cool breeze blew throughout the day and even made a cotton coverlet distinctly welcome at night in our open-to-sky bivouac. This was, and still remains, the only occasion it was possible to make a fairly accurate physical count of the population of Flamingo City in a peak breeding year, and to observe something of the nocturnal movements and behaviour of the birds, for it was a period of brilliant moonlight with a clear sky and optimal conditions. However, the lack of fresh water at the site, and of fuel for cooking and fodder of any kind for the riding and draft animals, made a longer stay than our two nights 'on location' impossible. This would necessitate elaborate and carefully planned previous *bandobast*. After measuring out the total area of the colony on the ground and randomly demarcating several 'built up' sample plots of about 90 metres x 90 metres each, and allowing for the bald (unbuilt) patches in between the nest clusters, I calculated the total number of occupied nests in the 'city' to be 104,758. On the basis of this figure, and taking two adults to each nest and two young to every three nests, plus the hordes of non-breeding adults and sub-adults around the colony, the total population would probably be of the order of half a million birds. This would undoubtedly make Flamingo City the largest breeding colony of the Greater Flamingo in Asia, and at least *one* of the largest in the world. I have long realized the potential of the Great Rann of Kutch as an area for biological surprises, justifying a full-scale scientific exploration, and regretted not being able to carry out a more thorough and extensive survey myself. On a subsequent visit to Flamingo City I was lucky to discover a colony of Avocets *(Recurvirostra avosetta)* breeding in its 'suburbs'—the first ever record for the subcontinent—and on another visit a few years later a nesting colony of Rosy Pelicans *(Pelecanus onocrotalus)*—also the first—among the worn-down disused flamingo nests on the periphery.

To make doubly sure that the camera he had lent me (to replace mine which had developed a last-minute hitch) behaved as it should in my hands, Maharao Vijayarajji had considerately sent out from Bhuj the state photographer, Ali Mohammad, with complete paraphernalia and a special assistant, whose function was not immediately apparent. The two photographers and their equipment made up two complete camel loads. The vintage apparatus—a full-plate studio camera of solid teakwood, enormous proportions and cumbrousness—looked like some antique piece of furniture from the period of William the Conqueror or thereabouts. It had no mechanical shutter but worked by smartly doffing and donning a cap over the lens with the photographer's hand. In open sunshine, despite the operator's lightning sleights-of-hand, the comparatively slow plates, and the diaphragm shut down to a pinpoint, the negatives were often somewhat overexposed. It was obviously a camera with a history, and quite believably the same as made the original picture published in the *Journal* of the BNHS by Maharao

Khengarji in 1896 giving positive evidence of flamingos breeding in the Rann. The apparatus not only needed two able-bodied men to rig it up for action on its massive wooden tripod, but also for its complicated co-operative operation. It was worked like a ship, and this is where the trained assistant became indispensable. The chief photographer (the Captain) had to enshroud his head in yards of black cloth, eyes glued to the focussing screen. From this position—the 'bridge'—he signalled orders down to the 'engine room', as it were, to the assistant in front, to twiddle the focussing knob a trifle this way or that to get the correct focus. The focussing knob was out of reach of the Captain himself and only a specially trained assistant could assist. The camera erected at the nest colony, 'on location', showed up from afar in the vast expanse as a fair-sized house, and, when a wind sprang up and the black shroud round the Captain's head began to flutter and flap, I thought there could be no earthly chance of getting any photographs of the birds. I am afraid at that point I also became rather uncharitably facetious at the Captain's expense, but he bore it all with surprising good humour. It was not until we got back to Bhuj and he produced the most unexpectedly good results from his dark room that I realized the laugh had really been on me, and that it needs something more than a good camera to produce a good photograph.

An edition of 1,000 copies of *The Birds of Kutch* with twenty colour plates by D. V. Cowen, fully funded by the Kutch durbar, was published by Oxford University Press for the Government of Kutch in 1945, under severe wartime constraints. It was acclaimed by reviewers in India and abroad. Five hundred copies of the book were retained by the Maharao for presentation to his state guests. Unfortunately, these copies were carelessly stored in a damp cellar where most were destroyed by white ants. The publication was priced at a nominal Rs 20 per copy and the edition was soon exhausted, second-hand copies fetching up to $100 thereafter.

One of our camps during the Kutch bird survey was in a tiny godforsaken desert village of a few down-and-out hovels called Rapar on the easternmost edge of the state, bordering on the Little Rann. The only comparatively substantial building within its mud-walled 'fort' was the police station manned by a couple of policemen and their camels for patrolling the area, and a single *puggee* whose main job was to walk round the village in the early morning and at evening dusk, eyes on the ground, to monitor the footprints of any strangers, human or camel, that may have entered or left the village since the last scrutiny. The station house had been cleared for our use by orders from above. It was at Rapar that we first came across this very remarkable tribe of hereditary trackers (*puggee* from 'pug', meaning foot, or footprint). They are as familiar with the footprints of the inhabitants of a village as with their faces, and can tell with absolute confidence whether particular footprints, human or camel, belong to a resident or to a visiting outsider. In desert areas where camel-stealing is one of the favourite local pastimes, this accomplishment is of the greatest help to the police in tracking down not only lost or stolen camels, but also camel thieves and other criminals. One or two such *puggees* formed the normal complement of every remote police outpost. The hereditary expertise these professional trackers have acquired through generations is phenomenal and truly amazing.

Khan Bahadur Malcolm Kothavala, the Inspector-General of Police in Kutch at the time of the survey, who had unmatched experience of *puggees* in the various desert states of Rajputana where he had served, related the case of a camel stolen from a border village like Rapar. This camel had a very slight limp in its left foreleg and its footprints were in consequence distinctive, but only for the local *puggee*. One night the camel disappeared along with a stranger who, as the ground monitoring had shown, had entered the village the day before. The village *puggee* got on the trail and followed the camel led by the stranger for several miles beyond the village till the ground became too hard and stony for any clues, and the trail was lost. Two years later this *puggee* took leave to go to his village miles away but in the same direction as the camel he had followed. While moving around his village, like a busman on holiday, he happened upon a camel's footprints which he confidently identified as those of the animal he had trailed two years before, but the footprints of the man leading it were different. Anyhow, he followed the spoor to its owner's house. On questioning the man it turned out that he had purchased the animal from its former owner a few months earlier. The seller was traced and from his footprints the *puggee* confirmed his identification as the person who had led the camel away from its native village. After the normal gentle third-degree persuasion, the thief confessed. Both he and the purchaser of stolen property got it in the neck, and the camel was restored to its rightful owner in its rightful village. The Khan Bahadur had many other stories of the phenomenal feats of tracking performed by these simple untutored folk, with the skill passed down from father to son through countless generations. It is a pity that, with increasing sophistication in methods of crime detection, the *puggees* are fast losing their importance as well as the skill and expertise they have acquired through the ages—and with it their jobs and livelihood.

In 1945, R. I. Pocock, who was revising the Mammalia volumes of the Fauna of British India series, wrote to the BNHS asking whether it could arrange to obtain a few fresh specimens of the Kutch wild ass for critical study, since adequate material was lacking in the British Museum (Natural History). Maharao Viajyarajji, with his accustomed generosity, offered to provide all facilities to the Society for a collecting expedition in the Little Rann, which is the stronghold of this animal. I was doing the bird survey of Gujarat at the time (March 1946) and was glad to avail of the opportunity for a closer acquaintance with this rare and interesting animal, the ecology and biology of which was so little known. It would also give me a chance to investigate the birds of the Little Rann which I had missed during the Kutch survey, and long suspected to be the only breeding ground of the Lesser Flamingo (*Phoeniconaias minor*) in the Indian region.

A narrative of the wild ass expedition with field notes on the habits and food, etc., of the species, together with measurements and other details of the five specimens collected, is published in the *Journal* of the BNHS [in 1946]. To weigh the animals in the field a rough-and-ready beam scale had to be improvised, hung from a tree with a wild ass at one end and three or four domestic ones (i.e. my camp followers!) at the other. The latter were subsequently weighed individually on a standard weighing machine and tolerably accurate weights of the animals obtained. The trip proved highly rewarding also from the ornithological angle. We fortuitously struck a vast open expanse of shallow brackish water in the debouchment of the Banas river into the Rann, where there was a heavier concentration of migratory ducks, waders and other birds than I had ever seen before or have since—duck by the million darkening the water for miles, the majority apparently Common Teal (*Anas crecca*) with a sprinkling of hordes of Shovellers (*Spatula clypeata*), and doubtless many other species not distinguishable in the distance. Besides these, there were some eighty Rosy Pelicans and three to five lakh Lesser Flamingo (*Phoeniconaias minor*) (*no* Greater), countless thousands of sandpipers, stints, redshanks, greenshanks and others; also thousands of Common and Demoiselle Cranes, all apparently collecting for the outward migration. Unfortunately I never had a chance to visit this place at the proper time again.

Excerpted from The Fall of a Sparrow *(Delhi: Oxford University Press, 1985).*

SÁLIM ALI

Stopping by the Woods
on a Sunday Morning

*For Sálim Ali, the joy of bird-watching in India lay not so much
in coming across rare species as in the incredible profusion of species
in virtually any garden, pond or patch of green; and it is this that
he celebrates in this piece, written in 1930.*

The island of Salsette, the potential Greater Bombay, is a veritable
Dr Jekyll and Mr Hyde. For the greater part of the year it sleeps
under the drab mantle of desiccated grass and dustladen foliage,
which is only lifted here and there in patches as the hot weather
advances, revealing gorgeous tints of scarlet and orange as the
various flowering trees, the silk cotton, the coral and the butea
(palas), blossom forth in masses of living flame.

But what a transformation the first few showers of the monsoon
bring about. It is as though some magician had, by a pass of his
wand, instilled fresh life into every object in the countryside. The
grass springs up everywhere, and with it a host of innumerable
monsoon weeds, till soon, the whole landscape becomes one great
fantasy in green.

Pools and puddles begin to form. The bull frog awakens to the
song of spring after his protracted underground slumbers, and his
croaking fills the air as he joyfully serenades his lady love. Soon she
will lay her eggs in some sequestered pond, where a few days later
innumerable multitudes of tadpoles will emerge to carry on the race
and save music from extinction.

We shall select some Sunday morning late in August for a jaunt
into the exquisite country surrounding the city. The heaviest blast
of the monsoon is blown over, and we may now look forward

without undue optimism to fine weather. The air is delightfully cool, the sky thinly overcast; banks of threatening nimbus drift across the heavens resulting only in occasional drizzles which help to subdue the uncomfortable steamy vapour that begins to rise immediately after the sun peeps out of his cloudy veil.

We leave our car by the side of the road, and loading ourselves with haversacks containing some sandwiches, a water bottle, specimen tubes and a camera, we commence the trudge into the interior. Creepers of that magnificent lily, *Gloriosa superba*, aptly named, are growing in every hedge. A few of the flowers are out, though the majority will bloom after a couple of weeks. Every monsoon, this creeper springs into life from the bulbs lying latent underground from the previous session.

The flower itself is a picture of loveliness, yellow, red and green. The delicately shaped tapering leaves terminate in tactile tendrils which readily entwine themselves round any object that comes within their reach. Would that colour photography were easier of attainment. No ordinary photograph can ever hope to do justice to this exquisite flower. The gloriosa lily is, as it were, part and parcel of the suburban countryside of Bombay in the rains.

Large numbers of a wild gentian are also out in the swampy grass fields now, while clusters of the dazzling red ixora flowers are present on all sides. Everything is calling out to the naturalist; would that this state of loveliness could survive the months to come, of dust and heat and desiccation.

We follow the path leading into the 'hinterland', the main object of our ramble this morning being to locate birds' nests. We turn our footsteps towards the hills, on the other side of which lies beautiful Tulsi lake hemmed in by verdure which might rival in magnificence that of any tropical rain forest.

The monsoon is the breeding season par excellence of insectivorous birds, and also of the numerous others who, though when adult, subsist principally on grain, yet require soft food in the nature of juicy grubs and caterpillars to nourish their young in the nest. Owing to the sprouting of fresh grass and vegetation, the caterpillars, which also appear at this time in devastating hordes, find easy sustenance. Thus, it is in birds that providence has devised the most efficient automatic control agencies. Were it not for the check exercised by man's feathered friends at this crucial period, a time would soon come when not only crops but all vegetation would cease to be. Such is the astounding rate at which insects multiply that no power of man's invention alone would ever be capable of stemming the overwhelming tide of their numbers.

There is warbling and song on every side; courting and nest-building are in progress everywhere, and a few early birds are already catching the worm, that is to say, those who have already undertaken parental cares are now busy feeding their chicks.

Finding a nest in thick cover is by no means a simple matter. There are people who will cover miles of a morning in the most promising-looking country and complain to you later that they did not come upon a single nest; that, as a matter of fact, there were no nests to come upon. Happily, there is a knack in locating birds' nests, and to hope to come upon them accidentally is futile. If this were not so, it would result in a very serious menace to the birds and be a grave impediment to their success in rearing families.

Nests are protected from their enemies either by being built in such secluded spots that without a clue of some sort, no one would think of searching for them there; or they are built of such material and design and with so much cunning and camouflage that to the untrained eye they either become totally invisible or entirely unsuspicious looking objects.

The nest of the Purplerumped Sunbird, common almost throughout India, affords a case in point. It is a pendulous pouch attached to the tip of an outhanging twig of the *ber* or *babool* tree, seldom more than eight or ten feet from the ground. The material employed in its construction is fine rootlets, and fibres, and the whole thing is so untidily plastered over on the outside with all manner of rubbish—spiders egg cases, pieces and shreds of pith, bark and paper, strings of caterpillar borings and droppings, and so on—as to resemble to perfection a mass of rubbish, and least likely to attract the attention of the casual passerby.

The simulation is further heightened by the fact that the entrance to the nest—a round hole near the top of the pearshaped structure, surmounted by a tiny little porch—is always on the inside, i.e., facing the tree, and therefore concealed from the intruder. Such camouflaged nests usually get detected only on account of the movements of their owners, their comings and goings with building material or with food for their young or, otherwise, by their inordinate fussiness.

The trick of locating nests, therefore, lies not so much in

traversing miles of likely country as in keeping an ever-watchful eye as you slowly saunter along, and patiently waiting for the birds to give away their secrets of their own accord.

An insignificant little brown and white bird, somewhat smaller than a bulbul, silently slips off a *karonda* bush at our approach, and flies into a neighbouring tree whence the field glasses disclose his apparent anxiety. This behaviour is distinctly suggestive. We walk upto the bush and peer inside. A pleasant surprise is in store.

There, concealed from view by the large green leaves and almost in the centre, is a deep cup made of rootlets and grass slung hammockwise between the stems of two monsoon plants. It is plastered on the outside with a supply of cobwebs. The cup is so deep that we have to bend right over for a view of the contents. It holds three beautiful roundish eggs, yellow-white in colour, with fine ruddy specks. Having photographed the nest, we withdraw behind a neighbouring bush and await the return of the unidentified proprietor.

Finding the coast clear, our friend approaches, he is too cautions to fly straight up to the nest. Alighting on the further side of the bush, he hops from twig to twig, peering through the tangle to assure himself that the danger is past. Soon, he comes into full view and in the twinkling of an eye, slips in and is settled on the eggs. Binoculars now disclose his identity.

He, or it may be she, for both sexes are alike and take part in incubation, is the Yellow-eyed Babbler, a chestnut-brown bird with white underparts and a conspicuous white streak over the eye. Close relatives of the well-known 'seven sisters', Yellow-eyed Babblers go about in small parties, searching for insect prey among bushes and under fallen leaves. During this, their bridal season, the males constantly clamber up to the exposed tips of bushes and tussocks of grass, and burst forth into a pleasant little song of several loud and melodious notes.

Leaving the yellow-eye to its parental cares, we proceed on our way. A great commotion set up by a pair of fussy little Tailorbirds draws us towards the thick tangle of a large-leafed creeper. The anxious couple hops around us from bush to bush, expressing the deepest concern in a series of alarmed 'pit-pit-pit-pits'. Their antics lead to a search which is soon rewarded by the revelation of that beautiful little sartorial masterpiece, the tailor's home.

A large pendant leaf is folded round in the shape of a funnel, and neatly stitched with thread of vegetable down along the edges. Within the cone so formed is a regular cup of fibres lined with cotton and down. The nest is fresh but empty, but we soon discover a trio of fluffy chicks, stumpy-tailed little mites, who have obviously just made their debut into the world. They sit huddled together on an adjacent twig, too innocent yet to have learnt anything of the wiles and treacheries of the world, and so, are perfectly fearless and confiding. Unfortunately, the light is far from satisfactory, and we have perforce to resume our tramp without having used the camera.

The Tailorbird is one of our three commonest warblers, and certainly the most accomplished nest-builder of them all. The other two are also tiny birds of about the same size with longish, loosely-set tails, and are known as the Ashy Wren-warbler and the Indian Wren-warbler respectively. Both these are also busy with family cares at the present time, and, as a matter of fact, we have not far to go before we alight on a nest of the former.

It is on the farther side of a nullah that lies across our path. We catch a glimpse of the occupant as he takes off from a chunk of the large leafed monsoon weeds now so abundant everywhere. Marking down the spot, we wade across and bend low to have a good look under the leaves. There it is, a structure not unlike the abode of the Tailorbird, which, to our delight, contains three tiny, polished, brick red eggs.

The remarkable thing about this nest is that it hangs directly over a used cattle path, on which the hoof marks still show—muddy puddles indicating that cattle have just gone over. Each time an animal passes this way, the nest must be brushed aside and shaken violently. The bird is undoubtedly an optimist; but it has at least the courage of its convictions, and is now well on the way to bringing up a family, mischievous herd boys permitting.

That dainty little fairy waltzer, the Fantail Flycatcher, whose cheery song and lively movements delight every resident of Bombay fortunate enough to possess a garden, has also turned his fancy to thoughts of love. In a lime tree growing in a semi-deserted garden, barely at a height of four feet from the ground, a marvellous little cone-shaped cup, two inches across, is marked down by following a bird carrying off a caterpillar. It is well plastered on the exterior with that approved cement of bird architects, cobwebs.

Three little baby birds occupy this nest. They are nearly full-fledged and will sally forth into the world in a day or two. Everybody acquainted with the fantail knows what a fury it can become when its nest is in danger. The parents promptly launch a violent attack, pecking at our hats and uttering feverish chucks of irritation, which, no doubt, are far from complimentary language.

The harmony within the fantail household is an object lesson in domestic give-and-take. We are astonished at the way in which three strapping, grown-up, hungry chicks can accommodate themselves amicably in this diminutive domicile. They are packed so tightly together that two of them have their wings hanging over the edges of the nest.

The Common Iora's nest is a very similar structure to the flycatcher's, with this consistent difference that while in the fantail's nest, strips of grass and rubbish are left dangling below, the Iora's is well rounded off at the bottom. Ioras also nest at this time of the year. They usually select a crotch formed by horizontal or vertical twigs, building skillfully around them so as to incorporate the supports into the wall of the nest.

The cup is composed of grass, fine roots and fibres, and here again, cobwebs play an important role in the lacing. In addition to binding the material firmly together, cobwebs serve as an efficient waterproof covering to prevent the water from seeping in through the sides of the nest. When the bird is sitting on its eggs, the plumage of the back is frowzled out and raised to form a dome. The fluffy feathers of the lower back, moreover, overhang the sides of the nest, the tout ensemble forming a most effective protection against the heaviest monsoon shower.

Birds are loath to allow their eggs to get cooled. While we are getting the camera ready to photograph the nest, the sitting bird is alarmed and leaves. Presently, a drizzle intervenes; the hen iora takes up her position on the eggs regardless of our proximity, nevertheless keeping one eye intently on our movements.

Although male Bayas (weaver birds) have begun to don their nuptial garb about the time of the rains breaking and quite a number may be seen playing at nest construction, they hardly give serious thought to parental responsibilities till the monsoon is well advanced. Around the end of August, operations begin in earnest and work is in full swing everywhere. Unlike the sunbird, the lion's share of the work appears to devolve on the cocks. The hens make their appearance on the scene only at a later stage. Their arrival invariably causes a great flurry amongst the lovelorn swains, whose strutting, impetuous advances must be quite embarrassing to the fair ones.

It is getting late in the afternoon, and we are a good way off from the car. Our way back lies through patches of open grass-land, where the cattle from the neighbouring village are turned out to graze. Amongst these we find numbers of large white birds with long slender necks and pointed dagger-like bills. They run freely in and out of the animals feet, darting forward every now and again with lightning rapidly at the insects and grasshoppers disturbed in their progress. These are the Cattle Egrets, found in attendance on village cattle all over India. They are now in their breeding livery; golden on the neck and the back.

A monsoon ramble through the woods will delight anyone who has the eyes to see and the soul to wonder at the romance and charm of this other world within our world. The electrification of the suburban railways has now thrown the delightful country in the environs of Bombay within comfortable and speedy reach of everybody. To the lover of the out-of-doors, the opportunities are such as might rightly be the envy of the less fortunate dwellers of almost every one of the other large cities in this country. Yet, how few are there who will sacrifice their Sunday morning sleep.

Excerpted from Express Magazine, *11 November 1984.*

KAILASH SANKHALA

Penitence

Born in 1925 and the son of a forester in Jodhpur state, Rajasthan, Kailash Sankhala was among the first trainees of the forest service in independent India. At the time, no one was put in charge of a division till he had shot dead a tiger. The Inspector General of Forests M. D. Chaturvedi had himself killed 50 tigers and was to argue at the time that the species was in no danger of decline. Sankhala's is a tale of a reluctant hunter gunning down his first— and last—tiger. By the time he wrote this account in his autobiography Tiger! *in 1978, Sankhala had done much to create an alternative tradition, having served as the first Director of Project Tiger, launched five years earlier. Even Sariska, the forest where he had gunned down the animal, had become a tiger reserve. This is a moving account from an era that is over, from one of those who helped usher in a new, more sensitive attitude to the tiger and its fellow inhabitants of Indian hill and plain. It is a tale of sorrow at having slain an innocent animal.*

My home State of Rajasthan in northern India derives its name from *Registhan*, 'land of sand', and indeed 50 per cent of it is part of the Thar desert. It is famed for its wildlife and for tiger hunting or *shikar*, and its hunting registers record all the well-known names of the British Raj, from George V to Queen Elizabeth and Prince Philip.

I was born at Jodhpur on the fringe of the desert where the first rains are greeted with feasting and ceremonial drenching. My people came from still further west, almost from the heart of the desert of Jaisalmer where the phenomenon of water falling from the sky has to be explained to children. Just when they left Jaisalmer is not known, but their exodus must have been in a year of exceptional drought, and they settled in the first depression which had even a trickle of water. This village, Chopsani, six miles from Jodhpur, featured in the history of the two world wars as the school of the gallant soldiers of the Jodhpur Risala.

My father was a forest ranger, and his area in the Aravali Hills was famous for sloth bears and leopards. In many of the villages it was not safe to be out after sunset as the paths were virtually taken over by leopards on the prowl looking for goats and dogs. We children had strict instructions to return home before dark to avoid encounters with wild boars or hyenas. Jodhpur was once the finest region for antelopes and often we would see a herd of blackbuck on the way to school. The richness of the blackbuck population, which lingers even today in some pockets (Dholi Sanctuary, near Jodhpur, for instance) was partly due to religious protection by the Vishnoi community, but the main protection for all wildlife in those days was by princely decree; only the Maharaja and members of his family could shoot. Instances are on record where the Maharaja pardoned a crime of murder but exiled those who shot leopards or tigers without permission. Even in cases of defence of property people would wait for the shikar officers rather than take the law into their own hands: benefit of the doubt was always given to the animals.

My father lost his father at the age of six, and was brought up by my grandmother, who earned a precarious living on our small farm. Although totally uneducated herself, she respected education and somehow managed to send her son to school. Afterwards my father trained in surveying and engineering, eventually becoming sub-overseer with a construction company which was building the Maharaja of Jodhpur's palace. Then the State Department needed a field surveyor, and to do this work my father was appointed Forest Ranger—even though he had had no training in forestry. My mother augmented the family income by keeping dairy animals, and I still begrudge her affection for the calves and our occasional neglect when it came to sharing the milk.

Foresters' sons do not settle down well. Partly this is due to living in primitive conditions with no educational facilities, or with frequent changes of village schools. The lack of playmates and social life make such children shy, which is not helpful when it comes to competing in life. My father earned less than Rs 60 a month (about £ 4) and it was not possible for his four children to board out, so my mother stayed at Jodhpur for our schooling while my father lived mostly by himself in the forests. I was the only one of the family who could go on to college.

Having failed to become an engineer himself, my father very much wanted me to succeed as one, for the profession had much prestige and was well paid. In order to study engineering at college I had to offer mathematics; I attended two lectures on trigonometry but failed to understand it so, without my father's knowledge, I changed to biology. By the time he came to know about this it was too late for the decision to be changed.

Biology I liked. My interest was in plants, especially the desert plants. Early in my college career an offer came to join an expedition to cross the Thar desert in May, the hottest month. The idea was to study the ecology in the worst period. I joined as botanist and photographer, and although the leader of the expedition was a fraud and the project collapsed I learned in that short time to love the desert. At first sight animal life appears to be non-existent, but late in the evening the desert comes to life. Hedgehogs, hares, rats and insects become active and their predators—foxes, both red and silver, and snakes—look for an easy meal. Even a small group of chinkara gazelles crossed the sand dunes with the same ease as they negotiate rocky hills and ravines. Already I had identified what was to become India's first and only Desert National Park; I had to wait until 1970 to initiate the idea, and I pursued it for another seven years, so my ultimate success in establishing it was particularly satisfying.

On my return to college I prepared an 8 mm film on vegetation types which I submitted as part of the course leading to a Master's degree. Although it gained me no credit at college it put me at the head of the queue for selection to the Forest Service. By that time the princely States had merged and appointments to the Forest Service, previously given to the chosen few, were extended to everyone. Overnight I became a potential forester. My father, whose interest in wildlife and plants had by then led him to become Director of Jodhpur Zoo, at last had a sparkle in his eye: his son was settled, and in his own old profession.

I joined the Indian Forest College at Dehra Dun and two years passed uneventfully measuring heights and diameters at 'breast height' (which seemed to me a curious word to use in forestry, since neither trees nor foresters have breasts). During my training period all that I learned about wildlife management was how to protect trees from animals and whether seven strands of wire, a deep trench or an electric fence would best hold back elephants or deer from plantations. But this training reinforced my love of outdoor life and gave me a clear understanding of forest ecology and the different habitats of India's wildlife.

At one time I was tempted to switch to history. In medieval times Rajasthan was divided into small principalities which were always fighting among themselves, and each one built forts for its defence. I became fascinated by these ruins. Overgrown with grasses and creepers, their wells filled with debris, these fortresses are now the haunt of tigers, leopards, hyenas and jackals; but they have witnessed forgotten events of history, feuds and atrocities and human sufferings. They seem to echo to the galloping hooves of horses, the rattle of swords, the cries of dying soldiers, and the melancholy wails of women ready to jump into the fire to save their honour rather than fall into the hands of the invaders. I was sorely tempted to try to unearth the hidden romance of these places, but Bora, my senior colleague, advised me not to be diverted from my chosen field. His advice was sound. A lifetime is insufficient to study the natural history of the living, which must surely be of more interest and importance than the history of the dead.

I have never regretted my time in the Forest Service, with its fine century-old tradition of conservation. This training, augmented at intervals by short courses on ecology and park administration both in India and the USA, made me a purist. The unlimited opportunities of studying nature under the sun and the stars I got only as a forester. And above all I was able to live with tigers in the wild for days and nights on end, often in full knowledge of each other's presence but probably even more often in ignorance of it.

My first posting was to Bundi, once a tiny princely State. In Colonel William Rice's book *Hunting in Rajputana* (1857) he mentions that there were more tigers in Bundi than in any other area where he shot, so I reported for duty on 1 April 1953 with even more than the usual enthusiasm of a young forester. In those days the maharajas, though without power, were still VIPs, and protocol demanded that I should pay my respects. I duly turned up at the Maharaja's palace in a loading truck and was conducted through his trophy room where tigers, tigresses and even unborn cubs were displayed along with antelopes' and deers' heads. The shikar registers were meticulously kept, recording details of all the specimens shot. Seven tigers were killed annually on average in that tiny State, extending little over 2000 square miles, with less than a quarter of its area under forest.

After my practical training was over I was posted to take charge of Khairwara, a small forest in the south-west of Udaipur. By that time I was married and my wife and baby son came with me. From the medieval city of Udaipur we proceeded by bus. The conductor used to collect a tax from each passenger to hand over to the bow-and-arrow man who was supposed to protect us from bandits. When I told the conductor of my destination he looked at me curiously; later I learned that in the princely days Khairwara was a place of punishment and the people still regarded it as such. Our journey of fifty miles took eight hours.

Khairwara is a small village with only a handful of people but it has a fine church. It was once the British cantonment of the Mewar Bhil Corps, and in the cemetery I saw the names of British soldiers who had died far from home. Although the place was named after the acacia forests of Khair there are no forests now. Hill after hill has been devastated, and wildlife is practically non-existent as the Bhils had wiped out even the pigeons. There were still a few leopards then, living mostly on goats and dogs; I was astonished at their powers of adaptation, living in a devastated land on tit-bits from the villages. Certainly there were no tigers.

After four months I was placed in charge of a forest division of Bharatput, a place which shaped me and my future career. The division extended over four civil districts and the finest wildlife areas had been passionately preserved by the ex-maharajas. There was no timber to fell and my main job was to collect revenue from whatever existed in the forest—firewood, grass, honey, wax, dry leaves, flowers, fruits, even cow dung—and to issue permits freely for shooting tigers, leopards and game birds. The licence fee was less than the price of a drink.

I knew little about the population of the game I was authorizing people to kill, and I became painfully aware of this when a man came to get a permit to shoot four tigers after he had already killed two. There were no regulations to stop me from signing the death sentence, but I decided to visit his camp. There I found every comfort, as well as a full armoury of heavy-bore weapons. There were two jeeps with blinding spotlights and a van to carry the carcasses, and two tiger skins were stretched out for drying. A couple with American accents were basking in the sun, but the applicant for the permit was a landowner with rights of revenue collection in Gwalior State who had become a shikar operator. Taking advantage of the absence of rules on commercial shikar I refused the permit. I felt guilty at having issued permits for the other two tigers, but I had the consolation of knowing that I had saved the lives of four more.

Bharatpur is famous for its fort; thought to be invincible, it fell eventually to the British in 1826 after a three-weeks' siege. Thereafter in the great Ghana marshes close by the epitaphs of thousands of ducks are testimony to the visits of all the Governor Generals. On 6 February 1937 Lord Linlithgow shot over 2000 birds in a single day. I am proud to say that I managed to get Bharatput declared a Bird Sanctuary, but the success was only partial: the Maharaja had exclusive rights, and he was jealous in their exercise. As late as 1965 when I took Sir Peter Scott to the Sanctuary the Maharaja turned up and opened fire to underline his privilege. Sir Peter was pained. We did not have to wait long: the Maharaja's rights vanished with the passing of an amendment to the Indian Constitution in 1972. Today Bharatput is a paradise for bird watchers, a feast for photographers, and a research station for ornithologists.

It was here that I made my own first attempts at wildlife photography, having been inspired by F. W. Champion, author of *With a Camera in Tigerland* and like me a member of the Indian Forest Service. By riding on a water buffalo or swimming through the leech-infested waters, holding my old box camera high with one hand, I was able to approach the colonies; but all I could photograph were nests with eggs or helpless chicks in the absence of their parents.

My father-in-law, appreciating that the distance between the nests and me was too great with such a camera, then gave me an old 35 mm Edixa miniature with a biotar lens but with its view-finder yellowed by age. The labour of creeping close to my quarry was still arduous and a telephoto lens was far beyond my means. But at last I found one in a junk shop, its surface scratched as if rubbed with sandpaper. It was a 12-inch tele-lens from some obsolete camera, and I took advantage of the dealer's ignorance and bought it for less than a pound. In spite of its not having a pre-set aperture I managed to get some good pictures, but my failures were many: animals, I found, did not wait for me to set apertures and I discovered that one has to surpass even the patience of the tiger to stalk a good picture. Trying to capture the wide spectrum of colours in the habitat proved to be just as challenging, but I gained immense satisfaction in trying to portray tigerland in all its splendour.

A condition of admission to the Indian Forest College is that every trainee is assured of a job so I had no worries on that score, but I was never promotion-orientated and it was always far more important to me to do the work I enjoyed. Photography became a passion and, as an alcoholic runs to the first pub with any money he has in his pocket, I would rush to the nearest shop for a film or a filter. I was fortunate in that my in-laws ran a chain of photographic studios and the facilities for free developing and printing gave me the opportunity to learn wildlife photography in the most extravagant way. Even so, my addiction severely disturbed the household budget, and here I must pay tribute to my wife's forbearance. We were married just before I entered the Forest Service, having been betrothed when she was only twelve years old. We both believe that marriages are made in heaven, and we did not know each other at all before our engagement was fixed. She says the only difference it made to her was that she got some new clothes, and she wondered why!

As I have already mentioned, my father had been Director of Jodhpur Zoo—where tiger cubs were like my half-brothers and sisters—and in due course I followed in his footsteps in the same profession. Next I became Director of Delhi Zoo, where for five years I spent many days and nights in the tiger house, munching my food near courting and mating tigers, watching tigresses in labour and giving birth. Then in 1970 I was awarded the coveted Jawaharlal Nehru Fellowship which enabled me to jump with both feet into the field of wildlife, and I exchanged vigils in the tiger house for malarial waterholes and malodorous kills.

For the next two years I travelled round the country to see with my own eyes the land where tigers live and how they use it. I walked through each major habitat from the evergreen forests of Assam and the deltaic swamps of the Sundarbans to the dry scrublands of

Rajasthan, from the foothills of the Himalayas to the central plateau and the Western Ghats, often repeating my visits in different seasons. I covered tracts in Nepal and in the forests of Bhutan, where I had the responsibility of setting up its Tiger Reserve as a joint venture of the Indian Government and the Royal Government of Bhutan. Ideally I would have wished to make a detailed study of the ecology in each of the tiger's habitat types, but clearly this was beyond the capacity of any single person. However, my two-years' walkabout did enable me to obtain first-hand information that could not have been collected in any other way.

The field stations for my main areas of study were at Sariska and Ranthambhor in Rajasthan. To supplement my work there I needed a somewhat different habitat and I chose Kanha National Park in Madhya Pradesh. George Schaller had worked there in 1964–5, and my own work in 1971 proved helpful in taking a second look at his observations and adding new ones. I found that the information he had collected was mostly from one family of conditioned tigers, which had been provided with baits for more than one-and-a-half years. The group included only one male and was confined to a small area of 10–15 sq km. Vital aspects such as reproduction and the behaviour of a tigress and her infant cubs had not been studied in depth. Schaller's work was valuable in being the first ever to be fully recorded in the field, but it was insufficient to justify wider application. At that time the real facts about tigers' distribution, numbers and the conditions under which they were surviving in other parts of the country were not known.

When I first decided to study tigers the large number of books written about them—over 200 since 1828—tended to damp my enthusiasm, particularly after the publication of *The Man-Eaters of Kumaon* by Jim Corbett (1944). E. W. Champion's book *With a Camera in Tigerland* (1927) and R. I. Pocock's *Tigers* (1930) made every effort to present the facts correctly (the former worked in the field and the latter in the museum). *The Book of the Tiger* by R. G. Burton when published in 1933 was considered to be the last word on the tiger, but it contained much unverified information and some which was highly subjective. A closer look at other books revealed that most of them related to how to place a bullet in a tiger's heart and how to measure a dead tiger. Stories recollected and reconstructed long after the event were invariably exaggerated and told far more about the hunter than the tiger. Thus my resolution to study tigers was not shaken for long by the number of words already written about them.

I shall never forget the first tigress I ever saw in the wild: she enchanted me: it was love at first sight. As apprentice trainees in the Forest Service we were supposed to spend at least 20 nights out of every month in the field. There is a tradition that a forester does not take the same route home, and one day I took a short cut back to camp by crossing a stream by means of boulders. Suddenly I saw something running, then I realized there were two animals, somewhat larger than dogs. They had stripes. The whole thing happened so quickly that it hardly registered in my mind, but a few steps further on I saw a half-eaten carcass and it dawned on me that they must have been tiger cubs.

I decided to climb a tree and wait for them to return to their kill. For an hour nothing happened and then, as the light began to fade, I heard quick steps on the dry leaves behind me. I turned my head and saw a sleek golden body with black vertical stripes, obviously the mother of the two cubs. Her movement created an optical illusion, causing her to appear strangely elongated. At the speed she was moving I expected her to be on the kill within a moment, but after a couple of minutes when nothing happened I looked back cautiously, moving my head in slow motion. She was right under my tree, hardly six feet below me, yet apparently she had not picked up my scent. My first wild tigress at such close quarters made my heart beat faster and a nervous movement produced a metallic sound from my belt. She looked up, jumped, and was off. Within a few days I heard she had been shot by a maharaja, who also captured the cubs.

During my period of training in the Forest Service I had to listen to gossip round the camp fire: how a certain officer got promotion for shooting a tiger during his first year of service; how someone was awarded an OBE for arranging a successful hunt for the British Governor; how another was summarily dismissed by a maharaja for failing to produce a tiger for his gun. The last lecture I had attended included a mock tiger beat. The instructor was the top brass of the Forest Service, the Inspector General of Forests, the late Mr M. D. Chaturvedi, who had been a celebrated tiger hunter in his day. 'Shoot your first tiger in your first year,' he told us, and eventually I steeled myself to obey. With a borrowed Express rifle and antiquated black powder ammunition I sat up one night over a buffalo killed by a tiger.

When I got up on the *machan* in an acacia tree the last rays of the sun were still lighting up the valley. In an hour it was dark and the temple bells of a distant village announced that the gods were ready to go to bed. Within minutes of the fading of the bells I heard sounds of a tug-of-war and the heaving of a carcass, then the animal settled down to eat. My companion, an experienced shikari and Forest Guard, pressed my arm to get ready. I levelled the 'cannon' and as he switched on his torch I fired. With a deep-throated 'Oonooh' the animal jumped into the bush. Peacocks called and langurs whooped, then after a time there was silence. The smoke of the black powder persisted over the *machan* as I flashed my torch over the buffalo carcass. It was not there. A moan came from the bushes; evidently the tiger had been hit. A thousand thoughts flashed through my mind: the tiger cubs which used to come to our house, the mock beat at the Forest College. Was it courage, or cold-blooded murder in the dark? The picture of the tigress's beauty haunted me, and with every groan from the bushes my feelings of guilt increased. Not surprisingly I did not sleep, and when the crows called and sunlight lit the valley once more I found it difficult to wear a brave smile when I saw the tiger dead, his legs up and his eyes open. He seemed to look in my eyes and ask the reason for his death. 'Is this sport, when all the rules are in your favour?' I could not even bluff myself that he was a man-eater or even a cattle-lifter. Humbled in guilt I touched his body to beg his pardon. Even today the scene is as fresh as it was that morning, and the open eyes of that tiger have haunted me all my life.

I never repeated that murder, and to overcome my guilt I have dedicated my life to the cause of tiger preservation. The first thing I did was to get the area of Sariska Sanctuary extended to include the Madhogarh forests where I shot the tiger so that no other should die in the same way. For the past 20 years no licensed gun has been fired in the Sariska valley and this is reflected in the behaviour of the animals. I derive immense pleasure in watching them at the waterhole and my heart gladdens when I hear a roar.

Excerpted from Tiger! The Story of the Indian Tiger *(London: Collins, 1978).*

KENNETH ANDERSON

The Big Bull Bison of Gedesal

Kenneth Anderson (1910–74) was a planter and often known as southern India's answer to Jim Corbett. Unlike the latter, he stayed on in independent India, tracking and hunting leopards and elephants, tigers and bears. But in this article, Anderson pays tribute to the gaur—the largest forest ox in the world, often incorrectly described as a bison. Gaur are among the most impressive of India's animals, jet black with white stockings, living in the forested hills of southern, central and eastern India. Anderson, as this account shows, was not only a hunter of the gaur: he was also an admirer of the great forest ox.

This is not the story of a regular hunt, concluding with the shooting or wounding of the Big Bull Bison I am going to tell you about. If you think that, you are in for a disappointment, for I never even fired a shot at this animal at any time, nor would I ever have done so. For I admire him too much.

He was a brave old warrior, and if he is still alive today he well deserves his title as lord and leader of the herd he cared for so faithfully. If he could understand me, I would be proud to call him my friend.

Gedesal is the name of a small Sholaga village standing at the head of what I call the 'bison range' in the forests of North Coimbatore District. A forest bungalow called by the same name borders the road as it reaches the top of the ascent on its southward journey from the town of Kollegal to the hamlet of Dimbum. This road runs down the side of a hill for five of the seven miles that separate Gedesal from Dimbum. For those last two miles it rises again. Dimbum is at the edge of an escarpment. The road falls steeply, in a series of sharp hair-pin bends, from Dimbum to the plains below it to the south, whence it pursues an almost level course to the large town of Satyamangalam.

Gedesal itself is flanked on the west by the towering range of the Biligirirangan Mountains, their slopes a scenic combination of frowning crags jutting out of a green background of lawn-like grass. In the folds of the hills, and along the beds of the myriad watercourses that tumble downhill, clumps of trees and matted jungle have sprung up. These are commonly called 'sholas', or isolated islands of forest, surrounded by open, grassy areas or out-crops of forbidding rock.

To the east lies another range of hills, much less in altitude, size and grandeur than the mountain range of the Biligirirangan to the west. These low hills are entirely covered by forest, consisting mainly of tiger-grass that grows to a height of ten feet, interspersed with thousands upon thousands of the stunted wild date palms. Towards the middle of the year these palms bear long clusters of the yellow wild dates at the ends of drooping stems—dry, tasteless fruit, indeed, but much favoured by birds and animals alike.

Thus the topography, the vegetation and the dates combine to make the area a favourite haunt for bison, sambhar and bear.

A long valley runs from north to south between the flanking ranges of mountains and hills, and along the side of this valley the road from Kollegal to Dimbum wends its lonely, southward way, passing between Gedesal hamlet itself and the forest bungalow of the same name.

This building is exceptionally large for a forest bungalow, and has a long line of outhouses at its rear for the occupation of the menials working for the Forestry Department. Moreover it has a big compound, where some nice specimens of the wild hill-rose grow, the flowers of which bloom in large clusters, resembling small bouquets.

Just south of the bungalow is a low-lying stretch of land, holding a small pond and some marshy ground. Because of the tender shoots of green grass that grow there—entirely different from the coarse tiger-grass in the surrounding area—a small herd of spotted-deer is almost always in residence. When I saw them last they were sired and led by quite a sizeable stag with a good head of antlers, his dark brown shoulders being almost black, against which the dappled white spots contrasted markedly.

I hope that no hunter, human or animal, has brought him down, and that he still roams at the head of his harem in that deeply green and refreshingly moist, cool glen—lordly and free as the jungle to which he belongs.

The low range of hills to the east of the road and the deep valley running along the base of the mountains to the west offer wide browsing opportunities to the many separate bison herds that inhabit the area. A perennial stream of considerable size flows down the length of this valley, the road being crossed every now and again by the various tributaries that feed it. A never-failing water supply, even during the hottest summer season, is thereby assured, which is the main factor that contributes towards keeping these animals permanently in residence.

These bison herds number from twenty to forty or even more, the majority being cows and calves of different ages, with perhaps about half-a-dozen sizeable bulls to each herd. The oldest and most mature bull automatically gains supremacy over his younger rivals and becomes the lord and master of that herd until such time as he in turn is overthrown by some younger and more vigorous male, or meets his end in some fashion that accords with the laws of the jungle. Occasionally a big bull will break away from the rest of the herd and pursue his own solitary existence.

Bison suffer severely from diseases such as 'rinderpest', which frequently attack the herds of domestic cattle belonging to the Sholagas, living in the forest or adjacent cattle patties. The cattle are let out to graze in the jungle and spread the infection to the bison. It is quite common to come across bison affected by the 'foot-and-mouth' disease which is so fatal to cattle, or to be led by the sight of vultures to the carcass of one that has succumbed to this most deadly of cattle scourges.

The big bull of which my story tells was leader of a herd of at least thirty animals. Very frequently have I seen him early in the morning when droplets of dew glittered in the rising sun, and sometimes round about 5.30 in the evening, grazing within sight of the road between the 39th and 41st milestones. It was easy to identify him by his crumpled left horn, which was clearly deformed and turned inwards and forwards.

Perhaps the old bull owes his long life to this deformity, as it renders his head worthless as a trophy, though the right horn is beautifully shaped. True it is that some hunter and collector of oddities might value his head as an unusual specimen, but he has been lucky in that such a curiosity-monger does not so far appear to have met up with him. In battle his deformed horn has proved an invaluable weapon, as I am about to relate. He has the natural advantages that would be those of a unicorn, if this legendary animal actually existed, in that he could transfix an opponent in a frontal attack or badly slash him with a toss of his head.

I have often motored along that road on a dark night, shining the sealed-beam spot-light on my car from side to side, to see what I could see and just for the fun of it. Twice or thrice on such occasions the widely-separated blue eyes of a bison have reflected the lamp's rays and upon closer inspection I have found them to be the eyes of the old bull.

My attention was first attracted to this veteran some years ago when I was out for a walk on the lower slopes of the Biligirirangan Range. There is a road running through the forest from the western side of the main road. It skirts Gedesal village, crosses the stream, and then starts to climb over the foothills of the mountain range to disappear eventually over a saddle-back and descend a valley on the other side. Finally it leads to a beautiful forest lodge, the private property of Mr Randolph Morris, who is one of Southern India's biggest and most influential coffee planters. He is also an authority on shikar and a hunter of renown, having contributed many valuable articles on the habits of big game and on big game hunting. He was the honorary game warden of the area, well known to the Viceroys and former Governors of British India, and the owner of some of the most beautiful and well-planned coffee estates in the south.

Long before this road makes its way over the saddle-back there is a pre-fabricated shed, the property of the Forestry Department, which has been erected for the convenience of its officers on tour and for the use of licensed sportsmen on shikar. Some thoughtful soul has made, or caused to be made, a ladder of stout twisted vines, which is kept in this lodge and comes in very handy for climbing up to and down from machans erected on trees, to those who are not naturally gifted or adapted to this arboreal art.

That morning I had passed this lodge and was walking along a ridge overlooking a bowl-like shallow valley when I heard a clashing and thudding sound, interrupted with snorts of rage. The evidence pointed to a bison fight, and I hurried along, taking what cover was available, in the direction of the sounds. Very soon I saw in the valley below me, but quite three hundred yards away, two large bull bison locked in fierce combat. With horns entangled and foreheads pressed together, they were pushing against each other with might and main, the outstretched taut legs of each animal indicating the tremendous effort he was making to push his opponent back. At intervals one or other would momentarily disengage his horns and head from his rival to deliver a short quick jab before interlocking again, and before the opposing animal could score a similar thrust.

Then it was that I noticed that one of them had a peculiar horn that gave him a distinct advantage over his antagonist, which was bleeding profusely from wounds in his neck, shoulders and side.

The fight raged for the next twenty minutes or so with unabated fury, till the gasps that took the place of the snorts of rage that I had first heard, and the glistening sides of the two bulls, soaked in sweat and blood that was clearly visible even at that range, showed that the gruelling pace and strain of the fight was beginning to tell. Froth drooled from the mouths of the bulls and splattered their bodies, falling in splashes to the ground.

I had never witnessed a bison fight before and was very curious to know how it would end. Fortunately I had come alone. Moreover, the breeze blew in my direction. Therefore the combatants were quite unaware of my presence and fought their fight under natural conditions.

The bull with the crumpled horn seemed to be getting the better of things, and his opponent gave ground, becoming reddened by the gore that flowed from the many wounds in his body. Of course, he had also inflicted some telling jabs on his enemy, but the crumpled horn was obviously giving its owner a decided superiority. After another ten minutes the severely injured animal began to falter. He fell to his knees several times, and at each opportunity that unicorn-like horn embedded itself in some part of the unfortunate animal. Eventually he broke, turned and ran at a staggering trot, the victor following up his advantage by pursuing him and butting his hind-quarters. The two animals passed out of sight at a point where the bowl of the valley merged with the surrounding jungle.

Out of curiosity I walked down to the site of the recent combat. The ground had been torn up by the straining hooves of the two contestants and was flecked with blood and foam in a rough circle some twenty yards in diameter.

It was a considerable time after that when I saw my bull again. The second occasion was on another walk one evening on my way to visit a water-hole situated on the eastern side of the road about a quarter of a mile from and almost level with the 41st milestone. A tiger had killed a couple of head of cattle belonging to the Sholagas of Gedesal village. They told me they had seen it on several occasions in the evenings, walking along—or crossing—the fire-line that leads past this pool and thereafter cuts across the road.

I went to the water-hole at about 4.30 p.m. that day, and walked around its edge to discover what animals had been visiting it. There were the usual tracks of elephant, bison, sambar, spotted-deer and of a few wild pigs. The tiger had also drunk there on about three separate occasions so far as I could judge by the age of his pug-marks, although the last time had been at least three days earlier than my visit.

Among the bison tracks were the pointed hoof-marks of what must have been a truly massive bull. The weight of his body had been so great that he sank almost a foot into the mire that bordered the pond. His tracks were also visible in many places in the vicinity, indicating that he was a frequent visitor to this pool. This was rather strange in view of the fact that he had the river, which I have already mentioned, at which to quench his thirst.

I asked the Sholaga who had told me about the tiger, and who had accompanied me, if he knew anything about this bull. He replied in the affirmative and told me that he and all the villagers had seen him many times, and that he had a deformed horn—the left one—which thrust forwards. Immediately my mind flew back to the scene I had witnessed in that memorable fight, in which a bull with a crumpled horn had completely routed his opponent. I wondered if this could be the same animal and thought it must be so, as such a deformity is extremely rare.

The Sholaga told me the bull frequented the pond, as he kept the herd under his care in that locality; probably because of the exceptionally fine grazing to be had on the low land around the water-hole. Then he went on to say that if I cared to take a walk with him, we might be lucky enough to see this animal for ourselves, or even come across the tiger.

At that time the tiger was my immediate quarry and I was not very interested in the bull, so more with that objective in mind I consented. In my case, stalking bison in broad daylight is a tricky business and depends upon the direction in which the wind is blowing, the cover available, and of course the lie of the land.

We set off on an aimless walk, following cattle trails and game paths and criss-crossing the fire-line several times. I remember we were ambling along a narrow track when quite suddenly the long grass parted before us, hardly thirty yards away, to reveal the head and shoulders of a massive bull bison which regarded us complacently and obviously without much concern. It was my friend, the bison with the crumpled horn.

He showed no signs of fear, but just stood looking at us. We advanced another ten yards then, with a loud swish of the reedy grass, he turned around and disappeared. After that day, as I have said, I saw him on other occasions, and then came the memorable event which drew him to me.

An unidentified hunter, who was also a poacher, came along the road one night and shot a cow bison. Before he knew where he was, a bull attacked his jeep and with a toss of his head tumbled the vehicle down a khud that bordered the road into one of the dry tributaries of the river. Fortunately the bison did not follow up its attack, so the poacher suffered only an injured leg and a smashed rifle. The Sholaga who was with him, and was sitting at the side of the jeep where the assault was launched, had clearly seen the bull and avowed it was the animal with the deformed left horn.

I heard about the incident some months later, on a subsequent visit, and felt pleased that the old bull had acquitted himself so creditably. No doubt the fact that he had tossed the jeep down the khud had caused him to think, in his own bovine mind, that he had disposed of his foe. Had the khud not been there he would probably have followed up his initial attack with another, found the men inside and eliminated them altogether.

It was some time later, in November, 1953, that I was visiting Dimbum. I had not intended to halt at Gedesal and was motoring along the road when I espied a lone figure walking. Drawing level,

I recognized the Sholaga, whose name was Rachen, whom I always employ when I camp at that bungalow. Stopping the car and returning his greeting, I asked him in Tamil: *'Yenna Sungadhi'*—which means: 'What news'?

Rachen replied that just two nights ago the villagers had heard the sounds of a terrific fight in the jungle, not very far from the village, between a tiger and some other animal. From the violence and duration of the combat, which appeared to last for hours, they decided that the tiger's opponent could not be a wild boar, which is the only wild creature of medium-size that fights back against a tiger, and thought it might be an elephant. But then again, had it been an elephant they felt sure they would have heard the trumpeting and screaming which an elephant invariably makes when in trouble or when fighting, or when otherwise excited.

Later in the night the sounds had gradually died away, but they had noticed before that time, from the great noise the tiger had been making, that it had been badly hurt.

Early next morning, impelled by curiosity, the Sholagas had gone to see what had happened and had come upon the scene of the marathon struggle they had heard the night before. The undergrowth had been torn up and trodden down by the combatants, and to one side of this arena lay the carcass of a tiger that had been repeatedly gored and trampled by a bison.

The Sholagas had then promptly removed the skin from the tiger and taken it to the village.

It was about noon when I heard this tale and, having time to spare, felt interested in visiting the spot myself. Seating Rachen beside me, I drove down the narrow track leading to Gedesal village and found the tiger's skin already pegged out on the ground to dry. The raw side was uppermost and had been liberally covered with dry ashes, which is the only preservative known to the Sholagas, salt not being available.

The tiger had been quite a large animal but, judging from the underside of the skin, it had been badly mangled and gored by the bison. There were no less than five distinct holes where the powerful horns had penetrated, and one of them, on the left side, showed where a fateful thrust had pierced the tiger's heart.

I was now more interested than ever and expressed a keen desire to visit the spot where the fight had taken place. Leaving my car, and accompanied by a crowd of Sholagas, I set forth. Less than half a mile away we reached the site of the incident.

'Arena' is the best word I can find to describe it, for indeed there had been a titanic struggle. Great gouts of gore were sprayed on the surrounding grass and bushes in all directions, which had been flattened by the weight of the contestants and were red with dried blood. The Sholagas pointed out the spot where the dead tiger had been lying.

It was obvious from the quantity of blood that the bison had also been severely injured. On a whim I decided I would like to follow him up if possible, to see if he was dead or dying somewhere in the jungle. In either case, I guessed he could not have moved very far from the scene of the fight in his present condition.

Even an entire novice would have been able to follow that trail, as the bison had left a wide path of blood through the jungle. He had passed downhill, heading towards the stream, and I felt certain I would find him there, very likely dead, beside the water.

We forged ahead, not troubling to keep silent. An hour and a half's quick walking along that tremendous blood trail brought us to the stream, and to the bison standing in shallow water and resting himself against the bole of a large tree that was partly submerged. Due to the noise made by the water as it rushed over the rocks, he had not heard us at first, and we were well out of cover before he turned around to face us.

It was the big bull bison of Gedesal, the bull with the crumpled horn.

From where we stood, with the breadth of the stream separating us, we could clearly see the awful wounds that had been inflicted by the teeth and the talons of the tiger on his face, neck, sides and rump. Even his belly was badly lacerated, and something red protruded from it and hung into the water. Perhaps it was a portion of his bowel, perhaps a piece of torn skin; I could not see clearly into the shadows where he stood.

But his eyes were clear and fearless, although pain-wracked, as he stood and faced us. Then he turned and staggered away into the jungle.

I had thought of shooting him to put him out of his agony, but somehow could not find it in my heart to do so after the gallant victory he had won at such frightful cost. In any case, I never expected to see him again.

But very recently I visited Gedesal, and great was my surprise and pleasure when one evening I happened to see him, surrounded by his beloved herd, browsing contentedly on the long grass that borders the water-hole on the eastern side of the road not far from the 41st milestone—his favourite haunt.

Long may he live in the jungle to which he belongs.

Excerpted from The Black Panther of Sivanipalli and Other Adventures of the Indian Jungle *(London: Allen and Unwin, 1959).*

ARJAN SINGH

From Killer to Conservation

*That Arjan Singh should have taken to the gun at an early age
was all too natural given the time and setting in which he was
born and brought up. Growing up in Balrampur state in the
United Provinces in the 1920s, he shot dead a tiger when he was
barely in his teens. His father was a senior officer in the state and
'Billy' as he was known joined the army. After 1947, he was one
of the early settlers in the* tarai—*but as the plough advanced and
the fauna vanished, his own attitudes underwent a change.*

*Arjan Singh, who has by now authored several books on tigers,
is best known for his role in working to establish the Dudwa
sanctuary, a stronghold of the rare swamp deer and for his
experiments with re-introducing big cats—a tiger and three
leopards—born or bred in captivity to the wild. This article
belongs to a significant chapter in his life—when he put away his
gun and became a watcher and a guardian of animals.*

The beauty and genius of a work of art may be reconceived, though its first
material expression be destroyed. A vanished harmony may yet again inspire
the composers, but when the last individual of a race of living beings
breathes no more, another heaven and earth must pass before such a one
can be again.

WILLIAM BEEBE (1877–1962)

The War had ended, and many people were looking for ways of
reordering their lives. Some were war heroes, others did not want
to make the army a career, and some were dropouts. I tried to get
a job with a couple of business firms, but nothing came of that.

It was now that destiny took a hand. Jaswant was eminently suited for a life in the armed forces, and he had found his niche. Balram should also have joined the Forces, but, thanks to some inopportune manoeuvrings to remove a somewhat meaningless hurdle to his recruitment into the air force, he had been compelled to join a business concern. In my case, circumstance, and the possible qualification of singlemindedness, or perhaps perversity of character, guided me from being a confirmed killer to become an ardent conservationist and a crusader for a lost cause.

If I had tried long enough I expect I would have landed a normal job. But I happened to meet Jai Singh, the younger brother of the Raja of Bijwa, a small feudal State near the Nepal border, who had just started farming on land leased from George Hearsey. He was a descendant of general Sir John Hersey who had tried quelling the 1857 mutiny in Barackpore by shooting Mangal Pandey. George was a pioneer farmer, and before the War had been using tractors, and also sowing soya beans, which was so in advance of the times that he was unable to find a market for them and went bankrupt as his warehouse filled with an unsaleable product. He called Palia 'the Chicago of the East', presumably because it was on a trade route from Nepal.

During the recently concluded war he had joined the army in some obscure administrative capacity, and, after demobilization, returned to resume farming. He had married a courtesan during the First War, but she had left him. This time he brought with him a young model from England, whom he had presumably inveigled into coming out to India inspired by the illusion of his vast acreage of rolling farmland. He tried to retain her affections by playing childish games, which involved hiding money and guiding her to find it! However, other predators were on the prowl, and an Anglo-Indian criminal lawyer named Walford was overheard by Hearsey making infamous proposals to her. Unfortunately, in his eagerness to eavesdrop, Hearsey fell over a flowerpot and, as Walford came out to investigate, he punched the latter on the nose, whereupon Walford instituted a case of trespass and assault. Younger aspirants were also lining up, and Jai, while paying nominal homage to his landlord Uncle George, was not averse to entertaining Hearsey's young wife. In the end, the lady found the situation too embarrassing to endure, and returned to the country of her origin, leaving a disillusioned Hearsey to his own devices.

In the mean time I was exploring the possibilities of farming as a career. I sought advice from a variety of people, and the consensus was that, as a farmer, you could not starve and that it was thus a worthwhile life. I went to stay with the Raja of Bijwa at Bhira, ten miles away from Palia, where he had·a farm. We visited the Sarda river between Palia and Bhira and heard the hooves of swamp deer thundering as they galloped through the tamarisk which lined the banks. In the evening we sat over a kill by a tigress of a bullock, which had strayed into the forest. At night we drank whisky from a toothmug, and farming under such conditions seemed an enchanting prospect. I went to Palia and selected a plot of 750 acres as farmland, and when I was warned of the depredations of a myriad wild animals, who competed with human beings for their agricultural crops, I foresaw my role as the holder of a thin red line. I bought myself a .275 bore Mauser rifle, and was ready to start my farming career.

I was on the passenger train from Lucknow, where my mother had now bought a house. The train drew into the Palia Kalan railway station at 3.30 in the morning of 1 May 1945. It was to go on to the Nepal border, a few stations ahead, which accounted for the extraordinary time of disembarkation. A small bullock cart known as a *lehru* was waiting for me and, as it was a moonlit night, I loaded my luggage on to it before setting off on the three-mile walk along the dirt track road which led to my farm site. Further north, another road known as the Prince of Wales Road ran a parallel course to the west, but it was now so overgrown with grass as to be unusable. Reputedly, this road had been made at some indefinite time when the Prince of Wales had come pigsticking to a place called Dhaka. The track was deeply rutted, and ankle deep in dust, but the stars shone brightly, and a waning moon lit the twin ribbons ahead. To the north, an Indian fox (*Vulpes Bengalensis*) gave a chattering bark, while in the copse a pack of jackals (*Canis Aureus*) sang their eerie falsetto chorus: 'Dead Hindu. Dead Hindu. Where are you? Where are you? Heree, Heeere.'

The sky was paling as I approached Jasbirnagar, which was what I had decided to call my farm, and further on a hogdeer (*Axis Porcinus*) fled with consecutive piping whistles of alarm. The sawing grunts of a leopard as it retired to its lair indicated what had frightened the deer. As I turned into my land, a vista of grassland stretched endlessly to the west. A herd of twenty Nilgai, India's large antelope (*Boselaphus Tragocamelus*) stood in an opening. The burly, slaty grey bulls with their sloping withers, contrasting with the more numerous, beige coloured females with their white stockings, and further on, a large herd of black buck (*Antelope Cervicapra*) cropped the short Imperata grass. The heads of numerous cattle, both cows and buffaloes, glinted in the light of the dawn. In front of me lay most of what I would have to contend with if I was going to make a success of farming.

As I had no place to live in I made my temporary headquarters at Jai Singh's, which also happened to be close to the village of Maraucha, where most of the cattle were owned by Gaddis, Muslim graziers. I got hold of some labourers to build me a grass hut, but as I had heard that the workmen were very slack, I stood over them, supervising their labour in the heat of the day, and went down with a bad attack of heatstroke.

On recovery, I bought some buffaloes and ploughshares to break the land and sow paddy as a monsoon crop. All the money I had was from my slender savings in the army, and I soon started running out of funds. However, my troubles were only starting, and they soon lined up in formidable proportions! Soon after the crop was sown, the young shoots were grazed by the numerous ungulates who had hitherto held undisputed sway over the area. The wild animals could be chased away, but the livestock was not so easily manageable. Moreover, the Gaddis resented my arrival to contest their right to indiscriminate grazing, though on the positive side they found their milch cattle were better nourished on succulent crops, and started to make a habit of releasing their unmanageable livestock to graze my agricultural crops.

I was soon embroiled in litigation with them. One day I found two bullocks grazing my fields. As they were very wild I was unable to catch and send them to the local cattle pound. I lamed one with a .22 rifle, and subsequently caught and tethered the cattle, but foolishly gave the sorrowing owner a note to the local veterinarian to say that, as I could not catch these animals, I had been compelled to lame them, and would he treat them? The owner promptly went to court and I was summoned before a magistrate at Lakhimpur, fifty-five miles away. After sundry negotiations, the matter was settled out of court, and I bought over the lamed animals. I subsequently sold them for more than I paid, and therefore won the first round. Numerous other cases were instituted, but by a mixture of cajolery and strong arm tactics I held my own, and gradually the cattle owners realized that agriculture had come to stay, and soon the Gaddis themselves turned their efforts to farming.

Wild ungulates were more controllable and shy and, unlike the voracious cattle, had smaller appetites, and would therefore graze on the move. But, when the paddy grain began to ripen a new menace appeared in the shape of wild pigs. They would devastate overnight a crop ready to be harvested, and to approach a field at night was like a gala occasion at a Latin night club, as the champing of the ripe grain sounded like so many castanets. I built myself a portable machan, which I used to set up in the middle of a field and where I spent the night. I brought out an old .500 Express which I had acquired before the War, and tried to shoot a record among the big, old boars. The biggest I could kill was one weighing 300 pounds, with tushes of eight inches, and I doubt if boars go a great deal beyond these dimensions.

As my farming activities increased, the competition from wild pigs became more acute. Sugarcane was their perennial delight, and they began their act as soon as it was sown. They would dig up the sets which were planted and covered with earth. After the sets had germinated they took shelter in the crop itself, and, as the cane matured, they would make shelters against rain and inclement weather by piling cane leaves in extensive heaps; getting under the pile of trash, they would elevate it to form a kind of igloo. They dug into the fresh earth to form breeding shelters, and bred outrageously large families, as is the wont amongst their kind. They lived in their larder, and ate at all hours. Their tribe grew in geometrical progression and increasingly competed with human beings for livelihood.

I employed a man as night watchman from the Pasi tribe. He was called Ram Dayal, but known as Dakua as he was an inveterate dacoit, and had been jailed a number of times. He was inordinately lazy and work shy, as behoves a man of his occupation who lives on the earned wealth of others, and the only recommendation which I found valid was that, as there was honour among thieves, no other miscreants would trespass on his preserve when he was ensconced. I found him quite amenable, apart from his obvious shortcomings. I gave him a thrashing periodically, which put the fear of god into him, and perhaps accounted for my immunity from larcenous activities.

One morning I was taken to where Ram Dayal was writhing in pain, presumably back from some thieving expedition, and was told that he had been bitten by a snake. I saw twin fang marks on his toe. It is known that a large number of snake-bites and deaths are caused by shock, under the presumption that all snakes are poisonous, but I felt this was the real McCoy. I tied a ligature above the wound, cut into the two fang marks with a razor blade, and sucked Ram Dayal's grimy toe. I sent him to the doctor who gave him some sort of injection, and he was well the following day. This act of mine may also have inspired a certain loyalty, for though he had the chance, he never stole anything of mine, and when he did disappear, unable to stand the strain of manual labour, he contented himself with removing my manager's watch and a few other sundry articles.

While Dakua had been with me he introduced me to other members of his tribe, as they specialized in netting pigs. The nets consisted of woven mesh made of stout rope, each net being the width of a tennis court. They were then stood up supported by unconnected stakes on the ground at right angles to the line along which the pigs were being driven, and behind cover. As the pigs rushed off, they got entangled in the nets which collapsed upon them as the stakes fell away. The pigs were then killed by belabouring with cudgels. It was said by these stalwarts that it took a whole night's belabouring to kill a big pig. The screams of agony, of course, were horrendous. I employed these professionals sometimes, and occasionally a tiger got caught. However, these animals were too powerful and heavily armed, and bit their way out of the mesh, while no human dared to come close, and their deafening roars on a dark night were forbidding sounds. Soon I came to terms with such adversities, and learned to live with them.

Gradually, I found that breaking up the land with animal power was an exacting process and, with help of Micky Nethersole, who was then what was known as the Senior Member, Board of Revenue, I took a loan from the government and bought a tractor. Unfortunately, the tractor was a small three-wheeler called a John Deere Model 'B', and not sufficiently powerful to control even a fraction of the 750 acres in my possession. By unfortunate hindsight I kept on discovering that, as in business, one should not under-power or under-finance in agriculture, though people are inclined to believe that farming is a poor man's enterprise and can be built up on a shoe string. However, even with my small tractor, which I drove myself, I found life was much easier. Micky Nethersole departed with Indian Independence in 1947, so further help from the government as a source of finance dried up. Also, I found that repayment under strict government regulations was rather more unpleasant than drawing a cheque on the Treasury. I therefore took a loan from a bank on the security of family investments.

Hitherto I had spent most of my time consolidating my venture into farming, but now, as crops started yielding a small income, I found time to look around. The North Kheri Forest Division was a commercial, working forest where a number of valuable timber trees were auctioned to private contractors by the Forest Department. Also, the Division was divided into a number of shooting blocks, which could be applied for on a roster basis, and where we were allowed to shoot a specified number of animals and live in one of the forest rest houses. I tried to get a shooting block every Christmas; this was more in the shape of a family and friends reunion rather than a serious shoot, though the old urge for slaughter was still smouldering and the destruction of the master predator dominated all desires.

My elder brother came from whichever air force station he was posted at, and would arrive in solitary splendour, much to everyone's amusement, whereas his wife, who was the daughter of the then Chief Minister of the North-West Frontier Province, would arrive the next day with the children and heavy luggage. Mariam was that ideal product, according to Kipling, of the marriage between a Pathan father and a Scots mother, with the virility of the one and the dourness and canniness of the other. Her marriage was the cause of a political upheaval as her father's political opponents made out that it was an out-of-caste union between a Sikh and a Muslim, though Jaswant was shaven and shorn and baptized a Christian, a kindred 'people of the book'. Mariam's heavily burdened arrival was accorded an extreme welcome, as she was very popular with all of us, and Jaswant was ribbed for shedding all responsibility while his wife bore the entire burden of travel.

Though Jaswant was the eldest of the family, he probably enjoyed himself the most, possibly because he was able to relax the iron discipline he normally imposed upon himself, which made him the most feared of senior officers on parade, and the most loved during leisure hours. He would appear in the early morning unshaven and unkempt, in an old balaclava to keep out the chill, and which we claimed he had pilfered from an ancient mechanic engaged in boring a tube well, and known as the 'Boring Babu.' He took great delight in identifying himself with the staff, and would drive the John Deere 'B', which towed the generator into camp. When the tractor broke down or got bogged, Jaswant would insist on going without his meals to keep the staff company, reminding one of the inscription in Chetwode Hall of the Indian Military Academy: 'The safety, honour and welfare of your country comes first, always and every time. The honour, welfare and comfort of the men you command come next. Your own ease, comfort and safety come last, always and every time.' Balram also arrived with convivial bachelor friends from Calcutta, and my sister Amar, who had married in London, sometimes came with her two children.

Our first Christmas was a modest affair, as the elephant which I had arranged to borrow never arrived, and the car which I tried to arrange developed engine trouble; but later, when I had acquired both forms of conveyance, the move out to Christmas camp was more elaborate. With Jaswant's help I bought a generator which had been used to light air force stations during the War, and the celebration of Christmas became a complex affair. Unlike deadly hunters who objected to the sound of the generating engine which disturbed wild animals, the noise and light added to the gaiety of the log fire, and the songs of earlier days were sung. It was Balrampur all over again, except that the *dramatis personae* was different.

One Christmas John Withnell, who shared a 'chummery' with Balram in Calcutta, arrived. He was a fine sportsman and rugger player, and one day we went to a marshy lake called Bhadi Tal. There we shot a couple of swamp deer, but on return were informed by the forest guard that it was a protected species and he would have to report the matter to his superior officer. In reality he was angling for a payoff, but we pre-empted his intentions by reporting our error to the Divisional Forest Officer, and got away with a good word for our honesty in confessing the mistake.

Later in the lake area we came upon a young chital fawn crouched in its form. As it got up to run, John made a fine flying tackle and grabbed the young animal by its leg. I unimaginatively named it Bambi, and brought it back to the farm at Jasbirnagar. It turned out to be a male and became so tame that it would follow me with my dogs, feed with them and even lick the milk from their jowls after they had emptied their saucers clean. Bambi was very gentle until, as a yearling, he came into hard horn, which is the timing of the rut, and the period during which deer get aggressive with their own species in the wilds. Soon I was accosted by a neighbour who complained that, when trying to drive the chital out of his paddy field he was grazing, Bambi, with his lack of female companions or male competitors and used to the human presence, had gored him. But his horns though sharp were small, and I was able to persuade the complainant that such an incident would not recur.

However, the following year as a brocket he assumed a more formidable presence, and though very affectionate with me—he slept near my bed—he took a violent aversion to my cook. One evening while dozing near the camp fire my subconscious registered a yelling, which seemed to be coming closer. It was the cook, who had abandoned my dinner and taken flight, pursued by Bambi. He was knocked down with rescue in sight, and would doubtless have suffered severe injury had I not leapt up and grabbed the chital by his horns. Blind with rage he went for me, and as we wrestled in the glow of the log fire his brow tine split my bicep, which scar I still carry forty years later. However, I was still the stronger and Bambi soon called enough.

The cook resumed his cooking of dinner, and Bambi, as if nothing had happened, came to his usual resting place at the side of my bed. Next morning we knocked him down and castrated him. Unused to such rough treatment he disappeared for two days, and just as I was mourning his loss, he arrived back on the third day and resumed life from where he had left off. The next, and third year, he grew a fine pair of antlers, but they never came into hard horn, presumably because of the castration. One morning he simply disappeared, and I searched everywhere for him. I thought that a predator might have got him, but then a few days later, I saw him running away. I called to him, and he stopped, looked at me in recognition, and resumed his flight. I never saw him again, and hope that he met others of his kind, and was accepted by them. Years later, I tried to reintroduce a young female to a local herd and she had been rejected. As in the lion pride, apart from males, herds are perhaps based on familial extraction.

I kept other pets, both chital and hogdeer, but they were all eventually killed by wayfarers on the look-out for easy meat.

Cymbeline used to share his roti with an elephant, but one day when I found him with his legs broken by gypsies, and mangled by killer dogs, I decided that as a human I had no right to take an animal from its environment for my pleasure. I had tethered an eighteen-foot python, but he too developed a sore on his back and died.

In the early 1950's the system of feudal rulers was abolished, and the State of Balrampur, faced with the imperative need of getting rid of its stable of elephants, had to decide what to do with them. My old guru, Lala Babu, had gone to the happy hunting grounds, and Butterfield had also passed on. I never discovered what happened to the great tuskers, Macdonald Bahadur and Kanhaiya, and presumably the skeleton of Chand Murat still collects grime in some government museum.

I had as my manager on the farm a man with whom I had played football in our youth, and one day I received a message through him that the State would like to present me with an elephant called Mabel Mala, who was supposedly named after my mother. How-ever, I was informed that the elephant offered to me was getting on in age, and I would do better to get another one in her place. Thus, after sundry negotiations, Bhagwan Piari ('the Beloved of God') arrived with her *Filwan,* and Jafar the *Fil Tabib* (elephant doctor) who had been the *Filwan* of Kanhaiya when I was a boy in Balrampur. Bhagwan Piari, a fine looking elephant, about nine feet tall, was reputed to be about forty-five years old.

During my days at University I had taken to weight training, as already noted. This activity had, of course, been interrupted over the war years, but when I settled down to my new vocation I took up the weights once more. The American weightlifting Olympic team paid a visit to Calcutta and I went to see them. Together with the Russian team, they were the leading performers in this form of heavy athletics, and there was much competition between them. There was also a Mr Universe contest of bodybuilders, which the Russians scorned as they claimed that they would rather be strong men than earn plaudits by posing with a rose between their teeth! Secretly I agreed with the Russians, and over the years they became the leading nation at this form of athletics.

The American team had many world champions. Paul Anderson the heavyweight, Tommy Kono, middleweight, Pete George a light-weight champion at the age of seventeen, and Chuck Vinci, a diminutive bantam who lifted over twice his body weight. I was fascinated by the ease with which these athletes handled enormous weights, and bought myself an Olympic barbell. However, I had started too late, and, moreover, had to train alone. I went to Calcutta to train at the Muslim Institute, and got to lift 220 pounds in the Clean and Press, which was close to the record in my weight in India. But sadly, I performed this feat only once!

I tried to visit Calcutta more often as, apart from being able to work out with other weightlifting enthusiasts, Jaswant was posted there as Air Officer in Chief, commanding Eastern Air Command. Balram was also there in a business house. We spent the Christmas of 1962 together, and the Chinese invasion had just taken place. Jaswant had been under tremendous strain flying unpressurized aircraft at great altitudes, and was in fine form, as was natural in the aftermath of the ending of hostilities. His achievements in the war were considerable. Whereas his class-mates from the Military Academy, who were supposedly commanding fighting formations of the army in the inhospitable mountains, had fled abandoning their ill-equipped troops, Jaswant had proved an example to his Command. He was decorated in 'the performance of a task beyond the normal course of duty.' We saw the New Year in to the nostalgic tune of 'Auld Lang Syne', but that was his farewell, for he had a fatal heart attack. Those the gods love die young. We were devastated, for he was only forty-seven years old. Calcutta, the dirtiest and friendliest city in India, now lost all its charm for me.

Some time later, Mohammed Ali, after his retirement, visited India. His three fights with Joe Frazier were in the legend book, and the 'Thriller in Manila' was the ultimate in punishment that one man could take from another. Ali had regained his crown in a fabulous fight with George Foreman at Kinshasa, and had retired disproving the theory that they never come back. He once came into the ring in Delhi, handsome and unmarked, with Jimmy Ellis for an exhibition bout. But a ring of fat showed round his midriff. Hawa Singh the Indian Heavyweight champion was given the honour of going into the ring with the Greatest and Prettiest of all time. He tried his utmost to land a telling punch, but as the round was closing Ali laid his hand on Hawa Singh's topknot and shook it as if to say, 'Well tried, Sonny'.

But for those whose meal ticket Ali was, he was immortal—the Legend that could never die, and they pulled him back again and again. He was thrashed by his erstwhile sparring partner Larry Holmes, by Michael Spinks, and by fighters not fit to lace his boots.

His features puffed and eyes dimmed, slurry of speech and mumbling platitudes, he now preaches the gospel of the Black Moslem.

Bhagwan Piari and I had many adventures during the twenty-five years that we were together, and I developed a great affection for her, and she for me, which she demonstrated by urinating copiously when I approached. While she was with me she eliminated a kidney stone weighing over half a kilogram, and narrowly escaped being crushed by a falling ficus tree during a thunderstorm. She attended all our Christmas camps, and I had my time cut out preventing her *Filwan*, Bhuntu, from purloining her Christmas rations to buy himself drink as he carried out parallel celebrations with his cronies. I often dismissed him for these misdemeanours; but he was good at his job, and I just as many times reinstated him. Eventually, smitten by asthma, his frail body wracked by indulgence in ganja and broken by an over-use of cheap alcohol, he abdicated in favour of his son. Bhuntu died shortly before Bhagwan Piari, and with their passing I too died a little.

Though elephants are nervous animals, Bhagwan Piari appeared unafraid of tigers, and I shot three so-called maneaters in her presence. She was present at the death of many more tigers, as well as assisting in the photography of others, and acquired a great reputation. April 1963 was a milestone in Bhagwan Piari's life. I had lent her to aid in the shikar of the Superintendent of Police, Kheri, who, unknown to me, passed her on to an industrialist from Kanpur. In early May she arrived at base with gaping fang marks on her left hind leg, where she had been mauled by a wounded tiger at Kiratpur about twenty miles north. Bhuntu considered this a suitable occasion for indulgence and, as I was supervising the medication of Bhagwan Piari's wounds, he related with elan that the tiger hunters, of whom there were many, had not bothered or dared to follow the ethic applied to the search for wounded animals, but had detailed subordinates to deal with the tiger. Bhuntu related with much bravado and probably little veracity that, when the wounded tiger charged the elephant, the mounted followers panicked, but that he had struck at the tiger with his Gajbag or ankus used to guide the elephant, and the tiger had then released his hold on Bhagwan Piari's leg, whereupon she had fled. A correspondence then ensued with the industrialist, from which I quote excerpts:

Every possible precaution was taken when attempting to recover the tiger. Nearly thirty dogs were used to trace it. On account of the dense foliage 'it took us two days to reach the brink of the nullah as we followed the blood which was found everywhere in gallons, with extreme caution.

On the third day, as was evident from his roars, the tiger could not climb the nullah, and when he did manage he could not move further and kept on roaring and roaring, when the elephant was asked to turn back. It was sheer bad luck that the tiger was lying somewhere under the dense foliage, and when the elephant came near he just attacked. From the above narration of facts it would be appreciated that it would not be fair to say that the tiger was wilfully abandoned, and that what was done was not against the ethics of good sportsmanship.

I am really surprised that you visited the nullah where the tiger was, the foliage was so dense and there were so many dry leaves, that the tiger would immediately detect the approach of anyone, and if alive would attack anything which comes near him. Anyway it is very nice of you to offer your cooperation.

The letter was in reply to one from me detailing my visits and accusing the industrialist of not following the wounded animal and, moreover, endangering my elephant which he had used without my permission. A second letter was more categorical, and elicited an acrimonious reply:

Thus the description of your valiant visits to the nullah, particularly the second when you once again searched it, where the tiger had been wounded, outwit even the story of Arabian Nights· entertainment.

Similarly your claim to the ownership of the carnivora stocked in the forest which made you suggest 'To forego my annual campaign' against what you call our carnivora, outclasses the story of King Canute, who claimed rulership of the waves.

Similarly your ideas of inadequacy of firearms, and shikaris must be indeed amazing. If one Hollands .465 D. B., two 450/400 D.Bs and two Hollands .375 Magnum, carried by as many shikaris as the number of rifles, and a host of other rifles carried by Nepali residents are considered inadequate, then perhaps a battalion, armed with mortars and cannon would be necessary to track a tiger hit by two .465 bore bullets.

You are at the fringe of libel when you say I can be charged with a heinous crime.

I wrote back to say: 'Your description of the armoury used against the tiger is impressive, but as you will agree, it is the man behind the gun that counts',... 'The Divine Conscience dwells in all of us, and though often obscured by self interest, and stunted by disuse, it does stand forth as a beacon for decent behaviour.' Correspondence then ceased, but I have given extracts in some detail because it illustrates the attitude of so-called sportsmen to the hunting of wild animals, the awe in which the tiger is held, and the animal's capacity for inflicting injury when aroused.

Subsequent events connected with this episode were as follows: a few days after the tiger was wounded, on 26 April 1963 the Range Officer, a forest guard and a number of Tharus from the village of Kiratpur, went to visit the place where the tiger had been hit, hoping it was dead; he charged out at the party. The portly Range Officer led the retreat, but the forest guard was mauled. Soon after the wounded Bhagwan Piari returned I took Bhuntu with me and went to the site where the tiger had been wounded. It was 10 May, and the tiger may just possibly have been alive as a kakar barked in the direction where the elephant had been mauled. The distance from Jasbirnagar was about thirty miles and we had started late. As it was turning into dusk, we came back from the mauling site. A week later we returned in the morning and, as we crossed the nullah, the rank smell of death assailed our senses. We came to a clearing which reminded me of a battlefield. Staves, shoes and clod hoppers littered the forest floor in profusion, and in the centre, as if still in authority, was the Range Officer's hat, and the bare bones of the tiger stripped of skin and flesh by scavengers, as he had evidently collapsed after his charge. I left the relicts where they belonged, and brought away one canine and a claw, and the Ranger's hat. I returned the hat to its owner and thought he looked somewhat sheepish. I have the canine as a souvenir, and was surprised to note that of its five inches as much as two-thirds were encased in the jawbone. The claw I gave to a woman friend, who has now disappeared with it, with my affection.

Bhagwan Piari's wounds healed slowly, as is the case with these pachyderms, but she now appeared to be more wary in the forest. Some time later I took her on a shoot in a nearby block. We were walking along a forest road when my companion turned and fired a shot in the undergrowth, and a tiger rushed away. He claimed that the tiger had been sitting sideways to us, but as we later discovered he had hit him low in the chest. We followed that tiger into dense grass, and suddenly he leapt on to the elephant next to mine and dug his claws into her head. Bhagwan Piari fled, and by the time she was brought under control, the man who had wounded the tiger and was on a third elephant, very commendably put a bullet into the enraged animal's brain. Bhagwan Piari, as so often happens with other elephants who are mauled, was now always nervous at the sight or smell of a tiger, and would not stand still when confronted, and fled many a time on later occasions. She died of old age when she fell into a shallow depression, and, with her head below the level of her body she was unable to get up. By the time we had dug enough to raise her head she was dead in the hot May sun. She was about seventy years old.

Though I was the original pioneer settler, other farmers started arriving towards the middle of the century. A large organization called 'The Collective Farms and Forests Ltd' started farming ten thousand areas. Other individuals followed suit as there was no restriction on the amount of land which could be leased. As crop damage by wild animals became distributed among other farmers, I bought two more, larger tractors to bring all my acreage under the plough.

But the landscape was changing. Whereas I had come to an endless vista of grassland, multi-coloured agricultural crops now shimmered on the horizon. Gone were the herds of Nilgai and blackbuck, and somehow the midnight cries of the fox and the jackal seemed muted. I conceived the idea of buying a crawler tractor to break up the land which was being settled by dispossessed personnel from Pakistan. Ahead lay extensive lands awaiting the plough: Majhra Singahi, the favourite hunting ground of Vizzy; and Khajuria, on the border of the districts of Pilibhit and Kheri—the haunt of robbers, of Kallan Khan who migrated to Pakistan and whose place was taken by Bashira, an ex-professional wrestler, and his gun-toting wife. Along the unending vista were grass hutments from where thin spirals of smoke snaked into the atmosphere. Some were the cooking fires of settlers who had arrived with the promise of large holdings. Others were funeral pyres for people from a dry temperature, enervated by recurrent malaria and the humid climate. Some gave their lives, but many stayed on, bolstered by the fact that they had nowhere else to go.

Once we camped at Mirchia Jheel, venue of the famous guber-natorial battues where forty trophy swampdeer stags would be gunned in a morning's shoot. Only a solitary female deer now splashed through the water, but further on a flight of mallard rose to the boom of a musket, leaving a couple lying in the water. On my return home I found that a neighbour of mine, one Boaz, had been raided by Bashira and his gun taken away. However, Boaz had been shooting tiger, so perhaps this was poetic justice. Another man named Agha, whose father had been with mine at Oxford, also took to shooting tigers on farmland, where there was no restriction on numbers. As his score grew, I suggested to the Chief Wildlife Warden that, as the end would justify the means, we should cook up a case against him. We did so, claiming that he had shot a tiger in the Reserved Forest. The Chief Wildlife Warden was unable to produce a witness, so I persuaded my tracker, who went by the name of Jackson, to give evidence. However, by threatening Jackson, the other side got him to refuse to falsify his statement, though I took him by the throat. But the case had a salutary effect, and Agha gave up his activities, alarmed by the notoriety, and migrated to Pakistan. Later, Bashira was gunned down in Pilibhit in an encounter with the police. His wife, the legendary gun-wielding Begum Bashira, turned out to be a nondescript and pregnant village woman; and the raid on my residence which was next on Bashira's list according to his diary, did not come about.

As though to underline that some wildlife was still left, two wolves raided my temporary premises at Jasbirnagar and took away a goat. I unashamedly shot one, but got no pleasure from this. The house that I was building was almost complete, but I felt no joy in occupying a building after over a decade of living in a straw hut. My feelings towards wildlife were at a stage of ambivalence, and killing no longer gave me a sense of achievement. I shot an old barasingha stag with antlers two inches off the world record given in Rowland Ward's book. The tamarisk brushwood lining the Sarda riverbed was being reclaimed by agriculturists, and no longer echoed to the pounding hooves of deer. Gaddis told me that barasinghas were still to be seen in large numbers in the area of Naudha Bhagar, a marshy river, where they took their cattle to graze every winter. I went there and saw remarkably large herds in segregated groups, their many tined antlers glittering in the morning sun. Land reclamation had already begun, and they were restless, and took off towards Ghola, an adjoining grassland of about three thousand acres with a lake in the centre.

On my return from this trip I determined to look for some land closer to the forest, for it seemed that overnight I had been smothered by cultivation. Khajuria and Majhra Singahi were also in the process of being reclaimed by a government colonization scheme to settle landless labour from eastern Uttar Pradesh.

Government officials interpreted the colonization scheme in their own way, depending on the posts they were occupying, and would visit the colonization areas as a means of boosting their travelling allowances, as well as indulging in forms of entertainment, chiefly shikar for which the area was famous, or smuggling from the Nepal border. One senior official had a tigress declared a maneater and it became known as the Maneater of Visenpuri; he shot an unidentified tigress and no doubt claimed a reward for killing the so-called maneater. The Commissioner of the neighbouring Nepal province of Dhangarhi was invited by his Indian counterpart to shoot a barasingha, though they were supposed to be protected in both countries. The Commissioner of Lucknow Division was brought a crocodile ensnared in a net which he was invited to shoot, and did so, believe it or not, from the safe distance of one metre.

I considered such incidents to be the lowest in depravity until I read in *Cat News 1991*, an official publication of the Species Survival Commission of the IUCN, the following nauseous extract: 'US Federal Officials are investigating more than a dozen ranches in the USA where "hunters" shoot tigers, jaguars, leopards and mountain lions. In some cases animals have been tranquillized and tied to trees and then shot, or released in areas the size of a football field to be killed by high-paying customers.'

A report in the *San Jose Mercury News* in California quoted Fish and Wildlife Service special agent Bill Talkin as saying one tiger at a Monterey Ranch was shot dead in its cage when it refused to move out. Witnesses said that another had walked less than thirty metres from its cage when it was shot. One of the ranchers charged, Floyd Lester Pearson III, told the newspaper that the 33 criminal charges against him were 'overblown'. 'The way they are talking about it like it was a crapshoot or something. It wasn't nothing like that. I am a hunter, and I lead guided hunts. There's nothing wrong with that!' Talkin said the Federal authorities confiscated photographs and videotapes of jaguars, tigers, leopards and mountain lions being shot on the Patterson property. The hunters came from all over the USA. The philosophy underlying such behaviour indicates a mental aberration.

Nepal was also changing direction. The King of Nepal shot a rhino in a Park to offer a blood libation to his ancestor. When I first arrived on the farm this Hindu kingdom was still in the thrall of the Middle Ages; with the King as the Divinity, the Ranas ruled the country, and its poverty was abysmal. Virulent malaria enervated the people, and wild animals competed with humans for existence. Sport hunting was the privilege of a few, and criminal punishment and procedures were primitive. The limited Rana rule had now gone. Everyone had Rights, and none Duties. The forests are going, and flash floods sweep down the great waterways. The Churia Range, traditional holding grounds of the tiger, is no more, and the harvest has been gleaned in India. The forests of Nepal, contiguous to the Dudhwa National Park, have been reclaimed for agriculture by ex-army personnel. Their cattle graze in our forests, and their fire arms decimate our wildlife. Buffer areas which were once pitted by tiger pugs and ungulate slots now only show signs of human occupation.

I had heard of land in an area known as Bilahia, which adjoined the Dudhwa Reserved Forest and which had been leased by a politician whose original plan was to use his location next to the forest to extract timber. He had indeed indulged in some illicit transactions, but he was handicapped by the fact that the Neora river ran along the escarpment which constituted the boundary of the valuable Sal timber tract, and the grasslands through which the timber had to be taken out were waterlogged for half the year. However, he had made a beginning, and a ford known as Chor Leek ('Robbers Path') had become a well-known entry point.

One morning we set off to look for some farmland closer to the forest and further away from human occupation. I rode Bhagwan Piari and Pincha, my faithful old mongrel dog, followed behind. We crossed a *bhagar* where the dog had to swim on occasions, biting his way through entangling weeds. The going on higher land was easier for him as he gingerly picked his way in the wake of the trampled grass left by the elephant. Coots skittered away in the occasional pools left by the flood waters, and occasionally a hogdeer rushed out, in the manner of the pig from which it derives its name. We came upon a large python coiled on a tree above the Soheli tributary, which we followed until its junction with the Neora. Above loomed the stately Sal trees on top of an escarpment, and way to the north, tier upon tier of mountains buttressed the ethereal peak of Nanda Devi. I was enchanted by the setting, the meeting of the waters, and the thought that I had reached the last bastion in my retreat from human settlements.

I leased 173 acres of land, and started clearing operations. Trees had to be dug out and huge roots pulled away by my crawler tractor and Bhagwan Piari. The area was subject to large-scale flooding during the monsoon, largely because enough outlet spans had not been constructed on the embankment of the railway, and partly because the meandering course of the river was choked by fallen timber each year. The condition was further aggravated when the construction of a metal road took place and the engineer in charge reduced the outlet spans from three to two in revenge after a Wildlife Warden and I had caught him poaching. It took me five years to shore the various cutaways into my farmland, as the embankments kept on collapsing and had to be rebuilt. My original approach to Tiger Haven, which I had originally called after my Air Force brother who was also known as Tiger, was over a tree which had fallen across the river. Later, I constructed a fairweather road connection. In the mean time I built myself another small one-room straw hut instead of the concrete structure it had taken me fourteen years to build at Jasbirnagar, and I was ready to start again.

I now lost Pincha. He was sixteen and a quarter, but his indomitable heart would not be stilled. He rolled down the bank of the river which he had swum in so often, and was too weak to get out, and there I found him. He was the founder member of the Tiger Haven Cemetery in which he has a headstone.

Retreating before the advance of cultivation, the swampdeer had now colonized Ghola, a 3,000-acre plot of grassland owned by L. D. W. Hearsey, and now under lease to three farmers. But a sword of Damocles hung over these leaseholders as well, for a ceiling on the possession of land was soon to be imposed by the government, and the area would then vest in the State. The land configuration of Ghola was in the shape of a cup, with a lake in the centre. We had estimated that about 1,500 swampdeer occupied this area, which adjoined the Reserved Forest Grassland of Sathiana. Bounded by the Neora which flowed along the escarpment about 50 feet high, a forest of Sal extended to the Nepal border. This formed the last refuge for the swampdeer of the marshy plains.

The State Board of Wildlife was constituted in 1964, and I was appointed a member. I submitted a resolution proposing that, in view of the fact that Ghola would lapse to the government with the imposition of a ceiling on land holdings, the 3,000 acres contiguous to the Reserved Forest, which seemed to be the last stronghold of the endangered swampdeer, should be taken into the North Kheri Forest Division. The Chief Wildlife Warden came to visit me and together we went round the area. We visited the Ghola lake where desiccated carcases of wounded animals who had come to the water to die lay submerged. The Chief Wildlife Warden left with great expressions of sympathy, and a seeming determination that something had to be done.

However, nothing transpired, and the arable land was gradually taken over by Naxalites and other landgrabbers. As the position continued to worsen, I determined to take matters into my own hands and try to entice the recalcitrant barasinghas into the Reserved Forest where they would be comparatively safe. For though their flesh was comparatively unpalatable there was a growing market for meat. I ploughed up some forest land under strong protest from the local staff, and planted barley and constructed some salt licks. As soon as the barley started sprouting I borrowed five elephants from a local shikar outfitters' establishment and staged a round-up towards the Reserved Forest. Some broke back, but the main herd which George Schaller had estimated at 600 earlier on crossed the Soheli and entered the precincts of the forest. Next day I was gratified to see a herd of about 450 grazing in the Sathiana Meadow.

However, the herd was greatly outnumbered by domestic cattle which lived in the grassland, and from which the Forest Department received a subsidy. With the cooperation of a sympathetic Divisional Forest Officer I set fire to the temporary hutments of the cattle station, and soon the barasingha were in and the cattle out. I watched with intense satisfaction as the number grew, and in 1972, after the IUCN Meeting of the General Assembly in 1969, Colin Holloway, their Chief Ecologist, visited me and estimated 1,200–1,600 animals in the Madrahia-Sathiana complex.

Though the swampdeer had colonized the area into which they had been driven, it was not prime habitat as far as they were concerned. They would migrate out of the Madrahia-Sathiana area towards cultivation, impelled by vicious biting flies, coarse grasses and the fact that the flooding of the grassland took place in the direction of cultivation, and away from the main forest on the escarpment—all of which coincided with their fawning. As a contrast, in the case of swampdeer occupation further east, where the flooding was towards the Reserved Forest, swampdeer herds would often be found in the Sal forest during the monsoon. Additionally, as their fawning period was May to July, this voluntary shift towards high land was an attempt to safeguard the highly vulnerable fawns, which returned in depleted numbers in January or February after the grasses were burnt, having run the gauntlet of high floods and poachers' bullets.

A further catastrophe now overtook the endangered swampdeer, when they were supposedly in sight of complete environmental protection. Dudhwa had been declared a National Park, and a Managing Committee with the senior bureaucrat of the State, appointed as Chairman. The Secretary of the Irrigation Department, as a member of the Committee, proposed that an irrigation barrage should be constructed on the Soheli river which formed the boundary of the Park. I submitted a strong note to the Chairman saying that the swamp deer, for whose conservation the Park had primarily been declared, would be greatly endangered. The very sympathetic Chairman agreed, and noted in the minutes that no structure of any description would be made on the Soheli. All seemed to be well, and the deer population continued to multiply.

However, I was unaware of the way the government functioned, and the enemy bided their time. The previous Chairman was no sooner transferred than the Irrigation Department started work on a barrage immediately outside the Park in the buffer zone. By the time the Park authorities discovered this construction, they claimed to have spent Rs 90,000, and, according to them, were unaware of the ruling which forbade the construction of the barrage. They pointed out the great financial loss which the State exchequer would be put to if the construction was abandoned. This story was accepted by the new Chairman, and when the Irrigation Department further compounded its duplicity by offering to construct safety walls, its work was allowed to proceed despite my strong protests. It seems that for governments ignorance of the law is an excuse for a fresh beginning.

From the 1,200–1,600 evaluated by Holloway, barasingha numbers are down to about 150 in the Madrahia-Sathiana area. High flood levels manipulated by the closure of the barrage outlets ensured that Tiger Haven had two and a half feet of water inside its tenements in mid-June 1988, when I also became an endangered species in my own country. It is doubtful whether the swampdeer will recover from the disaster in a hurry.

When Balram came on a visit from Calcutta in 1960 we went for a drive in the forest. There seemed to be more people than ever inside the forests on various errands, and we saw fewer animals than humans. It was dark, and we sat down to a cup of tea besides a log fire. A lapwing called across a depression, and soon after a leopard gave a succession of sawing grunts. He was objecting to the invasion of his territory. I drove my jeep to the edge of the depression, and saw in the glow of the headlights a lambent green pinpoint of light moving at right angles to our front. Resting my elbows on my knees I took careful aim from between the headlights at the moving pinpoint, and fired a shot. There was no sound, but the light went out. I advanced to the spot, and in the flashlight saw a leopard lying on the ground. A crimson circle welled behind the shoulder and, even as I watched, the fire faded from his eyes. I had brought off a spectacular shot, and acquired a fine trophy, but I felt nothing but an awful confusion—futility at the destruction of beauty and the taking of life for personal pleasure. I put aside my rifle as my father had done many years before. Soon after, the arrival of Prince [his own leopard], of whom I have written elsewhere, changed my life for ever.

Excerpted from The Legend of the Man-Eater *(Delhi: Ravi Dayal Publisher, 1993).*

M. KRISHNAN

A Day's Span of Life

*The death of the octogenarian M. Krishnan in June 1996 silenced
one of the most prolific and outstanding naturalist-photographers
of our time. Krishnan was always a 'lone wolf', preferring
watching wildlife to committee-room discussions. Trained as a
botanist, the 1913-born-Krishnan briefly worked in the princely
state of Sandur, Mysore, in southern India. In 1948, he began
a career as a freelance writer that lasted almost half a century.
In his 'Country Notebook' in* The Statesman, *Calcutta, he wrote
of India's creatures great and small, furred and feathered, wild
and tame. Only two collections of these and other pieces were
published during his life-time—*Jungle and Backyard *and* Nights
and Days. *Krishnan also wrote of encounters between prey and
predator in Kaziranga Wildlife Sanctuary in Assam, of aggression
among animals and about forest trees and plains wildlife. His
range was immense, his observations meticulous, his knowledge of
literature (English, Tamil, Sanskrit) always evident. These selections from his work only give a sample of his interests.*

About a kilometre from the rest-house at Kaziranga, there was a
small, shallow pool, fringed thickly on one side with 10-foot high
grass, and here I had set up a small hide. Early in the morning, I
was on my way to this hide to try and photograph a pair of
blacknecked storks that haunted this pool, and met a party of
tourists returning to the rest-house on elephant back. They informed me that a cow rhino had just given birth to her calf in a
spread of tall dry grass beyond the pool—the mahout said the calf
was less than an hour old, for on the way out with his party he had

seen this same cow, a heavily gravid cow he knew well, and it was then by itself with no calf by its side. Keen as I was on seeing the newborn calf, I had no wish to disturb that cow so soon after it had encountered this party of tourists; moreover, I was also keen on seeing the elusive birds I had set out to photograph. I had biscuits in my pocket and a flask of cold water, and asked the mahout to bring his elephant to my hide about noon, when he could take me to see the rhinos.

Well, the storks eluded me that day as well. They came to the pool all right, but seemed to know by some sixth sense exactly where they would be out of my sight, and went about their feeding, walking through the edge of the pool with their beaks plunged in and scissoring the water for prey, so that I could only glimpse them through the columnar culms around my hide—they never came to the middle. Past 11 o'clock the mahout came up, and I was glad to get out of the hide and on to the riding elephant.

The rhino mother was in an extensive spread of dead, dry, man-high grass, thick at one end and giving on to open ground at the other. I could not see the calf, but no doubt it was there, close by the cow, whose head and back alone were visible. I had the elephant moved to the thick end of the cover, so that the cow would be induced to move out into the open, and unexpectedly the calf came out to stare at us—many infant animals seem to find their first sight of an elephant fascinating and have still to develop a self-preservatory fear of men. At once the cow also came out and nuzzled the calf gently back into cover, and led it out to the other side. I took no pictures, for I was preoccupied with the calf: I had seen very young rhino calves, maybe only a few days old, in the Jaldapara sanctuary, but this one was only a few hours old.

Except that it had no horn, and that its hide seemed still tender and was pink in places, the calf was a replica miniature of its mother. It was already not too wobbly on its legs, and was able to follow its slow-moving parent without difficulty. I had heard a theory that rhino cows invariably preceded and led their young, but obviously this was not always so: most of the time the calf did follow, but was also ahead of its ponderous parent at times, however, on such occasions it always came back to give the cow the lead or to stay close beside her.

The noon lighting at Kaziranga in February, with the horizon still hazy and the sky leaden, was hardly congenial and after taking three pictures from a distance, I returned to the rest-house. The evenings are very short in this north-eastern sanctuary, but probably towards sunset, with the slanting yellow light upon my subjects, I could get much better pictures.

The calf was no longer there by evening. The cow was in that same patch of cover, visibly agitated, holding her head high and snorting, moving about restlessly. There was no possibility of my having mistaken another rhino for that cow, for she was quite distinctive, and both the mahout and I were sure it was the same animal; but noticed that the dead grass had been depressed in a long groove at one end of the cover, and that there was a heavy smear of blood in that groove. A little farther on, in a moist patch of open ground inside the tall grass, the fresh pugs of a tiger were deeply impressed and there was more blood there.

We hunted around but saw no other telltale evidence. However, what we had seen was sufficient for us to know what had happened. A tiger had sneaked up through the cover and seized the calf, perhaps when it had strayed a little distance from its mother, and taken it away, probably far away, for a newborn rhino weighs only around 50 kg., a deadweight that a tiger is perfectly capable of carrying over considerable distances.

Tigers are fond of young elephant flesh and will expose themselves to considerable risks from the great beasts in a herd to get at a calf if opportunity offers, and apparently they are no less fond of rhino calves. The mahout, a firm believer in the rejuvenating potency of all parts of a rhinoceros, wanted to collect the dry depressed grass with the blood on it, but I vetoed the move. We know that animals very different from ourselves can feel not only the same physical sensations like pain and hunger, but also many similar emotions, such as anger, high spirits and affection. That cow was the picture of disconsolate bereavement as she circled around restlessly, but sentiment apart, one would need to be both blind and unscientifically biased not to realize that she was in the grip of a powerful emotion, and that to disturb her further by collecting the bloody grass near her would be very wrong.

Excerpted from Nights and Days, My Book of India's Wildlife *(Delhi: Vikas Publishing House, 1985).*

M. KRISHNAN

Fights to the Death

Fights to the death are uncommon among animals of the same kind, but they do take place and seem less rare than is supposed. In mammals in which the sexes differ notably, as in the males possessing antlers or tusks but not the females (elephants, all our deer, and wild pigs), or being differently coloured or being horned (nilgai and blackbuck), or in the male being considerably larger (as among macaques and gaur), it is the males that sometimes engage in mortal combats with rivals. Not that the females never fight among themselves—they do indulge in bite threats and bickerings, but not in terminal combats, and as a rule the females never fight adult males.

How about animals like the tiger and the leopard, the dhole and jackal, and a great many others in which there is only a slight difference in size and power between the adult male and female? The position seems more fluid among them and less confined to male belligerence.

I know of two instances in which tigresses with cubs, attracted to the same live baits staked out by men, have fought till one killed the other, but in these instances there was the artificially imposed factor of the provision of the bait. An adult female will attack another that poses a threat to its young especially during their infancy, sometimes even a male of its own kind, but in such cases the attack seldom goes farther than the driving away of the potential threat. Note that I write solely of internecine fights between animals of the same kind.

To return to what I began with, intraspecific fights to the death being less rare than is thought by students of animal behaviour, two factors seem to motivate such fights—territorial feelings and the intrusion of a male into the established territory of another male, and among animals that live gregariously, the ousting of the dominant male of a troop or herd by another adult male belonging to the same association or from outside it.

These factors may be considered further with regard to particular animals, but before going on to that it would be just as well to stress the fact that in nature such internecine fights are generally avoided by threats and brief skirmishes resulting in one of the two antagonists accepting defeat or the dominance of its rival, and retreating. Nature's wisdom in this will be manifest when it is realized that otherwise, in addition to the destructive influences of diseases, predation and environmental hazards, frequent moral engagements within the species itself will result in its substantial depletion and the disorganization of social associations.

Purely as instances of such intraspecific fights, their occurrence among four widely different classes of wild animals, monkeys, elephants, gaur and deer may be briefly considered. In monkeys that live in troops, like the common langur, the dominant male whose powers are failing is challenged by another big male, often from outside the troop and sometimes from within it. A fierce fight for supremacy ensues, but usually the dispossessed male does not get killed but goes away to join an all-male troop and may even keep following its own troop keeping its distance.

Among elephants, which are perhaps the most stable in their herd association of our gregarious animals, mortal combats seldom take place between an aging dominant male and a younger bull of the same herd. When too old to maintain their status, dominant bulls go away by themselves or even stay in the herd occupying a subordinate position. But fights to the death occasionally do take place between a herd leader and a big bull from outside. Such fights are often prolonged over days, the rivals breaking off periodically to feed or drink but are usually sustained to the end.

[A photograph that I once took shows] the victor in such an engagement, unmarked except for the tusk wound (a lighter coloured weal) above the right hind knee. I also had a good look at the loser, though I could get no photograph of him, a great bull of equal stature and with equally well-developed tusks, gored in several places and covered with blood encrusted with earth through over the wounds. A few days later, this wounded tusker died. A close friend, whose personal knowledge of wild elephants was scientific and second to that of none, once witnessed a tusker goring a rival to death. Even herd bulls separate from their herd when engaging in such titanic battles.

Gaur, like elephants, form stable herds and, also like elephants, range far in their quest of fodder, and among them, too, there are old lone bulls. I have not come across an authentic instance of rival bulls fighting to the death, but have personally observed fierce fights between rivals. Once I witnessed a remarkable end to such a fight, between an older and bigger bull and a younger but more massive antagonist—they were clashing horns and going all out for each other when the entire herd (to which the older bull belonged) came galloping up between the two bulls, effectively separating them!

Chital, perhaps the most gregarious of our deer, are strikingly different from other gregarious animals in the instability of their associations. There is no permanence, even over a short period, in their herd associations or between stag and hind. In fact, only in the all-male herds of stags with regenerating antlers (most of them almost clear of velvet) does there seem to be some stability of association. Chital stags in hard horn sometimes engage in combats, but often these are only brief skirmishes and the lesser stag runs away. But on occasion the fight between evenly matched stags is deadly, the terrific force with which they charge each other, locking and clashing antlers, and the noticeable manifestation of sexual excitement during such fights, serving to distinguish them at once from mock combats and skirmishes. The defeated stag does try to run away, but is often badly gored as it seeks escape, sometimes fatally.

Originally published in 'Country Notebook', The Statesman, 11 December 1983.

PART III

The Living Landscape

Despite being home to more than a billion people, the Indian subcontinent teems with wildlife. The cycle of seasons in the forest is marked by the flowering of great trees—the candelbara-like trains of the *amaltas*, the dark red of silk cotton and the scarlet of the flame of the forest. The cheetah vanished half a century ago but the black buck, the *Krisna mriga* of the Sanskrit texts remains, protected by government rules in some pockets, by village communities in others. What were once staging grounds of hunts where viceroy or maharaja slaughtered ducks or geese, and dined on venison or partridge, have often become sanctuaries for wildlife. Though much is taken, much abides. The rhythms of nature have not all been broken: in fact, as many of the selections in this section testify, new links have been forged, bonds that give hope for the future.

Not all such links are new. The trackers of the Gir Forest earlier led hunters to their quarry: now they help tourists watch the great cats on foot. Scientists have rehabilitated even predators hated by sport-hunters. In India today, the wild dog for long shot at sight as vermin is a forest denizen who can live with dignity. The great Indian one-horned rhino and the lion, each down to a handful around 1900, have recovered and are regularly observed at close range by tourists. Even turtles and cobras now have their chroniclers and champions. Most amazing—certainly shikaris of yore would be surprised to know of this—we are even learning about the family ties and bonds of tigers and elephants in the wild.

M. KRISHNAN

Our Wildlife: A Great Legacy Dissipated

Krishnan's essay published in a special number of the now-extinct The Illustrated Weekly of India *traces the threats to and the salvation of our natural heritage.*

To have a fair idea of the present worth of our wildlife preserves (of all kinds: sanctuaries, national parks and other protected habitats) and to know what further steps need to be taken to effectively safeguard our heritage of nature, it is quite necessary to take a quick, overall look at the past. Many of these preserves were set up long before Independence, in British India and in the princely States—well-known examples are Vendanthangal in Tamil Nadu, Bandipur in Karnataka and Corbett Park (our first authentic national park, set up in 1934) in Uttar Pradesh.

Soon after the shikar battues that followed Independence, the Indian Board for Wild Life was constituted, a number of fresh preserves were created (some quite major ones) and conservation tightened. Illustrative examples of this are the metamorphosis of Keola Deo Ghana at Bharatpur in Rajasthan from a wild fowlers' paradise into the most important water-bird sanctuary in Asia in 1956, the Point Calimere and Anaimalai sanctuaries of Tamil Nadu and the intensification of conservation in the Gir Forest of Gujarat (the last home of the Asiatic lion) and in Kaziranga in Assam (the major stronghold of the Indian rhinoceros and the no less Indian wild buffalo). The trend has been continued right into the present: Sultanpur Jheel in Haryana, another favourite resort of wild fowlers, was converted into a fine sanctuary recently and the ambitious Desert National Park of Rajasthan was initiated earlier this year. We now have almost 150 wildlife preserves, big and small, all over India. But neither the old nor the new preserves have taken note of the basic fact that the wild vegetation is quite as integral and vital a part of the wildlife of any region as its fauna. In 1970, with the acceptance by the Central Government of the definition of 'wildlife' as the entire uncultivated flora and fauna of a tract, this profound truth gained formal official recognition—it still awaits recognition in the field. In fact, our wildlife preserves have all been set up solely for the larger animals, and a few for water-birds, and the flora has been considered purely incidental, as providing cover and fodder, and the lesser life not considered at all. Hydel projects have been sited close by, even right inside, some of the best preserves: with a few exceptions, diverse forestry operations (all highly destructive of the natural vegetation) are carried on in our preserves, and even the supply of raw materials at subsidized rates to industries from them undertaken: cattle-grazing, the collection of firewood and forest produce and other human activities are permitted, motor roads intersect the preserves, and human traffic on foot (highly unsettling to the wild animals) allowed. All our wildlife habitats (including all preserves) are solely in charge of our various governments: naturally, then, the responsibility for protection is entirely theirs, and even otherwise only governments have the sanction necessary for protection. It follows, inescapably, that by their permissiveness, our governments have been the chief depredators of our wildlife.

Actual, factual evidence in proof of every generalization made so far in this overall survey of the past is on record, but the detailing of even selected examples of such proof will take up this entire issue of the weekly, and the rest of the brief space available to me is needed for constructive suggestions for the future. But before going on to them, let me comment on the outraged defence of their past policy and administration that governments are likely to raise on this criticism, that they have been preoccupied with more important things, with providing for the elemental needs of our growing populations and industries.

SISYPHEAN TASK

Yes, I do realize that they have had that Sisyphean task right from the start, but then all our preserves together constitute only about one per cent of the total land area, and surely they could have provided for our populations and industries with the overwhelming percentage of the land not given over to wildlife at their disposal. Furthermore, conserving the wealth of nature we still have left is also an elemental national need. Much needs to be done towards more realistic conservation to rectify the apathy and wastefulness of the past, and it has to be done right now—to delay further is to be assured of not having enough worth the saving.

This is the counsel, not of despair but of hope. The depletion of the past 50 years *has* been staggering: places noted for their wildlife within my own recollection are now denuded and bare and their animals have declined to rarity, even to local extinction. But the wonderful, the heartening thing is this—in spite of everything, India is still second to no country in its wild fauna, and perhaps the richest in its flora. Though heavily depleted, our fauna is still there, and notably free from exotic introductions: that cannot be said of our exotics-ridden flora, but it will regain its pristine glory if conserved, that is, if left alone and allowed to regenerate.

The policy of leaving well alone and of manfully resisting the almost overpowering urge to improve on nature has been proved to be the best, actually the only sound policy in conservation. This was called trust in the balance of nature in the past, and is now termed total environmental conservation, and it will suffice to ensure the future of our wildlife. It means emancipating preserves of viable area from all forms of human exploitation, and the provision of strict protection (now sadly lacking) against human disturbance and depredation. That is all that is needed, but since natural regeneration is a slow process, patience and faith are also needed. Incidentally, it is only in the few reserves of Project Tiger that total environmental conservation is now being attempted, after a fashion.

RAVAGED OPULENCE

In the past decade, governmental cognizance of responsibility for the country's ravaged opulence of nature has displayed a certain nascent percipience. The Wildlife (Protection) Act of 1972 is constructive, if only for its insistence on a specific wildlife organization in each State, and it is the first realistic attempt at a national policy of conservation. There are other tokens for awakening governmental concern for our wildlife, even of awakening public concern in a minority of our people, but for the next generation at least governments must bear the entire responsibility for protection. Today, there is no informed popular interest in our culture, in our magnificent assets of nature. The human and natural curiosity of our children in the wild things around is sternly nipped in the bud by our traditions of life and instruction instead of being informed and stimulated. In the West, with a comparatively small store of wildlife, the great therapeutic value of such an interest in relieving the stresses and frustrations of civilized life has been fully appreciated after the last World War: wildlife recreation is widely organized and popular, and education at all levels features nature importantly. With no reliable natural history in the written or oral literatures of our languages, and no popular feeling for it, it will be no easy task to inform and stimulate this dormant interest in our people, particularly in the younger sections, but this is a vital national need and will endow future generations with a joy and a sustenance in life that we have been without.

PRIMARY PATRIOTIC DUTY

If I have only conveyed the impression so far that it is of national importance to conserve our wildlife and wildlife habitats, I have failed fundamentally in my argument. This is no matter of mere importance, but a primary patriotic duty, quite essential for the survival of the identity of this ancient country. Surely no country depends for its identity mainly on the conglomerate accretions of its cultural past or its mutable humanity—it depends overwhelmingly on its own peculiar physical integrity, its geomorphology and the flora and fauna that belong to it distinctively. Oddly enough, it is our poets and not our rulers or politicians who have realized this profound truth—it is they that have sung of our mountains and valleys and rivers, sounding seas and vast coastlines, great forests and lovely flowers, and of our birds and beasts.

The dissipation of India's physical integrity has now reached the stage where further indiscriminate demands on its natural resources will certainly erode its very identity. For this reason, it is imperative that adequate tracts, typical of the country's quiddity, should be freed from human exploitation and protected efficiently. Only that can ensure the continuance of India's identity. With our vast populations and growing industrialization, it will be unrealistic to ask for much territory even for this vital national purpose, but a modest five per cent of the total land area should suffice, in the circumstances. Naturally, this will include all existing wildlife preserves, so that no further demands need be made on our forests; for the rest it will embrace notable geomorphological features, and areas not provided for so far in our wildlife effort, such as swamps, estuaries, offshore islands, mountain tops and, by no means last, adequate expanses of plains for the wildlife of the open country, now so sadly lacking sanctuary.

Originally published in The Illustrated Weekly of India, *24 August, 1980.*

M. KRISHNAN

Buck

Few large mammals have declined in numbers in the last half century as rapidly as the black buck. Its range stretches as far south as Tirunelveli in the Tamil country, but it was most abundant in western India. It still holds out in several pockets. Krishnan had observed the species both before and after its decline. The black buck remains one of the most graceful of all antelopes; here, Krishnan celebrates its beauty.

Africa is the home of the antelope tribe. The smallest and the largest of them all, the strangest-looking and some of the handsomest, are all African: there are dozens of different kinds of antelopes there, most of them living in the bush country but a few also deep inside the great rain forests, and a few in the desert, too.

Here in India, we have only four kinds of antelopes, but the type-specimen of the tribe, *Antelope cervicapra,* the blackbuck, is exclusively Indian and anciently associated with our life and culture.

Even otherwise, the blackbuck has superlative claims to distinction, though only medium-sized. Many think it the most beautiful of all antelopes, It is sexually dimorphic, the buck differing from the doe not only in carrying horns but also in colour: the adult buck is a glossy black with white around each eye and the lips, a white chest and belly, and white on the insides of the limbs and tail, a most arresting colour pattern. The doe, smaller, hornless and more daintily built, is a sandy fawn where the buck is black and refined in its attractiveness. Further, blackbuck are the fastest long-distance runners of all animals, and can keep going over long distances at nearly a kilometre a minute. And taking bodily size into consideration, not even African antelopes can rival them in the magnificence and attractiveness of their horns—the decoratively ringed and sinuous horns of a big buck may be almost as long as the animal's height.

I remember seeing blackbuck in vast herds where now they are gone, or else survive in small remnant populations. The open country to which they belong being most open to occupation, has everywhere been invaded by human enterprise and settlements and been cut up, and needing extensive plains scrub for life, the buck have been wiped out from most of their old homes, where they had survived centuries of intensive hunting.

India has long been the paradise of sportsmen with guns, and professional meat-hunters with nets and traps and snares. And no animal here has been more eagerly sought by every description of hunter than the blackbuck. Nawabs and Maharajas hunted it by trained cheetahs, imported all the way from Africa when the cheetah declined to rarity and then became totally extinct at home; it was the favourite week-end quarry of army men and urban and suburban worthies, armed with an assortment of firearms from shotguns to high-velocity rifles with telescopic sights. For it was there around cantonments and towns; and hunters, uninhibited by the most rudimentary hunting ethics or humanity, encompassed its end by the most cruel means. I detail a mode of snaring buck practised in the central and eastern parts of the country, to show how callous and deceitful these professionals could be.

All herbivores, from the lordly elephant to the porcupine and even smaller animals, love the mucilaginous pulp of the *bael* fruit (whose leaves are sacred to Shiva). Hunters choose mature fruits and introduce a sharpened hook with a needle-point into each fruit through its base, where the stalk is attached, so that the smooth, firm rind is unbroken: a short length of thin, strong string is attached to the eye of the hook and its other end tied round the middle of a pencil-thin slip of tough wood. The fruits are then disposed miles apart in the open scrub where blackbuck live.

Locating the bait by smell and sight, the buck devours it eagerly. Like all oxen, sheep, goats and antelopes, it has no front teeth on its upper jaw, and seizing the fruit in its mouth, it bites hard with the front teeth on its lower jaw to break the rind. This drives the embedded hook into its palate, and at once it tries to rid itself of the tormenting mouthful by pawing at it with a foot; the dangling string gets into the deep cleft between the halves of the hoof, and gets firmly lodged there by the stop provided by the sliver of wood. It falls down, hooked foot to mouth, and the more it struggles to free itself, the deeper the hook is driven into its palate and the more tightly the piece of wood is lodged in the hoof. It may be days before the hunter comes round to end its agony.

Imagine my delight when in north-west India I saw blackbuck again in great herds, and not in the small, fugitive parties in which they are to be found elsewhere in the country. And what was more, these buck were much bigger and more magnificently formed than those I had known in the Deccan and in the far south—blackbuck attain their finest body and horn development in the flat, arid tracts of the north-west.

The buck here lived all around human settlements and were, in fact, protected strictly by rural sentiment: the Bishnois of these settlements are vegetarians, and protect all wild animals around out of their religious tenets. They suffer the buck to feed in their fields of millets and gram, perhaps keeping a watch by day to shoo them away but never hurting them. A Bishnoi of whom I made enquiries said that there was little risk of the buck damaging the crops at night, since they were diurnal creatures; in this he was mistaken, for blackbuck are also on the hoof at night, but it is true they feed only desultorily and lie up most of the time then—it is chital and nilgai that are rapacious nocturnal crop-raiders.

Anyway, it is a fact that the predominantly agricultural Bishnois get by in spite of their tolerance. Near Aska in Orissa, there is an agricultural village where, too, the people do not harm the local buck, but their numbers there are comparatively limited. Here, I saw a really big herd of over a hundred, with two dominant master-bucks (probably a composite herd), a great many adult does and some young animals. There were smaller herds as well, and one all-male party of 14, in which there were two old animals with broken horns, and four buck which had not yet taken on the blackness of maturity but were still a rufous brown, though they had well-developed horns.

In the week I spent here wandering around, I realized that for all their unmatched speed and ability to cover long distances, blackbuck are territorial animals and stick to their accustomed beats, though these may be extensive. It is not merely that the entire local population was to be found within a radius of about 10 kms.—even within this circuit, each herd and party stayed more or less within its own locality. Driven out of this by some compulsion as by being pursued, they return to it when they can. This, I think, explains two features about buck long known but little understood.

It has been proved over the past 60 years that when compelled by human invasion of their homes to restrict themselves to a lesser area, buck are unable to do so and decline rapidly. The need for expansive territory for the herds and parties of a local population explains this inability to cope with deprivation of territory. They are essentially animals given to roaming far and feeding on scrub vegetation, low, harsh grasses, bushes and herbs, and weak-stemmed plants like the wild bitter-gourd (whose fruits they love) forming small carpets on the ground. Because of this habit, they do not thrive and lose their virility when confined to too small a home ground, even if they can find the fodder in it for sustenance. They are not far-ranging animals given to periodical shifts of feeding ground like elephants or gaur, and so they need considerable *lebensraum*.

The second point is this: many have noted the tendency of blackbuck to run round in a curve when pursued. Dunbar Brander, commenting on this, suggests that being so fleetfooted and confident of their superior speed, they run across the line of the pursuer after gaining a lead because they like to feel that 'they have the legs of the enemy'. I do not think so. They flee in a curve because that way they can never stray too far from their beat. Moreover, they seem held to their herd by powerful ties—not a mere promiscuous gregarious urge as in chital, but a bond that ties them not only to their home ground but also to their own herd. This is why wolves are able to hunt them—not by outrunning them and overtaking them after a long pursuit, but by pack strategy, cutting off one or two animals from the herd and then waylaying their quarry as it runs in to rejoin the herd. Wolves are now extinct or completely rare in areas where buck still roam in large herds, but village dogs today are killing buck by adopting the same strategy—after all, even after centuries of domestication and being bred true to type, there is still wolf-blood in their veins, for all dogs were originally derived from wolves and jackals.

Excerpted from Nights and Days, My Book of India's Wildlife *(Delhi: Vikas Publishing House, 1985).*

M. KRISHNAN

Spring in the Forest

Spring comes with summer to most forests in India. In such a vast country, so diverse in terrain and climate, naturally the vernal urge varies with location. In rain forests and in sholas with a dominantly evergreen complexion, on herb-clad hilltops and in the scrub, the plants may come into flower earlier or even later than summer, but in mixed deciduous tracts it is soon after the hot weather sets in that trees burst into bloom dramatically—and spring, the season of resurgence, can only be known floristically by its flowers, for they are the means of the continuance of life.

No country in the world is richer in flowering plants than ours, and whatever their habit or stature, soft-stemmed or woody-boled, they flower seasonally. Many bear inconspicuous flowers, or only a few—some great trees have flowers that are quite small or else so greenish or dull that one must look for them to see them, and quite a few that are profuse and colourful in bloom are not common, or else rather local in their distribution—for instance, one of the most charming of our flowering trees, the scarlet-flowered *asoka* (*Saraca indica*), is seldom seen in gregarious stands outside the hill forests of Goa and a few other locations. Of course there are a great many Indian trees notable for their flowers, some like the *kumizh* (*gammar* in the north, *Gmelina arborea*), even celebrated in classical literature, but I write only of a handful of trees common in most wild tracts of ‚the country, whose sudden, prodigal flowering transforms the leafless, dark grey-browns of summer woods, lending them colour and beauty.

Perhaps the widest distributed of these is the *palas* (*Butea monosperma*) that is there even in dry forests and in saline soil. This is the authentic Flame of the Forest, a name sometimes misapplied to the planted and exotic *gul mohur* (*Delonix regia*). It is not a big tree, and often a few grow together in a clearing or at the foot of a hill. With the desiccating heat of February, it sheds its trifoliate leaves, and the bare twigs develop masses of flower-buds that open in a blaze of vermillion with the dark, velvety calyces splitting up the tongues of flame of the petals. The flowers cover the entire tree, and seen from afar a clump of these trees does suggest a raging fire—except that there is never a forest fire without billowing smoke. A close cousin of the *palas, Butea superba* is a liana, a woody climber ascending tall trees with its heavy clusters of brilliant red flowers hanging down from the treetops.

The red silk-cotton, I think, is the most magnificent of our flowering trees. It is a lofty tree with its bole buttressed as its base and rising clear to an imposing height before it branches, with the branches outspread to form a great canopy. Even when in green leaf it is notable; in summer it sheds its foliage and the entire vast spread of its crown is studded with big, deep crimson flowers, with their fleshy petals splayed out in a five-pointed star, and a mass of red stamens crowding their middles. It is difficult even to imagine a canopy more regal than this constellation of crimson stars, purple in their depths, against the hot blue of the summer sky.

This is an all-India tree, with many names in different regional languages—the north Indian name, *simal,* is the best known of them. It used to be termed *Bombax malabaricum,* but about twenty years ago the name was changed in the international revision of scientific plant names to *Salmalia malabarica,* to the delight of Indian botanists, for its name in Sanskrit is *salmali.* A famous botanist recited a sonorous passage from Bhavabhuti to me, and translated it (for unfortunately I have no Sanskrit)—a passage describing the contrast between the shrill green of parakeets in a *salmali* and its large, crimson flowers. How shortlived the joy of our botanists was over this change of name. Some years ago, in a further revision they have changed the name again to *Bombax ceiba.*

Red silk-cotton flowers hold nectar within them, and so attract a host of birds to themselves—mynas of different kinds, orioles bulbuls, sunbirds, babblers, drongos, even crows and squirrels. Other forest trees, too, draw flocks of many birds, but mainly when they fruit. However, none of those fruiting trees has the irresistible allure of the *mohwa* (*Madhuca indica*) in bloom, to 'both man and bird and beast'. Even before gaining a sight of the tree, one knows it is in bloom from the characteristic pervasive sickeningly sweet smell of its fleshy-petalled flowers. Men camp all night beneath it to scare away the wild animals, and collect the thickly strewn flowers from the ground at dawn—they eat it fresh or cooked, or dried and boiled with rice, and make a potent liquor from it. Bears love this manna from the treetop, and so do all deer and antelopes and the lesser herbivores, even cattle, and the flowers attract many birds as well, though their sweetness is inside their succulent petals and not in a nectary.

The yellow silk-cotton is wholly unrelated to the *simal*, and totally different in its looks, but has a no less vivid beauty when in bloom. It is a small, dark, crooked tree with thick branches and palmately-lobed leaves, and in summer the leaves are shed leaving it naked. In the stony, dry hill-tops in which it grows, they usually burn the ground vegetation as soon as it is summer to encourage fresh sprouts of grass, and all around the ground is black and barren and rocky, and the trees stand leafless and dead-looking. The gnarled boughs of the yellow silk-cotton end in dark, swollen twigs and on these the flower-buds open into fresh, big flowers of the purest aureolin, as large as a cupped hand, and are crowded with a mass of sinuous stamens of a darker yellow. Against the charred desolation of that setting, the opulent chalices of gold have a breathtaking loveliness, tinged with hope.

The Indian laburnum (*amaltas, Cassia fistula*) is another yellow-flowered tree that has claims to a highly distinctive and delicate beauty. It was commonly planted in the country till, with the craze for exotics, the comparatively coarse copper pod displaced it in parks and gardens all over India, but it is still very much there in all forests. In spring it sheds its foliage and the entire tree is draped in pendent racemes of lemon yellow, with the pale green of the calyces of the round, unopened buds lending a chaste coldness to its exuberance of yellow. Rounding a bend in a forest and coming upon the Indian laburnum in bloom, one is halted in one's tracks by the sheer impact of its almost luminous loveliness.

There are trees with flowers of other colours, lilac and purple and even blue, and trees like the *kachnar* (*Bauhinia variegata*) with the mantle of flowers covering the crown shaded in pink and white but no colour, however rich or brilliant stands out as arrestingly against the dry brown gloom of the forest in summer, as white.

In the less moist reaches of the Western Ghats and in hill forests elsewhere in the southern half of the peninsula, there is a white-flowered tree that has no common name in any language known all over India, but which is *Radermachera xylocarpa* botanically. It is common enough in these forests, but easily missed except in spring, unless one looks for the yard-long, drumstick-like sharply tubercled fruits hanging from its boughs. But when it flowers, one cannot pass it by without noticing it—the profuse clusters of brilliantly white flowers hold the eye even from far away, and when fresh they have a fine fragrance. However, they fade in a day or two and shrivel and are slightly discoloured, and when they have lost their freshness, langur guzzle them with avid relish—apparently, some irritant or poisonous principle in the newly-opened flowers becomes innocuous when they fade.

I shall mention only one other white-flowered tree. In clearings and on the firm surrounds of patches of swampy hollows, the *kare* (*Randia dumetorum*, Lamk.) grows, a small spiny tree, often only a large spiny bush, unremarkable except for its round, dark green fruits the size of guavas but with a smooth, hard rind, and the large white flowers an-inch-and-a-half across, decorating its spikiness here and there, with the angled corolla lobes most attractively twisted like pure white stars with contorted points. The flowers fade gradually to a delicate, pale, pure yellow ochre, when they are even more attractive. When fully ripe the fruits turn yellowish, but before then hold a poisonous principle that is potent to fish. Tribals crush a few fruits and throw them into a pool, and presently the fish come floating up to the surface, stupefied and resistless. Even when the fruits are ripe, men can eat the pulp within only after slicing and washing the fruits and then boiling them, but sambar and chital eat even the still-green fruits with patent zest, standing up on their hind legs to get at those high up the tree, and take no harm from the meal.

Excerpted from Nights and Days, My Book of India's Wildlife, *(Delhi: Vikas Publishing House, 1985).*

A. J. T. JOHNSINGH

Dhole: Dog of the Indian Jungle

It was not just in the pages of Kipling's Jungle Books *that the dhole or the wild dog was labeled as a voracious killer. Foresters and sport hunters had long seen the packs as competitors for deer. Until the 1970s, there were bounties for dholes even in the precincts of many wildlife sanctuaries. Only later did the species win a reprieve and get protection.*

Many tribal communities never harmed wild dogs; and F. W. Champion, the great photographer-naturalist raised his voice in their favour in the 1920s. But it was A. J. T. Johnsingh's research half a century later that first pinpointed the role of the wild dog in the cycles of life and death in India's forests. He worked in Bandipur, having first been a lecturer in zoology. As a pioneering wildlife biologist, Johnsingh practically re-wrote the ecology of this remarkable predator.

Ka ka khroo...ka ka khroo...A troop of common langurs, on their early morning foraging trip, mistook me, seated eight metres up in a tree, for a leopard and raised an alarm. A dhole bitch shot out from a rock shelter on a near-by hillock. I froze. Although it stood hardly 15 metres away, the dhole failed to notice me as there was no wind to carry my scent. Having verified that no potential danger lurked around the den site, and that the members of the pack had not returned from their hunt, she went back to the den and her new litter of eight pups. I relaxed. My fear stemmed not from any possibility of aggressiveness on the part of the dholes, but from the fact that they, being extremely shy, would move their pups to another den at the first sign of any disturbance. At around 11.00

a.m. the resting langurs again raised an alarm. This time it was a male dhole returning to the den to regurgitate meat for the nursing female and, as I watched, she ran after him through the rocks and dense thickets whining and wagging her tail.

We were a kilometre and a half from Bandipur, the major tourist centre in the Bandipur Tiger Reserve in South India which lies adjacent to the Mudumalai and Wynad Sanctuaries of Tamil Nadu and Kerala respectively. Gently undulating hills covered with dry deciduous forests and teeming with wildlife, are a constant source of delight to both wildlife enthusiasts and tourists. This area has a long history of conservation behind it dating back to the early half of this century, when the Raja of Mysore, a keen sportsman, photographer and naturalist, passed the Game and Forest Preservation Regulation and paved the way for its protection. Today, Bandipur encompasses most of Venugopal Wildlife Park, and covers a rough area of 690 square km. During my two-year study here as a biologist, my major concern was to assess the role of the dhole as a predator and estimate the effect of dhole predation on the deer population. Many Indian forest officials and naturalists continue to blame the dhole for the decreasing deer population. They conveniently forget that poaching is still prevalent in many areas, habitat destruction, in the form of firewood collection, is rampant and that cattle grazing in many of our jungles has increased dramatically. I also wanted to put to rest some of the many myths that surround dhole biology.

Dholes, or Asiatic wild dogs as they are known, are rust-sand coloured, weigh around 18 kg. and stand approximately 50 cm. at the shoulder. Their length—including a long, black, bushy tail, is about 135 cm. Females are somewhat slighter of build but cannot easily be differentiated from males at a distance. The distribution of dholes extends from Saghalien Amurland and the Atlai mountains (about latitude 50° north) over the whole of continental Asia (east of longitude 70° east). They occur on the islands of Sumatra and Java but not in Japan, Sri Lanka or Borneo. Of the nine subspecies recognized by Ellerman and Morrison Scott three subspecies definitely occur in India. They are *Cuon alpinus laniger* in Kashmir and Lhasa, *Cuon alpinus primaevus* in Kumaon, Nepal, Sikkim and Bhutan and *Cuon alpinus dukhunensis* south of the Ganges. The dholes found in the Namdapha area in Arunachal Pradesh could well be the *Cuon alpinus adjustus* from North Burma.

Despite numerous first-hand accounts, when compared to other pack hunting canids such as the wolf and the African wild dog, the dhole remains little studied and much misunderstood. Even now it carries a stigma with it and until 12 years ago a bounty on its head placed its worth at twenty rupees.

The field work I was doing, with support from the World Wildlife Fund and The Fauna and Flora Preservation Society, England, was the first long-term study of the dhole. However, the facilities and equipment I had, when compared to those normally available to wildlife biologists from the West, were highly inadequate.

I had neither a vehicle nor radio-telemetry equipment at my disposal. Only two tribals assisted me in locating the dholes and searching for the kills of other predators—the leopard and the tiger. Another major limitation was that elephants prevented me from working at night, at dawn and at dusk. So, early in the morning and evening, the two tribals and I, used to hike in different directions in an attempt to locate our subjects, with the help of the alarm calls of prey such as chital, sambar, langur and peafowl. We systematically combed the scrub on foot and often located the kills by the raucous calls of the ever-present jungle crows. Over a period of time, we assessed the abundance of such cover-seeking animals as sambar, barking deer and wild pig and were thus able to understand more about the predator-prey balance in the jungle. Life in the jungle, inevitably had its moments of danger—especially when in the excitement of following dholes, caution sometimes got thrown to the winds. Once, in a dense lantana scrub, I almost walked into a sleeping cow elephant which I mistook for dead! To verify the cow's condition I gently threw some hard earth at her only to have her come charging out at me with her calf in tow. Another cow elephant once opted to chase the forest department van as I descended from it and in the mêlée the driver drove off leaving me to deal with the cow! Only my familiarity with the area helped me escape as I jumped into a near-by stream-bed. On yet another occasion a tigress with two cubs remonstrated with a terrifying roar as I met them. Less dramatic, but infinitely more irritating, was the problem of ticks in the jungle. After the first few months my body was so completely covered with black itching dots that I looked as if I had had a severe attack of small-pox. All through my stay at Bandipur, much to my dismay, I was unable to develop any kind of antidote to tick-bites! When I started my study in August 1976, it took me six full days to just sight my study pack. During those six days I had walked nearly 90 km. through Bandipur, criss-crossing my study area of 32 square km. and finding nothing more than the tracks of five dholes which had unsuccessfully chased a sambar across a shallow pool. With so little progress, desperation began to set in. My colleagues and the local officials suggested that I had perhaps chosen the wrong animal for my Ph.D! On the morning of the seventh day however, the tension was relieved when one of my field assistants brought in the lower jaw of a chital stag which had been killed by dholes. That drizzly evening while I was routinely observing sambar from a tree, I suddenly spied my pack in action, 15 dholes in all, killing a chital doe which they had cornered after a chase. The long and slow process of gathering data had begun.

To a casual observer almost all dholes look alike. Nevertheless, there are variations in the rusty, sand-coloured fur and black bushy tail which makes the identification of a few individuals possible. 'Bent Ear' was one such individual I grew to recognize. Old, with a loose hanging scrotum, a bent right pinna (which gave him his name) and a bend in his tail, he appeared to be the leader of the pack. In typical dog-fashion he occasionally showed his dominance by raising one hind leg and urinating onto tree trunks in the presence of the other dholes. However, he never bullied them. On the contrary, the pack members often greeted him, sometimes even to the extent of crawling under his belly, forcing him to jump aside. 'Bent Ear' was extremely fond of pups and when the pack had made only a small kill the pups would run to him pestering him to regurgitate some extra meat. Like the African wild dog, 'Bent Ear' would oblige them even six or seven hours after he had eaten. I soon developed a strange affection for this aged hunter who flitted freely through the forest. He led a daring life. Alone and unafraid, he slipped easily through the thickets, which I entered with hesitation and, occasionally, fear. When he suddenly disappeared in April 1978, I felt a pang of sadness which stayed with me for a long time. I had lost a friend.

From the study certain interesting results emerged. I was surprised in the first year when, in the month of November, just prior to the birth of eight pups the pack of 15 was suddenly reduced to seven or eight animals. (Though there were three females only one gave birth to pups.) Later I realized that emigration of a part of the pack before the arrival of the pups, and also breeding by only one female, might be the major means of regulating pack size. Also, at no time were two packs seen operating in the same area; which suggested that dholes may be territorial. The focal area of my study pack was nearly twenty square km., an area I grew to know better each time I traversed it on foot.

The pups remained in the den until they were 70–80 days old and during this time did not visit the near-by water-holes. Pack life manifested itself not only in group hunting but also by the participation of all the pack members in feeding the pups. It was a thrill to watch Nature's miraculous learning process at work as the seven-to-eight-month-old pups first began to take an active part in hunting chital and sambar. The dholes' hunting strategies displayed perfect team-work. There seemed to be two basic manoeuvres to flush and kill prey—one by moving through the scrub in an extended line formation and the other by having some of the pack remain on the periphery of the scrub to intercept the fleeing prey disturbed by other members of the pack.

The pack cared for the pups even after they had left the den and until they were four-to-five-months-old, the adults treated them with special concern and solicitude. They would hunt either very early in the morning or late in the evening to avoid both the presence of man and the heat of the day. The pups were left in hiding during these hunts and the absence of a couple of adults in the hunting pack even suggested that some animals may have stayed behind to guard them. Eventually, even when the pups started following the pack on hunts, young stragglers were escorted by one or two adults. Pups were permitted to monopolize small kills like chital and, when food was insufficient, the adults who had eaten earlier even regurgitated meat for them. At larger kills like sambar which are over twice as large as chital, pups and adults often ate together. When they were seven months old however, and the food was inadequate, adults began to be reluctant to regurgitate food despite the fact that the pups were hungry. Often however, the young ones chased them and appealingly nibbled the corners of their mouths until the elders obliged.

During my many months in Bandipur I made many observations which clearly showed that dholes seldom hunt by relay. During the rush stage of the hunt, dholes are faster than their prey and with their speed and team-work most chases do not last long. Of the 48 chases I witnessed, 44 ended within 500 metres and only twice did the chase go beyond 500 metres. This data disproves the popular theory that dholes chase their prey over great distances in relays thus tiring the quarry but not the pack.

Dholes are not always the super efficient killers they are made out to be. One dry summer evening, while making my way back to Bandipur, a sambar doe trotted across my path followed by a dhole, trailing 70 to 80 metres behind. The dhole, however, appeared to have lost the direction of its prey's movements. I then heard other members of the pack, which had obviously lost sight of both prey and pack member, trying to renew contact with their leader, by their high-pitched whistling calls. The next day, with the help of some tribals, I combed the area thoroughly but found no kill. Neither did I see any jungle crows, which are good indicators of a kill. All this told me that the hunt had been a failure.

One March evening my attention was abruptly drawn to a silent struggle between a chital stag—with well-developed, hard antlers—and a group of seven dholes. Two or three dholes were biting and hanging on to the rump of the stag, thereby rendering it completely immobile, while the others worried the flanks. The stag was trying to fight off the dholes by swinging its great antlers which never once, however, came in contact with the dogs. Throughout the struggle the dholes remained silent although the deer vocalized its agony three times. Suddenly one dhole caught the snout of the stag and pulled it forward while those at the rump continued to bite and pull it backwards. Eventually, the helpless stag, was dragged down and the dholes started eating it even before it had died! Although predation is as much a biological process as grazing is, such incidents are often gory and repugnant. However, in defence of the dhole, I recount the opinion of Michael Fox, with whom I first studied this animal. He felt that since dholes lack the killing bite of the large cats, they can best kill prey, larger than themselves, by biting off chunks of meat. An animal thus weakened obviously became easier to overcome as massive blood loss and shock progressively lowered its resistance. Close examination of fresh kills clearly showed that dholes are particular about holding on to the nose of stags sporting hard antlers probably to prevent themselves from being struck by these potential weapons.

An amazing fact about the dhole is its ability to consume large quantities of meat. A pack of 15 could easily eat a yearling sambar male of about 90–100 kg., each animal consuming about five kg. After such a meal the dholes do not hunt for quite some time (even a two kg. morning meal would keep the animals away from another hunt till the next day). This capacity to gorge themselves is believed to enable them to live without food for a few days although this is yet to be verified in the field. One of the benefits of pack life is the efficiency with which kills are eaten. Even the bones and skin of a young deer are swallowed and when larger kills are made, the dholes may even come back to scavenge on the dry stiff skin. Such scavenging makes it possible for the dhole to appropriate kills of leopards and tigers and on many occasions leopards have actually lost their kills to dholes. This stealing of kills from other animals, however, may be dangerous; and I once saw a dhole pup, nearly six months old, killed and partly eaten by a leopard in Bandipur— the potential robber had become the prey.

In Bandipur there was no evidence, however, of either tigers or leopards regularly competing with dholes over a kill. The ability of each to kill prey of different ages, sex and size enables dholes and the larger predators to coexist. Over 42 per cent of the 19 tiger kills I counted, for instance, were above 100 kg., whereas out of 302 dhole kills only one per cent were of that weight. The obvious deduction is that the tiger prefers larger food items. Dholes also seem to show a preference for male sambar. Out of 10 dhole kills, seven were males. Tigers on the other hand seem to prefer attacking female sambar (this, however, was based on a small sample and before any real conclusions are drawn much more research is necessary). Young chital, being alert and agile, often escaped from dholes. They, however, seemed to fall easy prey to leopards which hunt by stealth and surprise. Another factor that seems to reduce hunting conflicts between the dogs and the great cats, is the fact that dholes are diurnal and prefer relatively open areas, while tigers and leopards are nocturnal and use dense cover from which to launch their attacks.

The dhole's whistle call (which can be imitated by blowing into a medium-bore empty rifle cartridge) would fascinate anyone who heard it in the jungle. How the dhole produces this sound is a complete mystery. Dholes separated from the rest of their pack whistle to reassemble after an unsuccessful hunt and even lone dholes may whistle occasionally to discover the position of other pack members. I have never, however, observed dholes whistling to maintain the cohesiveness of their pack while a hunt was in progress. Sounds play an important role in the lives of dholes and I found that they could be alerted, not only by imitating their whistle, but also by blowing air out through a leaf thus producing a shrill note similar to the distress call of a fawn.

Of the many unusual dhole behaviour patterns I observed, one was the use of communal latrines. One particularly eventful evening (I had the good fortune to spot both a leopard and a magnificent tusker that day) as I sat atop a tree close to a well-frequented jungle trail, I spotted two dholes which came out of the jungle followed by 14 more and they all lay at the crossing nudging one another and whining. *Nine* of them defecated at the crossing before they left the place in single file led by 'Bent Ear'. This feature of a communal latrine is peculiar to dholes and anyone walking in a jungle, frequented by dholes, will often come across their communal latrines on roads and animal trail crossings. This habit is not seen in the African wild dog and rarely in wolves; and may well be a display, warning neighbouring packs of the presence of the resident pack. Further, the scats probably aid pack members in tracking their fellow members as also in determining whether an area has been hunted in recently.

During the months of December 1976 and January 1977 I regularly watched 'my' pack caring for the pups and their mother. As February progressed the pups became stronger and their speed and agility increased. I thoroughly enjoyed stalking the playful pups and would freeze for minutes when I felt that the adults had become aware of me. On such occasions I would silently climb a tree to allow the wind to disperse my scent.

Until the evening of February 14, 1977, the dry weather held out and the sound of the pups running and playing over the dry leaves could be heard even 200 metres away. A good evening shower three days later made the leaves soft and damp and the next day I was able to crawl as close as 30 metres to the den to observe the pups, both in the morning and evening, without alerting the sharp-eared pack.

That evening, however, half an hour after my first 'visit' to the den, instead of the anticipated squeaks and whines of the pups and the soft growls of the adults, I was confronted with an ominous silence. I knew that the time had come for the pups to leave the den but such a sudden departure took me by surprise. In spite of the many common langurs, chital and grey jungle fowl feeding around the den site, I felt quite alone, almost abandoned in fact. Some alarm calls in the distance, however, suggested that the pack had not gone too far (their home range was around 40 square km.) and I was subsequently able to observe them several times before my departure.

Now, when I think back, I realize that my study, when compared to the magnitude of work done by others on pack-hunting canids, has merely scratched the surface of the vast potential information on dhole biology. Many questions still remain unanswered. Why do dhole populations periodically decline even when there is an adequate supply of prey as in the case of Kanha National Park? What happened to those members of the pack that had emigrated? What was the social status of the emigrant? Does the same dominant female breed every year? What explanation can there be for sambar chasing dholes (I actually saw this happen on more than four occasions) when dholes are capable of killing adult sambar?

The creation of Tiger Reserves has done much to protect the dhole as well, and we can be sure therefore, that like most wild animals, dholes too will do well if left undisturbed. However, a long-term study of two or three neighbouring packs, with each individual tagged and some radio-collared, is necessary to learn more about the social and physical characteristics of these, one of the world's most efficient predators. When I conducted my study, neither was I conversant with modern techniques like radio telemetry nor did Park 'rules' permit such vitally necessary know-how. Still I hope that the day for such research, which alone can answer the questions raised above, is not far off in India.

Originally published in Sanctuary Asia Magazine, *1984.*

LAVKUMAR KHACHER

'Lion Shows' in the Gir Forest: At Home with Humans

Gir Forest, the last home of the Asian lion, is also the only place in the world where it is possible to see wild lions on foot. This often provokes remarks about them 'not being truly wild animals'.

Lavkumar Khacher's defence of the Gir lion and the trackers of Saurashtra reflects his decades-long acquaintance with the region's wildlife. Khacher was from the former royal family of Jasdan, a small princely state in Saurashtra, Gujarat. He was a co-author of one of the early works on the birds of Saurashtra and an eminent ornithologist. But he is still more widely known as a nature educationist, and in this account he draws on experiences with nature camps in the Gir Forest.

During the several nature-orientation camps organized at Sasan Gir over the past 15 months, we have had ample opportunities of gauging the relationship developed between the lions and man. While, perhaps, a group of lions resting in the shade may not appear glamorous as a resplendent tiger may, and, standing on the ground, viewing the lazy creatures at close quarters might justify the criticism that lions in the Gir are not exciting, say, as in Africa. We pick up any refrain from a foreign visitor and run down what the Gir has to offer—the Gir Lions are tame...they are like dogs...the Lion shows are disappointing...and so on and so forth! Let us take a harder look.

At Sasan, the Forest Department shows many films to keep the visitors happily occupied. The film which draws the maximum 'Oohs' and 'Ahs' is the one on Elsa the lioness. Books on this lioness have become best sellers. All of us admire what Joy Adamson achieved with Elsa. Without in any way distracting an iota from the excellent efforts resulting in the close relationship evolved between Elsa and her human well-wishers, I would like to say that the shikaris* of the Gir National Park have achieved a similar success with a large number of lions and lionesses. The confidence that they have succeeded in generating among the lions of the Gir is a magnificent tribute to their fine work. Let us recognize a fine effort when we see one.

During our recent camp, the shikaris arranged for us to see a young lion, 'Bhagat', and his lady 'Mira'. The superb pair sat quite unconcerned as the school boys trooped past from their bus to settle down in a semi-circle before the regal couple not further than six metres. For a naturalist like myself, with my biological training, the acceptance of man by an animal, evolved over the years as a carnivore, is something to marvel at. There was a lazy grace as the two fine creatures relaxed; however, the lassitude was superficial for the tawny eyes recorded every movement. I gained an impression that we were accepted as long as the Forest Guards were with us.

Later we were taken to see two full grown lions (17 years' old) who were brothers—Akbar and Sultan—and roamed the forest together. They were resting at a distance near the shade. As I walked over to where the three Forest Guards were standing, Sultan got up and with superb grace walked towards us. His amber eyes, less than three metres away, looked into my eyes. He uttered a low 'Woof' recognizing me as a stranger. The guards softly assured me that it was all right. When the others joined us, Sultan settled down to be admired. Akbar, however, kept his distance and when a couple of us attempted to approach, he sat up, tail twitching and uttered a loud growl. Tabby cats and dogs indeed!

Perhaps the Forest Department's decision to set up Safari Park-type arrangements for average tourists is to be welcomed. The visitors can feel excited, viewing the lions from the vehicle as they do in East Africa, and these fine men can be freed from the daily task of locating the animals in thorny forests for an unappreciative audience and instead take on the work of making the Gir more

---

* The term shikari used for some of the men working with the lions stems from the days of the Junagadh Nawabs when they traced lions for the Nawab and his guests for shooting.

secure for all wild animals. Gujarat, India and all conservationists the world over must salute the Gir shikari who has done a fine job. Shaabash! Keep it up!

Originally published in the WWF *Newsletter,* Second Quarter, 1979.

KAILASH SANKHALA

Waiting for the Tiger

Sankhala's book Tiger! *was written in 1978 when he was Chief Wildlife Warden of Rajasthan. Earlier, he had served as Director of Delhi zoo (1965–9) and was a Jawaharlal Nehru Fellow for two years working on the status of the Indian tiger. As a young forester, he had managed many wildlife reserves in Rajasthan, in his home state, including Sariska.*

The machan *and watch-tower over the water-hole were, in the past, a place where hunters could sit waiting for their quarry. At no time were the shikaris as well-placed as in the bone-dry weeks of summer, when most streams run out of water and only a few ponds remain where animals can quench their thirst. The Sariska forests in the Aravallis were one of Kailash Sankhala's favourite locations for shooting—not with a gun, but a camera and telephoto lens. By patiently waiting for a long time, he got to see not just the tiger, the master predator of the forest, but an array of birds and animals. The valleys in the Sariska tiger reserve provide the ideal setting for this account: they have no major lakes or water-bodies, forcing all creatures to congregate in one place to slake their thirst.*

The tiger is an elusive beast who does not follow rules. Frankly, in studying his behaviour I used no specific method but welcomed all sources of information. I found evidence in old shikar notes kept by the maharajas, case histories of poaching offences, taxidermists' records, zoo records, and personal interviews with a cross-section of people living close to tigers. Sometimes I used baits by tying up a buffalo calf or a wild piglet, but only to study specific behaviour patterns such as feeding habits. To keep a particular courting pair or a mother and cubs in the area, or to study the interaction of predator and prey, I provided baits near waterholes in Sariska and in the Kachida valley in Rajasthan. Hides near waterholes in Sariska during the summer proved particularly rewarding.

While sitting at waterholes to watch the relationship between the tiger and his prey, especially when he was not hunting, I learnt a lot about water. Nature allows no one to hoard this vital commodity to the disadvantage of others, every animal gets an equal opportunity to drink and no one goes thirsty. Confrontation is met by tolerance, illustrating the marvellous discipline of nature. A hot summer day followed by a night of full moon at a waterhole is the most rewarding experience possible for a naturalist, who is able to see nature's encyclopedia open page by page in front of his eyes.

Animals possess the power of discovering invisible waterholes. The technique is simple. Every patch of water attracts insects, especially mosquitoes and waterflies. Their presence is conspicuous because their flight is noticed by insectivorous birds, and when these dive their calls attract the attention of small mammals which in turn lead the larger mammals to discover the waterhole. In the deciduous forests which form nearly 80 per cent of tigerland water becomes a problem—especially from April to June. The streams dry up and all that remains are a few scattered pools. The situation becomes acute in the dry deciduous forests of western Madhya Pradesh, Rajasthan and southern Bihar, and it deteriorates still further with the failure of the monsoon, which happens almost every third year. In the long summer days the water requirement of animals, especially the larger ones like elephants, gaur (*Bos gaurus*) and sambar deer (*Cervus unicolor*), as well as big birds like peacocks, is greater. They have to travel long distances to waterholes, which become the nerve centres of activity in the jungle.

I have spent countless days and nights at such waterholes, waiting and watching. A typical example will illustrate the routine—and the rewards.

Travelling by bus to my field station in Sariska I shout 'Kalighati' and the driver stops with a jerk; he hardly expected any passenger, least of all me, to alight as this lonely spot in the middle of the forest late in the evening. The bus goes on and I am left all by myself. 'Kalighati' means a black valley, and a long time ago the name was appropriate as the forest was thick and impenetrable and its floor was always dark. The fact that there are still tigers in the valley shows that its environmental quality has not deteriorated all that much. The landscape is one of well-clothed rolling hills, sheer quartzite walls of the Aravali range, hog-back crests and narrow valleys. I have returned to this fascinating country for the last twenty-three years, at different seasons and at different times of the day, even arranging to be there on the same day year after year to confirm my observations. In August the whole valley is lusciously green then as winter approaches the foliage turns copper-brown and the grasses become yellow. In spring the leaves dry on the trees and with a gentle breeze they start falling. By March the forest is leafless and bone dry, its floor covered with a cushion of fallen leaves inches thick.

On this particular occasion I looked around for help but there was none. On the lonely hut hung a padlock. Evidently the forest guard was out on his rounds, and I sat on my box to wait. A few peacocks arrived, and some tree-pies and red-vented bulbuls began to drink at the bird bath. Within minutes there were more than fifty peacocks around but they took no notice of me. The last rays of the sun were striking the hilltops and I was losing all hope of the forest guard's return: he might have gone on leave, or to collect his pay and rations. Then at last he appeared from behind a bush, a short man dressed in bleached khaki with an axe over his shoulder.

Bhanwar Singh, as later he introduced himself, has been there for 15 years, mostly entirely alone. His life is routine. In the morning he goes out to patrol his beat and look for poachers, including wood poachers, and drives the cattle away. In the afternoon he returns, cleans the watch-tower and prepares it for visitors. He pumps water from the well for the wild animals, provides carrots for chital, corn for pigs, salt for sambar; and he ties a bait for tigers. This duty he performs unwillingly as he dislikes the cruel killing of a tethered buffalo calf. Unfortunately the tourists expect it and it is part of his official work.

On the way to the hide he had made for me he told me all about what had happened since my last visit, about the tigers' kills, the tourists' luck in seeing tigers, petty quarrels with his officers, his home leave, the marriage proposal he had received from a neighbouring village, and finally his marriage. Bhanwar Singh—or 'Bhanwaria', as I call him—feels free with me because he comes from Jodhpur and we speak the same dialect.

Soon we were at the waterhole and I inspected the grass hide, which was cosy but flimsy. A few thorn bushes had been placed round it to discourage the predator from approaching too closely, but I insist on branches without leaves as otherwise they attract browsers and one cannot scare them away for fear of being discovered by the tiger. The game warden never approved of my sitting close to a bait in such a flimsy hide and was always anxious to know first thing in the morning if I was still alive.

It was impossible to stand up in the hide so I dived inside and made a soft landing on the cushions. The first job was to adjust camera angles, flash-unit positions and lenses so as to be ready in total darkness without making the slightest noise. For night work the lenses have to be focused in advance and fixed with Sellotape; the only adjustment that has to be made at the time is the diaphragm and I have familiarized myself with this by long practice. Winter nights in hides can be terribly cold, and frost often persists in these forest depressions even after sunrise, so I make myself as comfortable as possible with foam-rubber cushions, sleeping bag and extra quilt. Old clothing is best as it does not make a noise when rubbed, and gloves are necessary on frosty nights as it is too cold to remove the covering from lenses with bare fingers.

In the summer I have an ice box with soft drinks and oranges, but I avoid food and anything containing sugar as it attracts ants and makes the hide uncomfortable. Hides near water always attract mosquitoes and flies so I use an insect repellent. Other equipment includes a luminous watch to record the times of arrival of animals and their duration of stay, a counter, a stopwatch and a thermometer to record the temperature. For relieving oneself I keep a few bottles.

I always go alone and do not even take books to divert the attention in case a valuable opportunity is lost. Animals like chausingha, the four-horned antelope (*Tetracerus quadricornis*), visit water only once in 24 hours and stay for less than two minutes. They come during the day, but one never knows which two minutes they will choose, so it may involve a tense and tiring wait of many hours. I never carry a gun as it gives a false sense of security and one could be provoked to use it out of nervousness rather than need. Also, arms attract the attention of dacoits and other outlaws. Once in the Chambal ravines I had to explain the use of a telephoto lens to a group of dacoits; they did not believe me until one of them had triggered off my camera three times without hearing a bang.

On the occasion of which I was speaking, 'Bhanwaria' closed the hide with a thorn bush, passed me his axe (not for defence, but for making adjustments inside the hide) and left me. There was still some light, and although the animals had been disturbed by our presence they soon regained confidence. First came the peafowl with a 'honk, honk' to inspect the hide and, finding no disturbance inside, proceeded to the waterhole; I counted 32 peahens including a few chicks. A few months earlier when I visited the place the peahens had their August brood. The birds bring their chicks to the water with great caution and the slightest disturbance causes them to stop drinking, extend their necks and raise the neck feathers in excitement. Soon a few gorgeously feathered peacocks arrived and they were even more cautious. While the male went to the waterhole one hen came close to my hide and looked straight in; I did not even flicker my eyelids and, reassured, she proceeded to drink. When the peacocks lowered their heads to reach the water the beautiful metallic tail-feathers with their moons and crescents went up in the air, then as the equally lovely blue necks rose from the water the tails went down. This see-saw continued for ten to twelve times in each case, the fan-like crests adding grace to the movement of their bodies. Then more peahens arrived and the entire shore of the waterhole was filled with birds. Sariska has probably the highest concentration of peafowl in the world and Kalighati is the centre. Every day more than 100 birds arrive for their morning and evening drink. A few smaller birds such as partridges and quails waited their turn at a short distance and the whole scene was transformed with movement.

The sudden appearance of langurs disturbed the birds but soon they were sharing the waterhole. The monkeys came in small groups, mothers with babies clinging to their breasts, yearlings and adults; but the leader, a robust male, sat at some distance watching the troop. Langurs at a waterhole present an amusing caricature of human behaviour. The leader sat facing me, looked hard and bared his teeth, then he cautiously lowered his head, clasped the ground firmly and sipped. Except for drinking langurs have no use for water, but although they never take a bath they groom each other constantly and are the cleanest of all primates. The dominant male drank for over two minutes, raised his head and looked in all directions and then had another long drink. Hearing the click of my camera he gazed in my direction but was unable to locate the source of the sound, so all he could do was to bare his teeth again in protest. Confidently he walked off and disappeared. Langurs select a certain mud-free spot for drinking and all crowd together; they are tolerant of the presence of chital, nilgai and peafowl, but not of pigs.

The light was fading and only one peahen remained, then she too returned to the trees to roost. When it was almost dark a huge blue bull or nilgai (*Boselaphus tragocamelus*) arrived and stopped about ten feet from the water; although the waterhole was free he wanted to be sure that no predator was around. A massive, muscular beast, he stood on the shore and lowered his head but he could not reach the water. The blue bull has a backward slanting body and when the water is lower than ground level it is difficult for him to reach. He dropped on his knees and started drinking, but soon raised his head, the drops trickling from his mouth. This was the closest look I had ever had at the sharp, spiky horns, tufted beard and huge eyes of the majestic blue bull. After another short drink he was off, bouncing away like Humpty Dumpty. The whole visit lasted two-and-a-half minutes.

Next a jackal trotted to the waterhole, walked nervously around, then lowered his head and tucked his tail between his legs. After lapping up some water he remained half-submerged, presumably to quench the heat of the day. His mate joined him, and a large herd of chital watched and waited for the jackals to clear off. They stayed too long for a pair of red-wattled lapwing, who launched aerial attacks until the jackals left. Then the delicate-footed chital (Axis deer, *Axis axis*) approached the shore, a doe followed by another doe with a fawn. The three drank close together, almost touching faces, although the whole shoreline was vacant; probably in this way they gained confidence. Soon they were followed by does, fawns, yearlings and stags in such numbers that there was no room at the waterhole. For 45 minutes they drank in turns undisturbed in the darkness; chital are diurnal but here as in many other places they have become nocturnal owing to human disturbance.

All this time, of course, I had been taking notes. The recording of observations in total darkness is a problem. I tried talking quietly on to a tape, but even that is too loud. I tried using a small pencil torch under a blanket, but in the blackness of a moonless night in the jungle the slightest light is visible outside the hide. Eventually I had to resort to writing in a notebook in the dark. Once my pen is on the page I do not lift it until the sheet is finished and these scribbled notes can be deciphered next day to record a fair copy on specially designed punch cards. Although my friends laugh at my doing so, I prefer to use a roll of toilet paper when writing notes. It provides continuity, and while writing I get a philosophical feeling, as if I were preparing someone's horoscope on long rolls!

After the chital had left the waterhole a sambar doe arrived and, since the chital were still in the vicinity, she did not stop to verify that the coast was clear. (Wild animals are very much guided by signs, signals and alarms from their co-sharers of the habitat. Even the slightest signal is noted, and acted upon). She was joined by her fawn, and within ten minutes there were no chital on the scene. More sambar does arrived and then, very cautiously, a stag. More stags appeared and they formed into a stag party in a separate group from the does. There were five of them, yet there was no quarrel. Occasionally one of them raised his snout towards me and sniffed the air, stamping his forefeet on the ground and nervously raising and lowering his tail. Soon the waterhole was full of sambar. At first one entered the water, then two more who sat down to wallow. The first stag urinated into the water, unconcerned that he would be drinking it soon after. The full moon came out and I could count more than 20 sambar. Then a wild boar arrived and stood there snorting; he was joined by others and one started butting the sambar, who promptly left the waterhole.

Priority at a waterhole is obviously determined by the capacity of a species or individual to inflict harm on the others. Smaller birds yield to bigger birds, which in turn yield to mammals. Does and cows yield to stags and bulls. Among males the size and effectiveness of the weapon is the ruling factor, and even stags surrender to the wild boar's tusks. But he himself gives way to the bad-tempered porcupine, whose backward thrust impales his adversary with a battery of spears. Predators, including birds such as falcons and owls, take priority over all as they are equipped with claws, pointed canines, or sharp beaks.

As I waited in my hide and the jingling of crickets filled the air I suddenly heard a metallic 'dhank', the alarm call of a sambar. At that time of the evening the danger is 99 per cent certain to be a leopard or a tiger—most probably a tiger, I thought, as I knew that one lived on that hill. The cramped four hours I had spent in the hide were forgotten in my excitement. I rearranged and checked my photographic equipment, opened up the peephole, and reassured myself of the position of the flimsy gate. I had already fixed tapes on the lenses after focusing on the shoreline. A few sambar and chital were drinking normally and even when the tiger's roar from the near-by hill could be clearly heard there was no panic. Animals calculate the distance from the predator by the pitch of the sound, and react accordingly.

The moon rose higher and faintly I saw the forms of chital and a family group of wild boars. For more than an hour there was no further alarm call, but this did not damp my hopes as I knew the tiger was there. If he had left the valley the animals would have given fading alarm calls and their silence indicated that he was waiting somewhere in the vicinity. When a predator is resting, even in full view, his prey do not make a sound as a sitting predator is no danger to them.

My hopes further revived when a chital gave a low alarm call; since chital live on the plains the call confirmed that the predator had moved down from the hill slope. A few more chital took up the call, clearly demarcating their enemy's movements. Eventually all the animals stopped drinking and turned their heads towards the direction of the alarm. Then there was complete silence as if nothing had happened, and a whole hour passed. But the tiger could appear at any moment, and I slowly opened my water bottle and sipped to clear my throat, as a single cough could ruin everything.

At that moment the silence and darkness were shattered by a distant flashing of lights and with it my hopes disappeared. A mini-bus rolled in with a load of talkative tourists. Jai Singh, the game warden, had promised them a glimpse of a tiger and, failing to find one, he flashed his spotlight on my hide. He started talking about my research and told his audience about how I would spend a cold night in the company of tigers without any weapons. Some wondered, some pitied, while others wished me luck. Mercifully the warden did not know about the alarm calls so they left me to it, and I cursed them for ruining my chances.

I am not against people occupying the watch-tower while I am in my hide, but unfortunately many of the tourists are exhausted after a day of climbing steps to temples, or are suffering from jetlag, and within minutes of their arrival they start snoring. Generally they are elderly and cannot control their cough, and it is always difficult for them to refrain from talking, especially after an exciting day seeing 'Kama Sutra' carvings or buying jewels in Jaipur! A whisper is enough to make a tiger go elsewhere, and the glow of a cigarette bright enough to scare him away. We welcome disciplined tourists and those who are really interested in the wildlife, but many merely want to add the tiger to their list with the temples and the Taj. An influx of non-serious tourists is not what our reserves need.

After the noise of the mini-bus faded away, complete silence prevailed again. Sambar came back to the waterhole and the normal activity of the jungle was resumed. Suddenly—within ten minutes of the mini-bus leaving—peacocks called and the langurs with their 'Kho ka kookho' confirmed the movement of the tiger. In fact, the tiger had been waiting for the bus's visit, so he could finally come and drink in peace. Once I had realized this I was able to use this information to ensure that tigers came to the hole at an earlier hour. A blue bull which was at the waterhole stopped drinking and fixed his head in the direction of the calls, then he became very nervous, gave a muffled bellow and joined in the general stampede. The waterhole was deserted.

A muffled sound of rolling rocks and the flapping of a heavy bird came from behind the hide. It was a horned owl, and the resident lapwing cried 'Did you do it, did you do it?' and took to his wings. A moment later I saw a huge figure, of an animal larger than I had ever seen. The dim moonlight did not allow me to make out its contours precisely, but from my low angle it appeared bigger than a buffalo. It proceeded to the waterhole and, sitting on its haunches, lowered its forelegs and head into the water. The lapping sound continued for over ten minutes, then the animal rose and walked off. It was the tiger, and in the faint light and atmosphere of tension and excitement he had appeared enormous.

While I was watching tigers at the Sulkhan river pool in Kanha in April 1971 one arrived at 10 a.m. when the sun was beginning to get warm. He crouched, started lapping, then stood up, turned and lowered his hind legs and sat down half submerged in the shaded pool. After about an hour he sat down under a tree, and he repeated his visits to the water six times that day. This alternate drenching and drying keeps the tiger cool during the hottest hours.

I also saw a film with Maharaja Bhim Singh of Kotah which showed that tigers frequently visit water to soak themselves for an hour or so and then come out; the hot winds provide a cooling effect when they blow on the tiger's wet body. As soon as the water evaporates and the body gets dry, the tiger goes into the water for another long bath. Alternately wetting and drying himself, the tiger passes the hot day.

On another occasion in May 1971 I had spent the day in the same hide at Sariska. Evening fell and I was watching a bait when a tiger arrived. He lowered his body and rushed at the victim, there was a choked bellow and the tiger stood motionless with the head of the calf in his mouth. I could hear his heavy breathing, and after 20 seconds he opened his jaws and the lifeless body fell down with a thud. For a minute the tiger stood still, then walked away completely unconcerned for a drink. After ten minutes I heard repeated calls of a lapwing. The tiger came back to the kill, gave a few tugs and dragged the carcass a short distance. Next I heard the sound of tearing skin and the crushing of bones.

These sounds were clearly heard by some sambar hinds and a stag, who stood on the shore barely 45 feet from the tiger. They were nervous, but this did not prevent the stag from drinking for two minutes, pausing for a few seconds and drinking again, after which he trotted off. Similarly some chital drank and went away, and finally a porcupine arrived and was quite unconcerned. The tiger, busy munching, paid no attention to the juicy prey within his reach. Recently, in May 1977, at Sariska, I saw a sambar doe and two fawns sitting in an ash-patch absolutely unconcerned while a tigress and her grown-up cub fed in full view hardly a hundred yards or so away. Even when my jeep disturbed the tigers and they moved away this did not bother the sambar. Animals know that the tiger, unlike man, is satisfied with what he has killed for the day and is not concerned with tomorrow. He takes only what he needs and does not kill for the sake of killing. There is a perfect understanding between predator and prey. For the first time I felt ashamed of being a man, who is not trusted even by the jackals, much less the deer and antelopes.

After the tiger had eaten for an hour he had had enough. Leaving half his kill he went away, to return the next day. He could not stay to guard it owing to human disturbance by day in that valley. Within a quarter of an hour a hyena arrived and hurriedly tore at the open hindquarters, broke off the leg and carried it off. Then came a jungle cat who circled the carcass and climbed up on to it. She was nervous, but at last started nibbling. Meanwhile animals continued to come to the waterhole in ones and twos, unconcerned at the threat of death so close by. Another jungle cat tried to approach and there were growls at the kill. A resident ratel which lived in a near-by bush then punctured the rumen which released an awful smell, and I had to open the thorn cover of the hide for ventilation.

The moon shifted behind the western hills and shadow filled the valley. In the early hours just before dawn one small creature arrived, but I knew of its presence only from the sounds of something being torn. When the eastern sky began to lighten it was possible to confirm my suspicion that it was a jackal. He was busy pulling at the intestines, and was far more interested in offal than in solid meat. Every time he managed to pull a piece off he trotted away, returning after five or ten minutes, and soon after his mate also came out to feed.

Sunlight illuminated the kill and I saw that the buffalo was half-eaten. A big bird landed with a thud, then a few more landed and walked confidently up to the carcass and drove off the jackals. Any further attempts on the animals' part were repelled by a show of strong claws, and it was only after persistent begging by the jackals that after a while they were given a little room to continue feeding. Normally vultures arrive late as they have to soar high to discover a kill. If they are roosting within viewing distance they generally wait for the light, but sometimes they arrive for a moonlit dinner. Since vultures are so slow to get off the ground they avoid confrontations with a tiger on his kill, preferring to wait till the day is well advanced and the tiger has left.

More birds landed and I counted 42, but not all of them were visible at any one time as some were right inside the carcass. Soon there was no room at all for the jackals. The big birds shrieked as they gulped the meat, while the jackals looked on helplessly. The common vulture is not fitted with a cutting mechanism, so the whole process consists of tearing, stretching and pulling in reverse gear. After about half an hour the birds began to lose interest and sat basking in the morning sun. By 9 a.m. they had all left, and all that remained of the tiger's kill was the skeleton, head and hooves. All this time the tree-pies were anxiously awaiting their turn, and now that the vultures had moved off they started picking the fragments of meat still sticking to the bone, all fighting for the best place. The peafowl took no notice; all they were interested in was their morning drink at the pool, and I took the opportunity to photograph them with back-lighting to add depth to the scene.

As the day became warm activity slowed down except for visits by red-vented bulbuls, doves, rock pigeons and occasional orioles, green pigeons and parakeets. Sometimes a swallow would dive down swiftly to drink, or a kingfisher to fish. When the heat was dazzling a chausingha came along with his doe and fawn, but they were in view for less than three minutes. By 1 p.m. the heat in the closed hide became unbearable and I knew that nothing would happen until the stream of birds started arriving in the evening, so I called it a day. The first thing I did was to go to the nearest well and pour over myself buckets and buckets of water. I too needed a waterhole.

On some occasions in Ranthambhor and Sariska I was able to follow tigers in a jeep at night, and in Kanha on elephant back or on foot during the day. The tigers were not disturbed either by the jeep or the elephant and amply regarded my curiosity. I found elephant rides an uncomfortable and tiring exercise because, unlike horses, an elephant keeps three feet on the ground and lifts only one at a time. This results in the shifting of the centre of gravity with every step with consequent rocking movements. The ride is still more uncomfortable when the elephant crosses a watercourse: one feels as though one is in a giant whirligig every time it lifts its leg. Any attempt to resist the movement tires the rider in no time, but by leaving the body relaxed to harmonize with the elephant's movements the strain can be reduced considerably. When climbing or descending a slope the rider is thrown backwards and forwards respectively, and if he does not hold the rails of the howdah firmly he is likely to fall off. Although it is the elephant that does the walking, shoes are still needed to protect one's feet from the branches.

Even when standing the elephant is seldom steady, but shifts its weight from one side to the other, lifts its trunk to grip the nearest branch or clump of grass, then thrashes it on the ground or on one of its front legs before putting it into its mouth. Often when I thought the elephant was steady and was about to click my camera shutter it started inhaling or exhaling, resulting in camera shake. Successful photographs from elephant-top were a combination of instrument efficiency and a quick draw, but mostly good luck. After many failures I learned that if the elephant is made to sit one can take a shake-free picture.

However, in spite of these handicaps the ease with which the elephant wades through the water-hyacinth-infested swamps of Kaziranga, or the tall grasses of the Manas or Corbett Parks, crosses the ditches and ravines of Kanha and approaches grazing herds and sleeping tigers silently, all make it an ideal mobile *machan* for study and photography. In the majority of tigerlands there is no substitute for an elephant. To have a sitting elephant, incidentally, means there is a far more level position from which to photograph, and a greater opportunity to compose a photo with a feel of the natural background to it, but at the same time it is cruel to the elephant, who finds any sitting position particularly awkward.

In open forests and scrublands the jeep is a most versatile vehicle and is a great relief from tiring elephant rides. Wild animals get used to inanimate transport quite quickly and after a cursory investigation they ignore it and resume grazing. When it is necessary to drive across country through thick foliage or bushes one is dependent on the skill of the driver and I found Fateh Singh, assistant director at Ranthambhor, excellent at the steering wheel.

On one occasion he accompanied me when I was camping at the ruins of Jogimahal. At that time I was convalescing from heart trouble and was strictly forbidden to exert myself or get excited, but with a camera in the field this was impossible. I was following a herd of chital and a troop of langurs, and the light was giving excellent colour contrasts. The master stag left the herd to challenge an intruder and soon they were entangled. They were in a small, well-lit open patch, but my jeep was in the forest with no way out. I was in despair at losing this opportunity to photograph fighting chital as I watched helplessly.

Suddenly Fateh Singh virtually bulldozed through the trees and put me in the open patch in front of the stags. Amazingly, they completely ignored our approach and continued fighting for the next ten minutes, occasionally resting with antlers entangled, separating and fighting again. Eventually the intruder managed to push his tine into the shoulder of the dominant stag, causing the latter to flee. The victor triumphantly took command of the harem of does and the other stags accepted him as their new leader.

Driving efficiency is particularly important when you are sitting on the bonnet of the jeep to get a quick picture. Any sudden jerk is likely to throw you in front of the vehicle and may prove fatal. This happened in the case of the famous wildlife photographer Ylla [Koffler] who lost her life at Bharatpur in just such an accident. She was photographing a bullock cart race from the bonnet of a Land-Rover when the wheels hit a clump of grass and she fell flat on her head. After two days in a coma she died. I was at Bharatpur at the time. Photography while the vehicle is in motion is never satisfactory, and it is essential not only to stop but to switch off the engine at the right moment. Animals ignore a uniform noise but allowing the vehicle to roll with switched-off engine scares them: probably they take the silent monster to be some curious animal moving towards them. An open jeep is not ideal, as the animals note one's hand movements, so I prefer a closed jeep which provides suitable cover.

My classmate from the Forest College, Jagdeesh Mishra, had an amazing mastery of the art of approaching wild herds with a jeep. When he took anyone round Palamau Park he always tried to give them the closest possible view of the elephants. He knows most of them by name and never forgets those which have given him trouble. I once tried to frame a cow elephant which was busy pushing trees down and Mishra put the jeep in reverse and backed a few metres. The animal stopped her activity and looked at us, raising her trunk to try to catch our scent. Then she advanced a few steps and stared, at the same time making a drumming sound. All of a sudden the entire herd stopped grazing and the cow elephant charged. Our jeep was already in reverse and Mishra continued to drive backwards rapidly. Meanwhile another elephant appeared from a depression and tried to block our way, and the slightest hesitation on the driver's part would have been fatal. One of the elephants of this herd had made pulp of a Fiat not long before. The charging cow followed for some distance and then stopped, staring at the retreating jeep and thumping her front feet in anger.

Early next morning I returned to find the area littered with broken trees, looking as though it was the site of some inefficient forestry operation. Apparently one of the cow elephants was about to give birth and was looking for a safe maternity ward, so her companions were helping her by clearing the ground to fortify her hiding place. The trees had been pushed all to one side, giving us a clue to the direction of the elephants' movements. The morning was completely silent except for a faint sound coming from a thickly covered ravine, where evidently the herd had retired to rest. This road-blocking behaviour by pulling down trees is a peculiarity of the elephants of Palamau, which number only about 30 and are a recent invasion of the late 1930s. They are believed to have escaped from the elephant camp of the Raja of Sirguja, a famous tiger hunter.

As there was no chance of elephant photography we were discussing the next move when I heard the distant roar of a tiger. It was repeated twice at an interval of 30 seconds. The night before we had left a buffalo calf as bait, and the sound we heard might have been the last call of a tiger which had eaten a good meal and was about to retire for a day's rest. On investigating the place where the bait had been tied we found that the calf had indeed been carried off. Christian Zuber, the wildlife photographer, was busy filming the drag mark and remains of the calf. It seemed that the tiger had come to the bait after Zuber and his charming wife had abandoned the hide the night before, and the animal must have been watching them the whole time. Zuber was not the only one to be duped like this; the then Chief Conservator of Forests, Shri S. P. Shahi, and many others had been the repeated victims of the tiger's cunning. The villain had taken more than 60 baits without obliging even the Park Director.

On examination I found several causes of their failure to film or photograph the tiger. One was that the hide was not properly located and designed. The first principle of hide-making is that the hide should merge with the landscape, and for that purpose only local material should be used. Thus on river banks or on rocky areas local stone is vital; similarly grass should be used in meadow hides and brushwood in scrublands. In open country one needs a 3 ft deep pit with local thatching to merge with the environment. On one occasion the hide was a massive structure, with three big windows for projecting the cameras, and these openings gave the tiger a clear view of the inside of the hide and any movement within. He could also hear all sounds. I advised them to close all three windows and to leave open only a few very small peepholes, just sufficient to project a lens at eye level in a sitting position. Another defect I noticed was the manner in which the bait was tied; the tree could have created an obstruction between the cameraman in the hide and the animal attacking the bait. We solved this problem by anchoring a wire loop round a log buried two-and-a-half feet in the ground. This done, I elected to try my luck and sat there the next evening, but unfortunately the herd of elephants decided to graze in the same area. The tiger was scared and did not turn up. With burning torches, my rescue party escorted me back to camp.

Certainly I had more failures than successes. There were occasions when I travelled hundreds of miles along dusty forest tracks without meeting any wild animals except a hare or a jackal. Even in the famous tiger forests of North Kheri in Uttar Pradesh driving through the night I saw only a few chital. Cruising for over 1000 km in creeks around the islands in the Sundarbans, spending sleepless nights, I failed to see a tiger even though I found fresh pug marks on almost every island. For days on end sometimes I waited at hides in the hope of getting a glimpse of a tiger without success. On such occasions I had to be content with collecting corroboratory evidence such as disturbed grass, footprints, droppings, drag-lines of kills and the carcasses of prey which showed individual methods of killing, even claw marks on three trunks. There were also noises: the alarm calls of chital and sambar, the nervous dog-like bark of a barking deer, the muffled bellow of a nilgai, the snort of a gaur, the sneeze of a chinkara, the hooting of an owl, the cough of a peacock or a langur, and occasionally the great roar itself coming from a distant hill. Even when I did see a tiger it passed so quickly that few details registered in my mind, much less in my notebook or camera film. Attempt after attempt proved frustrating, but success when it came dispelled all the previous depression. All the same, I came to realize that failure could be as important as success from the ecological point of view, negative information being just as much a record very often as something positive.

There were times when luck was on my side and I would find myself spending days in the company of a tigress with cubs, or of tigers relaxing in streams or pools or guarding their kill. On one glorious night after another tigers would come to dine on their kill and keep me company till dawn. I made many thrilling discoveries, such as the times when I photographed courting tigers, a tigress carrying a cub in her mouth or one bringing up a record litter of five cubs.

Successful photographs are distressingly rare, sometimes owing to the presence of tourists, sometimes (which is worse) due to my own fault. Once after a hectic day I rushed to Kalighati waterhole and entered my hide to see the usual stream of chital and sambar coming to drink but no sign of a tiger. The cool breeze lulled me to sleep and the next I heard was a lapping sound. It was dawn. I looked around and there was the tiger. His pug marks showed that twice he had come close to my hide and I knew nothing about it. My wife tells me that when tired I snore heavily and no doubt the tiger was puzzled at such curious noises in his land.

There are worse things to look into than the eyes of a tiger. In my Kachida hide in May 1971 while I was observing sambar at the waterhole I found that a stone was obstructing my view. After the sambar had gone I pushed the stone out of the way and was getting ready for a fresh shot when I saw a cobra face to face through the lens opening and hardly 20 inches from me. Movement in the cramped hide was impossible so I gave a hiss and the reptile raised its hood. It turned away, but I hardly had time to breathe before it had dropped into the hide from the other peephole and there it was behind my camera box. I do not recall what I did, but the snake must have slunk away. I have never been so frightened in my life even when facing tigers at close quarters, such as the time when a tigress with three cubs surrounded my hide and tried to take the roof off to discover the source of the flashing light.

Studying a tiger is always thrilling, but if not carried out with sufficient care and knowledge it can be dangerous. I had some very anxious moments in Kanha Park when for a whole day I hung precariously from a tree while a tigress with two small cubs prowled below making angry attempts to get at the outsize 'vulture' up in the branches. My choice had been a bad one as the tree forked not very high above the ground and the branch on which I perched was almost horizontal. The tigress discovered my presence while her cubs were feeding and she stood under the tree with murder on her mind. I froze and made no attempt to climb higher for fear of catching hold of a dead branch and falling. The tigress raised her forelimbs on the trunk, scratched the bark in frustration and then sat down. I wondered how long I could remain in this position, and whenever I made a move the tigress rushed to the tree. I had an eight-hour ordeal until the camp elephant came and lifted me off.

On other occasions I had to hold my breath when a tiger, to confirm his suspicions, came close to my flimsy grass hide. Some of my close-up pictures are the products of sheer foolhardiness; but then, it is just these risks that give tiger-watching its special thrill.

I enjoyed every minute of my stay in stuffy hides, sometimes sweating in a temperature of 46°C, at other times shivering beside a frozen pool. Perhaps my most uncomfortable experience was while watching birds rather than tigers, sitting on floating hides in the fresh-water swamps at Bharatpur to observe the behaviour of Saras cranes on their nests. The atmosphere was almost unbearably hot, humid and oppressive, and any movement shook the raft and made it conspicuous. I watched from sunrise to sunset, seated precariously almost on the surface of the mosquito-infested marsh; but I forgot the glare of the August sun and my discomfort in the fascination of watching the cranes' nest-building activities, their share in the duties of incubating the eggs, and the dance and trumpeting calls in unison at the time of the changing of the guard. The cranes put me to shame for my own shortcomings as a father.

The technique of photographing from a hide was unknown to me until I met Dr Salim Ali, the greatest living authority on the birds of India. At our first meeting I invited him to lunch and noticed that he was only nibbling salad. To my horror I saw that the main dish was green pigeon: it was August, the close season. My wife tried to pretend it was a small chicken, but Salim only smiled. After that I saw him almost every year, and in 1969 when he got the Phillips Medal from the IUCN went to congratulate him and presented him with a one rupee coin. In Rajasthan tradition such a gift conveys the highest respect, and Salim valued it. When I saw him later after he had been presented with the Paul Getty award of $50,000 I reminded him that this was not the first gift of cash he had received.

By photographing and taking notes over long periods of time in some places I came to know the animals and birds almost by name, or at least by their morphological peculiarities such as deformities, injuries and battle scars. I saw them when they first came with their mothers, then as youngsters, then with their mates, and finally with their own young. Sometimes when I missed a certain individual I would be afraid it had been killed or trapped, only to be reassured by seeing it the next day or on the next trip. Such encounters always make me happy and I experience a sense of family reunion.

Although I identified with these creatures they never trusted me: the understanding was all one-sided. Even my scent sends them bolting. I have wondered whether it was my fault, but then I tell

myself that it is nothing personal but an inbuilt fear of man which
the animals have developed because human action has exceeded the
natural limits of predation. Man is the embodiment of unpredictable danger, so I could never be accepted as part of the ecology of
tigerland and can only remain a secret witness to the animals' lives.

Excerpted from Tiger! The Story of the Indian Tiger *(London: Collins, 1978).*

The Rhino of Kaziranga

E. P. GEE

The Assam tea-planters were a small, select group, with a love of the outdoors, camping, angling and shooting. Gee as a conservationist had a big-game hunter's world-view—his only book The Wildlife of India *is skilfully woven together from several articles written over three decades travelling across wild India. He surveyed the status of lions in Gir Forest and the wild ass in the Rann of Kutch, rode an elephant in Kanha in central India and watched wildlife along the shores of Kerala's Periyar lake. But it was the great Indian one-horned rhinoceros that perhaps ranked first for him both as a writer and a photographer. The Kaziranga national park in Assam, set up initially as a reserve in 1908, was and still is the most significant stronghold of a species that once ranged across the Indo-Gangetic plains. The wet savannah grasslands along the river Brahmaputra showcase an array of wild animals that now exist nowhere else in one place: the wild buffalo, the elephant, the swamp deer, the tiger and the great Indian one-horned rhino.*

Gee's account is especially interesting on two counts. It reflects how 'amateur' naturalists, in this case a tea-planter were often closely associated with particular national parks. Further, it shows how a small group of Englishmen who stayed on in India carved out a new public role as conservationists.

The history of the Indian rhino is also the story of the changing vegetation and climate of this sub-continent. Rhino existed during the Mohenjo-Daro era about 5,000 years ago, in the plains of the Indus river of what is now West Pakistan. Some rhino seals, relics of that ancient civilization, are preserved in the Indian National Museum, New Delhi. That region was then green and fertile: it lost most of its natural vegetation due to cutting and over-grazing by the local population, as happened in many parts of North Africa and the Middle East. The climate there has also gradually changed.

It is recorded that the invading Emperor Timur hunted and killed many rhino on the frontier of Kashmir in A.D. 1398. In the sixteenth century there were rhino in parts of the west of the sub-continent, and as far north-west as Peshawar. In his memoirs the Emperor Babur describes how he hunted rhino in bush country near the Indus as late as 1519. About that time the King of Cambay (in western India) sent a rhino as a present to the King of Portugal, and this was shipped from Goa. This was the first Indian rhino ever to be seen in Europe, for the ones brought to Egypt, Greece and Rome in ancient times were most probably African white rhino, from the Nile in Sudan.

Partly due to capturing and killing, and partly due to the clearing of the habitat for settlement, cultivation and grazing, the rhino gradually disappeared in the west. Even in the Ganges valley rhino became extinct during the nineteenth century. By 1900 they only survived in southern Nepal, northern Bihar, northern Bengal and Assam.

The Brahmaputra valley in Assam in the last century was mostly covered with thick grass and jungle. Then came the tea industry, with labourers imported from other parts of India; and a lot of clearing was done for opening up of plantations. At the end of the century the railway in Assam was constructed, and vast numbers of settlers and graziers entered the valley. Wild life gradually became scarcer, and in particular the rhino was very much hunted by sportsmen and poachers alike.

A special reason for the persecution of the rhino is the fanciful belief in the wonderful properties of its horn. The rhino horn is not really horn at all, but consists of compressed or agglutinated 'hair'; or, more scientifically, keratin fibres cemented together in a hard compact mass. It is not fixed to the skull, like the antlers of a deer which grow on pedicles, or like the horns of an ox or antelope which grow on central cores of bone connected to the skull, but is epidermal and rests in the flesh and can be knocked off by a hard blow. When a rhino's horn is thus struck off, the wound bleeds profusely but within a year a new horn will start to grow there.

Medical properties have long been attributed to the rhino's horn. It was supposed to be a good insurance against poison, as it was believed that a drinking cup carved from rhino horn would split in twain if poison was added to the contents! Another belief was that a drink served in such a cup would start frothing if poison had been added! Kings in eastern Asia, therefore, used such drinking cups, one or two of which are still preserved in museums and elsewhere.

Even now rhino horn finds a ready market in eastern Asia, especially in China, as an alleged aphrodisiac for 'restoring lost manly vigour'! Thirty years ago it used to be worth half its weight in gold: now it is priced even higher. At a recent auction in Gauhati which I heard of, a party of Bombay merchants came in a chartered plane, and purchased the whole lot at Rs 2,525 (about £189) per lb.! The present price of African rhino horn in East Africa is only £2 10s. per lb.

The Survival Service Commission of IUCN has for some time been considering the possibility of putting some kind of artificial 'substitute' for powdered rhino horn on the market in large quantities, to forestall the demand for real rhino horn at the expense of the few surviving animals. But I think this idea has now been dropped on the grounds that it would be most unethical to put such a spurious 'drug' on to the market however worthy the ultimate objective might be.

I understand that tests made in chemical research laboratories in Basle (Switzerland) have conclusively shown that rhino horn has no biochemical or hormonal properties whatever. Investigations as to its potential effects as an irritant, I believe, show that any possible temporary results would be offset by injurious side effects.

Another fanciful belief in some parts of eastern Asia was that a rhino horn placed under the bed of a woman at the time of childbirth would assist her in her labour! Persons owning a horn would rent it out to expectant mothers for the equivalent of about £30 each time! Yet another absurd belief was that a rhino horn left to soak in a filled bucket turned the water into a sort of elixir of life, of which members of a family would sip a spoonful every day!

It certainly seems extraordinary that, even in this space age of science and technology, such absurd beliefs still persist. It is to be hoped that there is some truth in the report that legislation has now been introduced in China prohibiting the use of rhino horn for alleged aphrodisiacal and other 'benefits'.

Cow rhino in India carry horns as big as seen on bulls, in fact the sexes are almost indistinguishable at first sight. The record horn of an Indian rhino, in the British Museum, is twenty-four inches. The largest I have ever seen in Kaziranga is one of eighteen inches recovered by the Forest Staff from an old animal which had died, and I have seen and photographed one of an estimated length of sixteen inches on a live rhino. The average horn to be seen in Kaziranga would be about eight inches, I think.

Apart from the horn, almost any part of the body of a rhino can be marketed. Even the urine is drunk by some persons, tiny pieces of hide and bone are worn as charms against sickness, and the meat is believed by some to be not only palatable but also a combined passport and ticket to the land of eternal bliss!

One of the last unspoilt and unoccupied grassy areas of the Brahmaputra valley was the one which is now Kaziranga Wild Life Sanctuary. It stretches for some twenty-five miles along the southern bank of that huge river, just to the north of the Mikir Hills in the centre of Assam. It was a sportsman's and poachers' paradise until 1908 when it was realized by the authorities that there were only about a dozen rhino left.

After being constituted as a Forest Reserve and closed to shooting, Kaziranga become a 'Game Sanctuary' in 1926. And in the late 1940s its name was officially altered to 'Wild Life Sanctuary' because the word 'game' refers to those animals and birds which are shot for trophies and for meat, whereas the term 'wild life' embraces all living creatures and implies their conservation.

In the early 1930s Kaziranga was a closed book, a sort of *terra incognita* completely left to itself by the Forest Department. I remember trying to get permission to go there in 1934, but the rather lame excuse of the British DFO was, 'No one can enter the place. It is all swamps and leeches and even elephants cannot go there.' Shortly afterwards the very fine Chief Conservator, A. J. W. Milroy, thought otherwise, and decided to clean up the poaching which had recently started again and to open up the sanctuary for visitors.

I have talked to the Forest Officer who was the first to be deputed to survey Kaziranga in the mid-1930s. He found poachers' camps at every *bheel* (small lake), and about forty carcasses of rhino with the horns removed. The Mikirs, the simple, peaceful but very interesting tribal folk who dwell in the Mikir Hills just on the southern boundary of the sanctuary, were among the many poachers. And when they ran away from the Forest Staff their 'tails' (the ends of their embroidered loin-cloths) were caught hold of by the pursuers. The Mikirs would then draw out their sharp chopper knives and cut off their own 'tails' to facilitate their escape.

When Kaziranga was opened to visitors in the year 1938, I was one of the first to go and see it. Two friends and the Range Officer accompanied me, and we had a most exciting time on our two riding elephants. When I first saw rhino, they appeared to be most improbable-looking and prehistoric-like with their quaint features and thick armour-plating. Our party carried two rifles, one on each elephant, for 'self-defence', but this practice of taking defensive weapons into a sanctuary was soon discontinued, and since then I have never taken a rifle or gun with me in self-defence at any time anywhere in India.

Rhino were then unused to seeing human visitors, and often their reaction was to charge those intruding into their haunts. At that time the Forest riding elephants were not trained to stand their ground in the face of a charging rhino. Their instinct was to turn tail and flee; and as the *mahouts* felt likewise, the result was sometimes headlong flight through the tall grass for a mile or so. I remember writing my remark in the visitors' book, 'Twice charged by rhino, and the elephants each time bolted for some distance.'

A few months later some planter friends of mine visited the sanctuary, by which time the rhino of that vicinity had become more accustomed to visitors. After paying the fees for entering the sanctuary and for riding elephants, they wrote in the same remarks column, 'Rather disappointing. Charged only by the Forest Department!'

Nowadays the rhino which inhabit the areas frequently entered by visitors on elephant-back are 'well-behaved' and rarely charge unless there is a cow with a young calf. In the other parts of the sanctuary, however, where visitors seldom go, one is liable to be charged. But the elephants are now staunch and trained to stand their ground, and in any case a charging rhino will very rarely press home its attack. Nearly always it suddenly stops short, wheels round and eventually trots away, snorting all the time.

On the very rare occasion when a rhino actually presses home its charge at a riding elephant, or attacks a man on foot, it does not use its horn as a weapon of offence. Unlike African rhino, the Indian rhino has never been seen to use its horn thus: instead it uses the tushes (large incisor teeth) in its upper and lower jaw, especially the latter, and bites its victim with an upward thrust of the head. Consequently the lower tush nearest to the victim will often make a single gash, which has given rise to the imaginary belief that it has used its horn. African rhino have shorter jaws and lack the powerful tushes of the Indian rhino.

Moreover I have never heard of an Indian rhino sharpening its horn, or even rubbing it, in the wild state, as African rhino do. So when you see an Indian rhino rubbing down its horn on the walls and iron bars of its enclosure in a zoo, it is probably because of parasites which cause itching and therefore rubbing. Ralph Graham, Assistant Director of the Brookfield Zoo in Chicago, found this out, and managed to cure his pair of Indian rhino of rubbing their horns by applying mud which had been suitably medicated for killing the parasites. After this treatment, the rhino stopped rubbing, and their horns grew properly.

In their wild state Indian rhino are nearly always found during the heat of the day resting in wet muddy wallows, a sure protection against external parasites, and against the flies which try to lay their eggs between the folds of the thickly armour-plated skin.

There is an old legend as to how the rhino got its armour-plating. Once upon a time Lord Krishna decided to give up elephants as battle animals, and to use the rhino, because *mahouts* were too easy a target for enemy archers. So a rhino was captured, dressed in armour and trained. But when the animal was brought before Lord Krishna, it was found that it was too stupid to learn and obey orders, so it was driven back to the forest—with its armour still on it. And so to this very day rhino still have on them the armour-plating of that particular animal.

As a matter of fact, rhino were actually used by some of the old kings in Indian as front line 'tanks' in warfare. They had iron tridents fixed on to their horns when so used, and this implies a certain amount of training.

It is interesting to speculate whether the great Indian one-horned rhino, whose scientific name is *Rhinoceros unicornis,* was the origin of the legends of the unicorn. Certainly the ancient popular belief that the unicorn could detect poison by dipping its horn into a liquid tallies with the alleged magical properties of the rhino horn. Also the belief that the unicorn was the only animal that ventured to attack the elephant seems to have something in it.

Considering that both the elephant and the tiger are afraid of the rhino, this latter creature could with justification be termed 'the king of beasts'. A tiger will hunt a baby rhino and often succeeds in snatching away a very young one when the mother is off her guard. No single tiger would dare attack an adult rhino, as the following story shows.

In 1886 a certain 'sportsman' went out on elephant-back in the area which is now Kaziranga to shoot rhino. He encountered one and fired about a dozen shots at it from very close range. The wounded rhino made off, and as it was late in the evening the hunter returned to his camp. Next day he followed up the bloody trail of the badly wounded rhino and came across it while it was actually engaged in fighting and keeping off two tigers. 'One tiger,' the account says, 'had his neck fearfully lacerated, evidently by the rhino's teeth; the other was also covered with blood.' The 'sportsman' fired at both tigers, which escaped, and then finished off the unfortunate rhino.

This episode demonstrated the boldness, powers of endurance and agility of the Indian rhino. It can easily outstrip an elephant, and can gallop, jump, twist and turn quickly—none of which things an elephant can do. For an elephant cannot run, but can only shuffle along at a fast walk at about twenty miles per hour; and an elephant cannot jump, in fact it cannot cross a crevice or ditch of more than six feet in width, which is the maximum length of its stride.

All of the world's five species of rhino, the two in Africa and the three in Asia, are in peril of becoming wiped out by man; and because of this danger a world committee has been appointed to try and save them from extinction.

The two African species are in less immediate danger: the African black (or hook-lipped) rhino are now believed to number 11,000 to 13,500 while the African white (or square-lipped) rhino are fewer, about 2,500 to 3,500. Both of these rhino are two-horned, and the former is a browser while the latter is a grazer like the Indian rhino.

The three Asiatic species are much fewer in numbers. My own estimate of the great Indian one-horned rhino is as follows: Nepal 185, Bengal 65 and Assam 375, making a total of 625. The Asiatic or Sumatran two-horned rhino are now believed to number about

170, mainly in Burma, Malaya and Sumatra, and there is a female
of this species in the Copenhagen Zoo. The Javan or lesser one-
horned rhino is now confined to the Udjong Kulon Reserve in
western Java and number somewhere between 25 and 50. There are
no Javan rhino in captivity anywhere.

In size the African white rhino is the largest. Then comes the
Indian, and then the African black. Next comes the Javan, and
smallest of all is the Sumatran. It is interesting to note that in the
case of two grazing species, the African white and the Indian, when
a mother and calf are on the move the baby goes ahead in front,
while the mother follows behind—presumably as a precaution
against a prowling lion (in Africa) or a tiger (in India) in grassy
country. This precaution would not be so necessary in the case of
browsing rhino in scrub tree forest.

All three Asiatic species used to be found in India. The Javan
lesser one-horned rhino was once 'fairly common' in Bengal,
especially in the Sundarbans, but became extinct in India about
1900. The Sumatran two-horned rhino still existed in the Mizo
(formerly Lushai) Hills of Assam up to about 1935—when it was
exterminated. Although this rhino is two-horned, the anterior horn
is small, while the posterior one is often very insignificant indeed.

The great Indian one-horned rhino also would undoubtedly have
ceased to exist, but for the strict protection given to it when its
numbers fell to a very low level at the beginning of this century.
What are the reasons why rhino cannot survive the battle of life?
Some people say it is slow of hearing and short-sighted, but I am
not so sure of this.

I myself think that it is generally slow-witted and foolhardy. Most
wild animals in India instinctively run away from danger and seek
concealment in thick cover. The blundering rhino does the opposite. It continues grazing till danger is quite close, and then instead
of retreating and hiding it is liable to expose itself still more by
charging. Also it has the habit of depositing its dung at certain fixed
places, and a would-be slayer can wait for a rhino at one of these
large dung heaps, to which the animal finally approaches backwards.

Some people have suggested that these rhino dung heaps may
denote 'territory', but I do not think so. I have observed that any
rhino will deposit its excreta at any heap, and that rhino do not
usually stay in a particular locality, but move about from place to
place according to the availability of grazing. I think that individual

animals, while passing near a dung heap, will decide by 'association' to make use of it. Quite a number of other herbivorous animals deposit their droppings at particular spots, for example nilgai and other antelopes, without necessarily demarcating territory.

Although the rhino is a solitary creature, I have seen as many as seven of them all together in one wallow; but these came from different directions and departed from the wallow, when disturbed, in seven different directions. As an Indian poet has said:

> 'Fearing nothing, caring for nothing,
> Wander alone, like the rhinoceros.'

Several writers on animals have described the Indian rhino as only uttering one noise, a grunt! I have heard four noises: a roar or a bellow when newly captured, a snort when excited or disturbed, a grunt when not disturbed and a peculiar whistling sound at the time of courting and mating. I think it is the female which makes this whistling sound, while the male grunts; but I notice that several sportsman-writers of the old days have described a whistling noise made by a mortally wounded rhino.

A curious thing about Indian rhino is that old animals, mostly bulls, on reaching a stage at the end of their life when they can no longer defend themselves against stronger ones, often 'retire' to the edge of the sanctuary. They then sometimes live for years close to where villagers provide a certain amount of protection for them, because younger rhino will not venture outside the sanctuary in such a manner. These old rhino usually carry the ugly gashes of conflict when they first come; and later on become a welcome tourist attraction of Kaziranga because if no rhino can be seen in the sanctuary, a visitor can generally be certain of finding one of these old ones which can be approached very closely.

Perhaps the most famous of these old half-tame rhino was the *boorra goonda*, which was admired and photographed at close quarters by many thousands of visitors during the fourteen years he lived just outside the entrance to the sanctuary. I once photographed him on the ground at a distance of only nine feet from his nose with impunity, much to the disappointment of a certain professional TV cameraman who was hoping for a charge—at my expense!

The *boorra goonda*, 'old big bull' in Assamese, died a peaceful natural death in 1953, and was much missed by all. But his place was soon taken by another 'ousted' bull called *kan katta* or 'cut ear'.

A number of rhino have been sent from Kaziranga to zoological gardens in different parts of the world for exhibiting to the public. Among the very first were Mohan (in 1947) and Mohini (in 1952) which went to Whipsnade. I assisted in the arrangements and care of these two young animals from the time of their capture to their loading in the planes which flew them to Britain.

Rhino are captured by the pit system. A pit about ten feet long, five feet wide and six feet deep is dug in the middle of a much-used rhino path, and then thinly covered with sticks and grass to camouflage it. A rhino, sometimes a calf walking in front of its mother, falls and is later removed in a wheeled cage dragged by an elephant to a stockade, where it stays for about a month before being taken to its final destination. This is all done scientifically and humanely by experienced men of the Forest Department.

When first captured a rhino, like a newly caught wild elephant, will display a wildness and apparent ferocity which has to be seen to be believed. This is because it suddenly finds itself in a position in which it has never previously been and in which its freedom of movement is totally restricted. It is purely due to fear, and this is proved by the fact that newly captured rhino and elephants become remarkably tame within a few days. Once they find that they are being well treated, their fear quickly disappears. I will always remember how Mohini, a baby rhino, after a very short spell of savagery, became devotedly docile and used to lick my hands whenever possible!

Mohan and Mohini at Whipsnade and the pair at Basle in Switzerland have successfully, reared two and three calves in each place respectively, and have provided us with much valuable information about their breeding habits. This information is of particular use when interpreted in the light of what can be observed in the wide open spaces of Kaziranga.

For instance we now know that when we see one adult rhino chasing another, it is probably not a case of a stronger bull pursuing a weaker one, or of a bull trying to catch up with a cow. It is almost certainly a cow 'in season' running after a 'reluctant' bull! A cow rhino comes 'into season' once every forty-six to forty-eight days throughout the year, unless it is served by a bull. Bull rhino are also believed to have periods when they are 'in rut', and the 'seasons' of both cow and bull must coincide before mating can take place. The gestation period is 16¼–16½ months. A rhino probably lives as long as an elephant, about seventy years, though we have no definite proof of this yet.

For the last twenty-five years, ever since it was opened to the public, I have been visiting Kaziranga. I remember what it looked like before all the streams and *bheels* were invaded by that beautiful but terrible pest the water hyacinth. This was introduced into India from South America about fifty years ago as an ornamental plant. One tiny bit of it can spread over an area of 600 square yards in a few months, and it does incalculable damage. At first no animal in Kaziranga would touch it, except wild pig which grub up the roots in the dry weather. Nowadays elephants, rhino and buffalo sometimes eat a little of it, apparently with reluctance.

I have seen Kaziranga so many times when the strong, dry winds of February and March sweep the roaring man-lit fires through the elephant grass, leaving bare black patches of charred stalks. I have seen it often in April and May when the new freshly-growing grass attracts swamp deer and hog deer, now resplendent in their bright new summer coats.

I have boated through it during the peak floods of the monsoon months, and have secured what is probably the only photograph of a rhino swimming in deep water. The time I like best of all, however, is the end of the monsoon, October and November, when the floods have receded and the rains with their heat and humidity give way to cool, sunny days. It is then that most of the many kinds of grasses and reeds burst into flower, and in the distance to the north can be clearly seen the snow-capped peaks of the Eastern Himalayas, over a hundred miles away.

During a visit on elephant-back there is always the chance of a thrill, when an angry or frightened rhino may snort and charge. It is equally exciting whether the *mahout* makes his elephant stand its ground and thus call the rhino's bluff, or whether the elephant turns tail and flees through the tall, treeless grass, without any danger of overhead branches hitting you.

Apart from such minor thrills while on elephant-back, I can only recall two occasions on which I have had to retreat from a rhino when I happened to be on foot.

Rhino can be very dangerous, and every year a few people get killed by them. Because of this danger, visitors are not allowed to dismount from their riding elephant in the sanctuary, but being a person not without some experience and an Honorary Forest

Officer I have always been given some latitude by a co-operative Forest Department.

The first occasion was when I was determined to secure one or two steady cine shots of a rhino in an open place. An elephant is a most unsteady form of transport to do cine photography from. Accordingly when I reached a dried-up *bheel* (small lake) where a large bull rhino was grazing on the short grass, I signalled to the *mahout* to stop and make the elephant kneel down. Then I and a man, whom I had brought to assist me with photographic equipment, dismounted and cautiously approached the rhino on foot with the cine camera on its tripod.

When I got within 'shooting' range, I placed the tripod in position and started to film the rhino, which was now slowly coming straight towards me. I sent the man back to the elephant, while I continued to film the oncoming beast at a closer range. As soon as the rhino more than filled the frame of the view-finder, I thought it was time for me to quit. There was no time to take the camera and tripod with me.

As I was nearing the elephant, I turned round to look back. There was the rhino closely examining my camera. I mounted the elephant the usual way by standing on its bent hind legs and climbing up the rope under its tail, and there was the rhino still very interested in my camera. It occurred to me that if it had known anything at all about how to use a cine camera it could easily have obtained a very good shot of a man hurriedly scrambling on to the back of a frightened and trumpeting elephant!

The other occasion was when I was trying to photograph a pair of Pallas's fishing eagles at their nest high up in a *simul*, or Indian silk-cotton tree, in Kaziranga. I had built a *machan* about forty feet up another tree near by, so situated to make the best use of the morning sun from about 8.30 to 9.30 a.m. As there was usually a rhino of rather unpredictable temperament living in that neighbourhood, I had asked for an elephant to take me and my two men out there each morning, and bring us back a couple of hours later.

One morning the elephant did not turn up. I was in a quandary as to what to do. The sun was shining in a cloudless sky, and I could hear the eagles calling to each other with their loud and melodious *kooroo kooroo*. I just could not resist the temptation to risk a journey on foot to the site of the lofty tree with its nest.

'The elephant has not come,' I explained to my two men, 'but I am willing to go there on foot. Are you willing to come with me, or do your want to remain here?'

'Where the *sahib* goes, we will also go,' came the not unexpected reply.

We cautiously walked along the narrow track through the elephant grass, and I remember reflecting on how small and vulnerable we were and how very much higher than usual the fifteen-foot grass was. We reached the *simul* tree safely, and then followed an hour's photography. When the angle of the morning sun made further work impossible, it was time for the return journey through the tall grass.

We had not gone more than a hundred yards when there was a noise near by, and with a panicky 'Rhino coming!' both my men, who were aged about twenty, disappeared down the track, seemingly breaking all Olympic records.

At their age I could have run even faster. But I knew that a rhino can soon catch up with the fastest of humans. However, I also started to try and escape. The track was wet and slippery and much depressed in places by three-toed rhino and large circular elephant footprints.

After about ten yards, I did the best possible thing I could have done. I slipped and fell down, flat on my face, with the rhino very close at hand. I knew that an Indian rhino, unlike a wild elephant, will not continue its attack on a fallen victim, and I quickly rolled sideways off the track into the grass and remained perfectly still.

The rhino thundered past. After about twenty minutes the grass parted and one of the men, who had come back by a long detour, asked if I was all right. We then together went along the track, on to the main road and called to the other man. After a long time he emerged, too frightened to talk. Then, at last, he described how he had eventually thrown himself into a thick clump of grass, and how the rhino had stood over him breathing heavily before going on its way.

Excerpted from The Wildlife of India *(London: Collins, 1964).*

M. KRISHNAN

Did-he-do-it?

Krishnan, in the brief nature essay that was his forte, invites attention to the red-wattled lapwing whose cry is so common in the evenings across the length and breadth of the land. As was so often the case, Krishnan found the commonplace as fascinating as the rare creature, the small just as much as the large.

All over India the most familiar of the vast tribe of plovers and other shorebirds is the red-wattled lapwing, always there along shallow streams and small spreads of water, and distinctive in its livery. One needs to look narrowly at the white bars and spots on the pinions, pale or dark eye-streaks, and subterminal or terminal tall-bands of most birds of this teeming clan to distinguish between one another, but this lapwing can be known at a glance.

A pigeon-sized bird with very long, yellow legs, a black head with a white streak down the neck of each side, prominently red around the red eyes (in the wattles and the red, black-tipped bill), a glossy black bib and black wings with a flashing white band in the flights, a bronzed olive brown on top and white beneath, can be nothing else. And unlike most birds which flee at the approach of men it flies around them in frantic, high circles, screaming its reiterated alarm call, a shrill, insistent 'Did-he-do it?'. In Tamil we have a highly indicative name for it: it is called the 'aal-katti-kuruvi' which, literally translated, means 'the bird that points out men'.

Perhaps no other bird is so heartily disliked by the small-game hunter, furtively stalking the watersides. In an old bird-book the author says of this lapwing: 'Though it can hardly be called shy, it is nevertheless a very wary bird and seems to be gifted with a marvellous faculty for accurately gauging the range of a shotgun; for what sportsman, when quietly walking up some marked-down game, has not been exasperated at the persistent way in which these birds wheel and circle overhead and round him, always just out of range, uttering, their shrill cry of "Did-he-do-it", "Did-he-do-it" thereby giving warning to all and sundry of his approach.' Regretfully he adds, 'They are quite worthwhile shooting for the table if one can get near enough to them.' There should be a question mark after the well-known syllabization of the bird's alarm call, for it has a definitely interrogative sound.

It is not only men at whose approach the bird sounds its loud alarm, broadcast to the neighbourhood as it circles around. It knows which visitors to its water are predatory and which harmless. It ignores the visit of chital, sambar and other herbivores to the pool it haunts, but mongooses, monitors, jackals and the like are instantly mobbed, with shrill imprecations. I have actually seen a jackal, mobbed by a pair of these lapwings, turn tail and retreat, to seek a less bothersome drink elsewhere.

I do not know whether it demonstrates at tigers, but it is definitely excited to a frenzy by a leopard in the open. It is as vigilant by night as by day, especially when there is a bright moon. Years ago, cycling home along a country road through the scrub jungle one full-moon night, the frantic calls of a pair of red-wattled lapwings just ahead of me alerted me to the presence of a leopard crouching on the roadside.

Like most birds of their clan, these lapwings build no nest but lay their eggs in a scrape on the ground, usually on the shingly bare banks of a stream or pool. The eggs are wonderfully blotched and speckled obliteratively, so that they look exactly like the pebbles on the bank—so much so that if you take your eyes away from them after locating them, you cannot spot them again at once. The nestlings too depend on camouflage for survival. They can run soon after they are hatched, but cannot fly, and when alerted to the approach of some predator by the alarm calls of their parents, they just stay put, with the head resting on the ground at the stretch of the neck, utterly immobile—and they are so hard to spot that usually they escape.

Like many other plovers, the red-wattled lapwing also indulges in a broken-wing display to distract enemies when its young or fledglings are approached. It flies around the intruder screaming, flying much closer to the enemy than it usually does, and then flies some distance away to subside on the ground trailing a wing, as if it was broken. A purely instinctive display, of course, but highly effective.

That dependable observer and gifted painter of birds, G. M. Henry, says that this lapwing's food 'consists of ground-dwelling insects such as beetles, grasshoppers, termites etc. It is never found far from water but, although it wades quite freely, it takes most of its food on dry ground.' I have seen it taking prey from shallow water too, water insects, and even tadpoles and probably small crustaceans. Once I saw a red-wattled lapwing seize a mass of algae and swallow a bit of it, dropping the rest. And picking up what it had dropped, I took it home and examined it under a powerful magnifier. The thallus of that algae was literally swarming with minute, pin-head snails!

Originally published in 'Country Notebook', The Statesman, 31 July 1983.

R. SUKUMAR

In the Company of Elephants

In his foreword to Sukumar's Elephant Days and Nights, *the veteran wildlife biologist George Schaller remarks how the author has made 'a major contribution to helping elephants endure as icons of India's culture'. Sukumar's doctoral thesis at the Indian Institute of Science, Bangalore, on the Asian elephant and his subsequent research on this, the largest land mammal in the continent, yielded many insights into how best to protect and manage it. His decade-long study also enabled him to gain so much more than a passing acquaintance with individual wild elephants. The nicknames he gave them are a sign of his easy familiarity with the animals; this in itself is a relatively recent feature in India's forests. It might even point to a new phase in the centuries-old relationship of* Homo sapiens *with the Asian elephant. Such an intimate knowledge of the family ties and the genealogies of individual wild creatures may not be new to researchers in Africa; it certainly is in India. And Sukumar's work captures the magic of those moments.*

Tender, copper-coloured, with soft down on his fore-limbs, drowsy, marked by a blotchy trunk, having limbs undeveloped in form, seeking the breast, in the first year he has the name of *bala.*

With toenails getting thicker, with the tongue, lip and the rest (the seven 'red parts') very red, drinking little milk, somewhat inclined to eat creepers and grass, reddish between the foreparts; he capers constantly for no special reason, is generally frolicsome, very fond of sugar, with down-turned eyes, causing delight to the sight, in the second year he is a *puccuka....*

Up to the twelfth year his age makes him worthless; before the twenty-fourth year he is of middling value; up to the sixtieth year this noble elephant is called the best in respect to age.

Nilakantha in *Matanga-Lila*

The morning of 31 March 1982, Setty and I were on our way to Karapallam. During the previous two months we had been busy here once again watching elephants, after several months of trudging through trampled *ragi* fields and listening to the woes of the farmers. It was over a year since I had arrived at Hasanur. Now, looking back at that period in retrospect, I feel that I learnt as much about elephants during that year as I have since then. It had been an eventful year and I still have vivid memories of all my early encounters with these captivating creatures. I can recall exactly where I saw the elephants, how many there were, and what they were doing.

The road from Hasanur to Karapallam goes over a small hill about two kilometres before the inter-state border, from where one gets a sweeping view of the Araikadavu valley to the east and the steep granite hills beyond. That morning in March was as dry as it would get, the brown landscape enlivened only by the orange splash of *Butea monosperma* flowers and the evergreen trees lining the Araikadavu. All along the road were the signs of elephant-broken branches of *Acacia pennata, Capparis sepiaria* and *Zizyphus xylopyrus*.

A herd of elephants was moving up from the valley towards the road. I could only see their backs and hear the crackling of the defoliated bush as the huge beasts otherwise moved silently to cross the road. I have often marvelled at how silent a group of elephants can be as they move through the jungle. They seem to glide on their padded soles without any of the tramping that one usually associates them with. The only way to detect elephants in the jungle is to listen carefully for the flapping of their ears, the rumbling of the stomach, or the crackling of dry bush.

I recognized the old cow, who was not particularly tall but who had ears completely folded over at the top, as Tara. She was leading her family of eight elephants, including a young calf of her own, as they briefly paused to pull at a trunkful or two of the dry plants before moving over to the west of the road.

Accompanying the herd was the tuskless bull, about twenty years old, whom I called Makhna. I had seen him with the family three days earlier and he was obviously joining them. His cheeks were lightly stained as he was coming into musth. As usual with Makhna, he kicked up a fuss, swinging his head threateningly and scraping the ground with his foot before moving off with the rest of the group into the jungle. The herd began feeding and moving slowly towards me parallel to the road. The subsequent events unfolded rather quickly.

At 8.35 a.m. a six year old cow crossed the road from the west to the east, and without noticing me came very close to my jeep which was parked near a small bridge. When it was almost within touching distance it panicked and, emitting a distress call, disappeared into the bushes. Immediately there were deep rumbles from the rest of the herd. Setty and I jumped out of the jeep and went under the bridge to watch. Five elephants including Tara, her young calf and Makhna came rushing out to see what was wrong. They stood at the edge of the jungle, bunched together with their trunks up, the tips swaying from side to side like the raised hoods of cobras, trying to locate where the danger came from. Upon seeing them, the young cow hurried across the road with a squeal of relief and the herd went back into the jungle.

Makhna, however, stayed back, pacing up and down the road angrily. Finally he began dusting himself with red soil from the roadside. Whenever he heard the sound of an approaching vehicle he would wait until it came up to a curve in the road before quietly hiding in the dense acacia bush. After the vehicle passed by he would resume the dusting. Three vehicles passed by him without noticing him. The third time he made a sound that I can only describe, at the risk of sounding too anthropomorphic, as one of sheer exasperation. He was obviously a very shrewd creature.

At 9.05 a.m. the herd led by Tara came back to the road and they all went down to the Araikadavu.

This is a classic example of how an elephant herd would react when one of its young members was threatened. Even the otherwise peaceable Tara had a streak of aggression in her, and rushed to the aid of one of her family members. This, after all, is what elephant society is all about.

In 1982, the same herds I had seen in the Araikadavu valley during the previous dry season moved there somewhat earlier. From the first week of February I began regularly seeing Meenakshi, Tara, High Head and the Mriga sisters, and their herds, in the valley. They stayed there until the end of April or early May as usual. This was another productive period of elephant watching for me. The Karapallam pond did not attract elephants as frequently as it had the previous year because it did not hold as much water, but this did not really matter. The herds were there in the Araikadavu valley in full strength, busy moving between the practically dry stream bed and their favourite feeding grounds, stripping the bark and breaking the stems of *Acacia suma* at Karapallam.

I too was kept busy observing and photographing them. My file of identified elephants grew and I was pleased to see that the measurements I had made of adult elephants the previous year matched closely with those made this year, while the juveniles grew as expected.

Some bulls which I had not seen earlier began appearing in the Araikadavu valley. Hardly a kilometre from Hasanur I photographed a large bull with a blunt tail and a pair of short tusks that looked very lethal indeed. When I calculated his height I was shocked at the figure; he stood 322 centimetres at his shoulder. None of the other bulls either here or at Mudumalai came anywhere near this size. At first I could not believe my estimation, so I went back to the location where I had photographed him and once again measured the distance (I knew precisely which path he had come along and from where I had taken the shot). The figure was correct. I turned to the prints again and recalculated the height. The height was indeed accurate. Could this have been the much-dreaded Akkurjorai Bull? I had never actually seen him before. If it was him, what was he doing near Hasanur? To these questions I simply did not know the answers.

Two other bulls, Cradle Tusks (who also had a blunt tail) and a younger bull with beautiful incurved tusks which I called Cross Tusks, also came to the valley. One busy morning Setty and I had photographed a number of herds, as well as Cross Tusks who was trailing the Mriga family. He was in musth and in some hesitation came up to us before disappearing into the jungle behind the others. After the coast was clear of elephants, we got out of the jeep, took out a tape and began our distance measurements. We were engaged in this for a few minutes when, glancing back, I noticed Cross Tusks approaching the jeep from the opposite direction! We retreated in a hurry not wishing to mess around with a musth bull, however harmless he might seem. Cross Tusks slowly walked up to the jeep, stopped in front of it, and ran the tip of his trunk over the windscreen. Then he moved over to its open side and put his trunk into the jeep. My camera (and his undeveloped picture) was lying on the seat and I wondered if he would become the first elephant to trigger the shutter and take his own picture! Not satisfied, he went to the back of the jeep and again stuck his trunk inside, no doubt absorbing the human smell that still lingered there. His curiosity finally satisfied for the moment, he walked over to an *Acacia suma*, pulled down a branch and headed to the shade of the Araikadavu.

I was to eventually meet Cross Tusks at Kyatedevaragudi that November but, apart from him, I did not see any of the other elephants I had identified in the Araikadavu valley whenever I went north to the Biligirirangans. I could have certainly missed some of the bulls, but all the herds I saw here seemed to be different ones. These ranged over the moist deciduous forests of the Biligirirangan Hills Temple (BRT) Sanctuary during the dry months and the early wet season. Of these, Champaca, with a large tear in her left ear, was the most easily recognizable. I could recognize a few other groups by identifying a large cow or a sub-adult bull with peculiar tusks, but I never got around to naming them as my sightings of them were not too frequent.

By now a picture of how elephant society was organized was beginning to crystallize. I was, of course, familiar with the descriptions of African elephant society based on more detailed research and I found that Asian elephants were organized in similar fashion. There were differences in specific detail, such as group size and so on, but basically the structure was the same.

Elephants live in families led by the oldest female. The shikar literature is replete with references to the alleged 'master bull' of an elephant herd. If the term master bull implies that a bull is the unquestioned leader of a herd then it is no doubt a figment of the male chauvinist's imagination; the human male, and that too a macho hunter, cannot perhaps think otherwise. This is surprising because, as early as 1878, G. P. Sanderson had observed that 'an elephant family is invariably led by a female, never a male'. The truth is that among elephants it is the lady who gives the marching orders. No bull, however formidable he may be, can usurp her authority.

A family typically has one adult female and anywhere from one to five immature children. The term family has also been applied to larger groups. In a group there may be three generations, where the matriarch has mature daughters who have their own offspring. A group may also consist of two or more adult females, presumably sisters, and their children.

Ian Douglas–Hamilton felt that elephant groups with more than one mature female could be termed 'extended family units', but he retained the term 'family' in view of their cohesion. In Lake Manyara he found that the extended families were remarkably stable. Whenever he saw an identified family its composition was practically the same. Later studies in Africa, including those of Cynthia Moss at Amboseli and Rowan Martin at Sengwa in Zimbabwe did not confirm this, however. The splitting and fusion of different families were common even over short time intervals.

In southern India, both in the Biligirirangans and later in Mudumalai, I observed that the only really stable elephant unit was that of one mature female and her immature children. The matriarch Meenakshi sometimes moved with only her immature daughter and two sons. At other times she was seen with her entire family, including her two mature daughters and their children. Presumably her mature daughters also spent time on their own with their children. On yet other occasions Meenakshi and her family, larger or smaller, were seen in the company of another family led by the old cow Tara, who may have been Meenakshi's younger sister. Other well-identified families also behaved similarly. Champaca either moved along with only her three children, or with a larger group consisting of her sisters (presumably) and their offspring.

In view of these observations I propose that the term 'family' should be restricted to a single adult female plus offspring, and the term 'joint family' is used, in the Asian tradition, to describe groups with more than one adult female, even if these are reasonably stable.

Above the family and joint family are other levels of organization. A family or joint family may show strong ties with one or more families in the area. These may well be related families which have separated at some time in the past. Douglas–Hamilton called them 'kin groups'. If relatedness is not necessarily implied it is better to refer to them as 'bond groups', as Cynthia Moss does.

A still higher level of organization seems apparent among elephants during the dry season. While searching for elephants at this time of year I noticed that if I came across a herd in an area there would almost invariably be many other herds nearby. At the same time, there were other areas that were practically free of elephants. In other words, elephants distinctly congregate in certain places. Each of these clusters, made up of several elephant families, seemed to represent a 'clan', as has been described of some African elephant populations.

In my study area each aggregation had between 50 and 200 animals. To the north, the clan I named after Champaca, ranged over the moist deciduous forests of the BRT Sanctuary. Meenakshi's clan, meanwhile, occupied a more central location in the Araikadavu valley. From density estimates in the valley during the dry months I figured out that about 125 elephants made up her clan. A much smaller clan was seen to the west near Talamalai. A large aggregation of some 200 to 300 elephants occurred early during the dry season to the south in the Moyar valley and the jungles around Bennari, though there may have been more than one clan there. Another clan ranged to the east in the vicinity of Gaddesal. There were thus five or more clans which used my study area at least part of the year. Indeed, the families constituting a clan seemed to be broadly co-ordinated in their seasonal movements. The home ranges of adjoining clans did overlap to some extent, though not necessarily during the same season.

These clans were part of the larger population of over 5000 elephants that range over the Nilgiris and the Eastern Ghats.

Unlike female elephants, who remain with their families even as they grow older, the male elephants leave their families when they are on the threshold of sexual maturity, usually between the age of ten and fifteen years. The process of separation is a gradual one. The young, maturing bull spends more and more time away from its family, either alone or in the company of other young bulls, until it has for all practical purposes separated from its family.

One young male in Tara's family, which I named Dancing Bull (because of his peculiar manner of shuffling sideways whenever he saw me), seemed in the process of breaking away from his family in 1982 when he was an estimated thirteen years old. One of Meenakshi's sons, who was invariably attached to her during 1981 and 1982, was not seen with the family in 1983, when he would have been about eleven years old. Although I have never seen it happen, others have reported that the adolescent bull may even be physically pushed out of the family by its mother.

In terms of the survival of the species, it would be adaptive for the members of one sex to leave the family into which they were born and to go elsewhere to breed. This would lessen the chances of close relatives mating and producing children. Inbreeding can have many undesirable consequences. The offspring have greater chances of inheriting genetic defects, while the population suffers a loss of its genetic diversity.

After leaving their families, the bulls wander on their own or seek the company of other bulls. There is no evidence from any study on elephants to indicate that associations of two or more bulls are anything but temporary. No special bonds seem to be formed by the bulls in an all-male group although, as I had observed earlier, two or more bulls may associate for up to a month at a time for raiding agricultural fields.

Most of the adult bulls I saw in the jungle moved alone. There were very few times I saw two bulls together and just once I saw three young bulls keeping each other company. The large bull groups described of many African elephant populations did not occur. This was partly because there were, relative to the total population, far fewer adult bulls in my study area, ivory poaching having eliminated many of them. Even in Sri Lanka, George McKay had observed bull groups of up to seven animals. The males here, which were mostly tuskless and, therefore, immune to ivory poaching, constituted a much larger proportion of the total population than do those in southern India.

Adult bulls join the family groups temporarily for mating with oestrous cows. Here again there is no evidence that a bull always associates with a particular family group. The associations are opportunistic and depend upon other factors, such as dominance hierarchies among bulls or even the choice of the cows. The adult bulls spend 20 to 25 per cent of their time on average with family groups.

Since male elephants cannot 'recognize' their children, they show no interest in taking care of the young. The opposite is true of families. The members of a family form very intimate bonds. Mother–child ties are the strongest, but close bonds do exist among all the members. Not only the mother but also her sisters and older siblings participate in the care of the young. If an adult cow does not have a young calf of her own she may even allow another's calf to suckle, an act termed as 'allo-mothering'. Such altruistic behaviour would be in an animal's own self-interest. By helping a close relative, with whom it shares a significant proportion of genes to survive and reproduce, the seemingly altruistic individual also ensures that copies of its own genes are passed on to the next generation. This argument, known as kin selection, was first explained in clear mathematical terms by biologist W. D. Hamilton in 1964.

Elephants have evolved a complex and sensitive system of social interaction. Members of a family or bond group communicate through touch, sound, and scent. It is common to see elephants rubbing their bodies or pressing their foreheads against each other, placing their trunks into each others' mouths, intertwining trunks, or just going into a huddle. Such interactions may occur in different contexts—when sub-units of a joint family or bond group meet after a temporary separation, when the animals are in a playful mood, or when they are under some stress. These interactions reinforce the social bonds.

When elephants are under stress they may seek reassurance through touch. A common expression of nervousness is seen when a younger elephant goes up to an adult cow, entwines trunks with her and places the tip of its trunk in her mouth. On 7 April Meenakshi's family seemed unusually nervous as it crossed the road to go down to the Araikadavu river near Karapallam. Along with the family were Meenakshi's sister Tara and her younger children.

9.05 a.m.: The elephants cross the road facing me with their trunks lifted. After they reach the other side they are still bunched together. Meenakshi is in front with one of her adult daughters to her right. The old cow, who could be her sister, is behind. Her daughter places the tip of her trunk in Meenakshi's mouth. Meenakshi reciprocates. After a few minutes the herd turns around to go to the Araikadavu. Meenakshi now goes up to her sister and places her trunk in the latter's mouth.

Elephants also use a rich variety of sounds to communicate. A low rumble seems to be used for making contact at short distances, while a full-throated roar may be used for calls over longer distances. The latter can be more commonly heard during late evenings or night when sub-groups of a large family may wish to come together.

A series of short squeaks that can be rendered, 'kook, kook, kook...' seems to indicate a state of conflict plus, perhaps, an alarm signal. I have commonly heard this call when I have surprised an elephant when it has strayed from the rest of the herd or when it has retreated after a half-hearted charge. A more determined charge may be accompanied by a shrill trumpet. An elephant making a threat display may scrape its foot on the ground, at the same time hitting the ground sharply with the tip of its trunk, which produces a booming sound not unlike that of a muffled explosion.

The most intriguing of elephant vocalizations is the throbbing, '*phut, phut, phut...*' like the sound of a motorcycle. As I previously mentioned, I really did mistake this sound for a motorcycle when the Karapallam Bull was coming up from behind my back! Recent research indicates that this is merely the audible part of an infrasonic vocalization.

An early as 1972 the Indian naturalist M. Krishnan stated that elephants may communicate at sound frequencies that may not be fully audible to humans. He had variously described these sounds as 'throaty, hardly audible', 'low-pitched but clearly audible from a distance', and 'a throbbing purr'. These are very apt descriptions of the phenomenon. Unfortunately, he did not have the necessary instruments to record and analyze the sound frequencies.

It was left to Katharine Payne and her associates working at the Washington Park Zoo in Portland, Oregon, to record and precisely characterize infrasound. While observing Asian elephants at the zoo one day in May 1984 she sensed a throbbing sound that puzzled her. Later the thought occurred to her that it may have come from the elephants, which could be communicating among themselves with calls that the human ear is incapable of hearing. She had been trained in music and had earlier worked on infrasonic communication in whales. With the aid of recording instruments she confirmed that certain calls of elephants have frequencies that may be as low as 14 hertz. A human with perfect hearing can catch sounds from 20 hertz upwards to about 20,000 hertz; those living amidst the din of modern civilization can probably only hear sounds above 30 or 40 hertz.

The discovery of infrasound among elephants opened up entirely new vistas for investigation. The remarkable co-ordination in movements of related families of a clan could now be explained. A cow in oestrus could silently advertise her condition to bulls in the surrounding area and they would come flocking to court her. By means of experiments, Katharine Payne and her associates actually found this to be true of African elephants in the wild.

This discovery also raised other disturbing questions. Could an elephant herd which was being hunted, either during official culling or by poachers, communicate the message of death to other herds in the region?

Infrasound could perhaps be even more important as a means of communication to the forest-dwelling Asian elephant or the African forest elephant than it is to the savannah-dwelling African bush elephant. Infrasound can travel long distances through forest without attenuation. The same would not be true of scent in dense forest. This could provide a clue as to why the temporal glands of the female Asian elephant do not seem to secrete temporin, that serves as an agent of communication, as do the African savannah elephants'. This communication function of the temporal glands could have either been lost in the course of evolution or not have developed sufficiently in the forest-dwelling Asian species. Actually, as I have mentioned earlier, they do secrete occasionally, and this could be because the populations I have observed in southern India live in habitats that are relatively open, like the savannahs of Africa. The crucial evidence as regards this will come from further studies on the African forest elephant, a sub-species whose biology and ecology is very poorly known.

The elephant family is superbly geared to confront any predator other than man. The older elephants are too big to be seriously challenged by even the largest predator such as the tiger, though the juveniles are certainly vulnerable. Indeed, elephant calves are known to fall prey to tigers. To protect the young ones the older cows in the family make up a formidable defense—offense system. When any danger confronts the young ones the cows can be very aggressive indeed.

A herd may also be agitated by even a small predator such as the dhole or Indian wild dog that hunts in packs of four to eight animals. One morning in August 1982, Tara and four others of her family were standing out on the rocky bed of the Araikadavu, sucking up water from a small pool. The monsoon had failed to live up to its promise during the previous two months and the elephants were in poor condition. Tara's bones stuck out through her skin and her temples bulged prominently. The animals were quite listless as they stood out in the open under a fierce sun. After drinking for a while, Tara put up her trunk in the air, testing the breeze. She became quite agitated, scraping the rocks with her feet and making low growling noises. The herd bunched together, with the calf secure in between the larger cows. I first thought they were agitated after getting my smell, but a few minutes later a pack of five dholes emerged out from the jungle. The elephants wheeled around to face the dogs and even took a few steps forward, but the dogs just turned direction and vanished. They were certainly not after the elephants!

It would be rare to observe a direct confrontation between elephants and a large predator such as the tiger; in most places where tigers can be easily seen in India, such as at the Kanha or Ranthambore national parks, elephants are absent, while in areas where elephants are abundant, the tiger is elusive. One outstanding place for observing both the species together is the Nagarhole National Park. I was once fortune enough to witness the interaction of elephant and tiger in the company of wildlife biologist Ullas Karanth, who was studying tigers and leopards at Nagarhole.

Ullas and I were sitting up one of his favourite watch-towers located some 200 metres away from a water-hole. At about 3.00 p.m. a herd of elephants made its appearance at the pond.

'Oh', groaned Ullas, 'your elephants are a positive nuisance! They will keep my tigers away.' However badly I wanted to see a tiger, I could not but disagree.

The elephants did not sojourn for long, but departed after drinking only a few trunkfuls and without even bathing. Soon another herd of nine elephants entered the water and they too came out and huddled together amidst the bamboo clumps, some of them trumpeting half-heartedly. Only a young male, about five years old, still lingered in the water. We thought this to be rather strange as it was a hot day in March at the peak of the dry season. Added to this the spotted deer grazing nearby were sounding an alarm. Ullas was sure that a predator was close by. He knew these signs well.

At 3.25 p.m. Ullas suddenly grabbed his camera, whispering excitedly, 'Tiger!' Sure enough, a large tiger walked up to the edge of the pond in full daylight. The young tusker, who was still drinking, rushed out in alarm upon seeing the tiger. The other elephants did not seem unduly worried as they could now actually see the predator. The tiger did not seem to relish the idea of a sauna with the elephants nearby and quickly disappeared into the jungle.

For once Ullas had not brought along his radio-tracking gear, as he was not expecting one of his collared tigers to be present at that place and, in the excitement, neither of us had noticed whether or not the tiger had a collar or not. In frustration Ullas went back to the camp to pick up his equipment. When he returned half an hour later along with K. M. Chinnappa, the indefatigable Ranger of

Nagarhole, he confirmed that the tiger was Das, one of his collared males, for whom we had been searching without success for that entire morning.

At 6.15 p.m., when the pond was free of elephants, Das returned to sink into the warm, relaxing water. Chinnappa could not resist getting down from the tower and sneaking up to the pond through a circuitous path that ran through the jungle. After ten minutes or so Das turned around and began paddling, as if he wanted to come out of the water.

'Watch out, he is going to charge at someone', whispered Ullas. Seconds later, a bull elephant, not more than fifteen years old, charged into the water and Das in sheer frustration turned around to beat a hasty retreat. Upon reaching the edge of the pond all that Chinnappa saw was the elephant drinking victoriously.

The defence–offense behaviour of an elephant herd towards a predator resembles its reaction to a perceived threat from people. The elements of aggression can be described in the classical terms of conflict behaviour: threat display, displacement activity, redirected aggression, attack, and retreat. When an elephant smells or hears humans its immediate reaction is to suspend all activity for a while and to concentrate on locating the source of disturbance. The trunk may be half-raised and the tip moved in an arc to detect the direction of the scent. The ears stop flapping and are held half or fully extended. In most instances, the entire herd retreats in the opposite direction. On occasion, an elephant may approach the source of the stimulus in an aroused state even without seeing a person.

Makhna was a particularly aggressive bull who charged practically every time he saw me or even when he smelt me. On one occasion he had finished a bath and was rubbing himself against a tree on the farther side of the Karapallam pond as I watched him from behind a bush.

The wind was unfortunately carrying my scent towards him. While still rubbing himself, he put up his trunk to get the direction of my scent. Though he had certainly not seen me, without warning he ran around the pond towards me, trumpeting twice only after crossing over. I had retreated to my jeep and was moving away where Makhna burst out into the open. At the same time a bus was coming along the road in the opposite direction. The bigger object caught Makhna's attention and he ran straight towards the bus, which managed to squeeze past him as he came up to the road. Frustrated he began a typical 'displacement activity' of dusting himself in an exaggerated fashion with soil. Finally he went over to a large tamarind tree to resume the activity he was originally engaged in, that of rubbing his hind leg against the trunk, before heading back to the pond.

When an elephant notices a person there may follow a period of conflict. A nervous elephant may place the tip of its trunk inside its mouth or, if a tusker, drape it over its tusks. Elephants may seek reassurance from one another through trunk or body contacts. The elephant may then stage a mild threat display by fully extending its ears so as to appear even larger, swing its trunk rhythmically, shake its head, or sway its whole body. It may scrape the ground in conjunction with displacement activities, such as gathering mud and grass with its trunk and throwing it over its body. Sometimes the displacement activity takes the form of a rapid feeding upon grass.

An agitated elephant may run a few paces first towards and then away from the enemy, making trumpeting sounds, in an attempt to scare the intruder. If this fails it may launch a more serious attack—a mock charge culminating in an impressive display within a short distance from the enemy.

It is not always the largest female elephant or matriarch that puts on this threat display; very often it is a younger cow in the herd. I have generally found the oldest and most experienced cows to be relatively calm, while sub-adult cows were often more agitated and charged.

An elephant may even charge without any warning or threat display. During a determined charge the trunk is coiled inwards and the ears held back close to the neck. For all its seeming clumsiness, an elephant can run pretty fast. I have clocked a charging cow on my jeep's speedometer at about thirty kilometres per hour, although it cannot sustain this speed for long (an olympic sprinter completing 100 metres in ten seconds is doing only 36 kilometres per hour). Considering that an elephant can bulldoze its way through bushes, even an athlete would be hard pressed to outrun a determined elephant over short distances.

At the end of a charge an elephant spreads out its ears and unfurls its trunk, delivering a sledge-hammer-like blow to any object unfortunate enough to be close by. There is considerable variation in vocalization during a charge. A charge may begin and end in complete silence. On occasion there is a warning trumpet before the charge, but more often a shrill trumpet is let out either during or at the end of the charge.

If an elephant decides to retreat after a charge, it turns sharply to one side with its head raised and its tail up, and moves away at a tangent, keeping the enemy in view until it reaches a safe distance. It may then enter into a phase of 'redirected aggression' by thrashing the bushes or breaking a branch from a tree. One cow even broke a dried branch from a fallen tree and flung it in my direction.

Actual physical contact with a vehicle is rare, although this possibility must be always borne in mind. It is wise not to fool around with a three-ton missile which is programmed to seek out and destroy you. A five-ton missile armed with a gleaming pair of weapons, the tusks, can be even more lethal. In the northeastern Indian state of Arunachal Pradesh, an army truck was once pushed off a mountainside by a tusker, resulting in many casualties.

What do you do if you are faced with an angry elephant? If you are on a steep slope, it is better to run down hill as the elephant will be afraid of losing its footing. If there is a ditch sufficiently deep, the best course would be to quickly get across it. As a last resort, an elephant may even stop if you shout loudly. Many of these rules, of course, break down when an elephant is actually chasing you. Then all that one can think of is to merely run away.

I have known of cases where, upon running away from an elephant, the people have fallen down and, expecting, to be crushed at any moment, have found to their surprise that the elephant stops near to them and proceeds to cover them with mud and leaves, burying them with due honour! Arun Chandrasekhar, a young wildlife enthusiast from Mysore, had a remarkable escape after being attacked by an elephant in Kerala's Parambikulam Sanctuary in February 1983. After observing an adult bull for several hours from the safety of a watch-tower, he came down in the evening to return to his camp. The bull noticing him charged, caught up with him and lashed out with its trunk. When Arun fell down the bull retreated and stood some distance away. After regaining his senses Arun, who had fractured a collar bone, managed to crawl up to the watch-tower. Fortunately for him, a jeep with some officials soon came by and put him on a bus to Coimbatore. Here he contacted Tilaka and Theodore Baskaran, keen naturalists whose house was a favourite meeting place for all wildlifers in the region, and with their help was admitted to hospital. The very next day the same bull killed a man from the local tribal settlement.

This behaviour of 'burying' the dead has also been described in the African elephant. Elephants are especially curious about the bones of dead elephants and will examine them, pick them up with their trunks and even carry them off some distance. Sometimes they pile up leaves and mud over a carcass. There are also anecdotes about cow elephants standing guard over their dead calves or even carrying the carcass around for several days. We have no reason to disbelieve these accounts. Concern for the dead is not solely a human prerogative. The elephant is a remarkably sensitive creature.

The significance of this behaviour has been a puzzle to elephant observers. I think a perfectly rational explanation is available. I base this upon a brilliant deduction that one of my graduate students, Milind Watve, made with regard to burial behaviour among humans. Milind was actually tackling the question of why tigers indulge in man-eating in certain regions. He approached it by asking the opposite and more relevant question as to why tigers and other predators do not kill many more people than they actually do; after all humans are pretty frail creatures. He reasoned that it was because humans retrieve and bury the dead. It would be a waste of a tiger's energy if it were to spend time in killing people only to find that it was not possible to consume the carcass at leisure without it being taken away by other people. The earliest evidence of burial among humans is seen in the Neanderthals about 70,000 years ago. Once this practice spread it was no more very attractive for predators to kill people. Primitive humans had taken a giant step in freeing themselves from the continual fear of being preyed upon by large beasts. Where man-eating occurs at present times, it is usually in remote places such as the Sundarbans, where dead people cannot be retrieved easily, or in places where 'modern' state laws make it imperative that people wait for the police to arrive before removing a dead person killed by a tiger in the jungle, thereby providing an opportunity for the animal to completely devour the carcass. Man-eating, or avoidance behaviour, in predators could be culturally passed on from one generation to the next.

It is, therefore, reasonable to think that the behaviour of elephants guarding carcasses or attempting to bury them is adaptive. Although a tiger (or a lion) cannot bring down an adult elephant, it can certainly cause panic in a herd sufficient to allow it to grab a young calf that would provide it with meat for several days. However, the fact that adult cow elephants refuse to easily leave a dead calf behind and to move on makes it unattractive for tigers to prey upon elephant calves in the first place. The behaviour of inspecting carcasses or picking up the bones of a dead relative reinforces the strong social bonds that exist among elephants of a family. In the course of evolution such behaviours that improve the chances of survival of a creature would have no doubt been favoured.

The family setting is thus indispensable for the normal growth and development of the young elephants. Within the family, the calves are protected, nourished, nurtured, and taught the rules of living. At birth the calf is a pretty helpless creature and needs all the help it can get from the elders in the family.

To follow the development of various behaviours over time in a particular elephant calf in the wild would be a rather tall order, unless one were to radio-track a family. I had to be content with making casual observations on the behaviour of calves of different ages. Around the time I was beginning intensive work at Hasanur, my colleague Vijayakumaran Nair was concluding a study on the development of behaviour and calf-mother relationships in captive elephants held in the forest camps at Bandipur and Mudumalai. I have drawn upon his observations to fix the precise age at which different behaviours appear.

The first few days after birth the calf walks with an unsteady gait, keeping close to its mother, searching between the mother's legs for its source of milk. When it does find a nipple, it suckles briefly for a minute or two. The herd is considerably slowed down by the calf, for it rests frequently with its mother. Sometimes others stand guard and provide shade. Although unable to pick up anything, the calf inspects its surroundings with curiosity, touching objects with its trunk and placing the tip in its mouth.

After a week, the calf is bold enough to enter a pond along with the rest of the herd. It cannot yet suck in water with its trunk but drinks directly through the mouth. The rubbery, flexible trunk is a source of puzzle to the young calf and one of amusement to the human observer. Wriggling it about, twisting it around in the air, placing the tip in its mouth or even tripping over it, as yet the calf seems unsure of what to do with it.

Mother and calf stick close to each other, in continual contact with each other through their trunks. The mother reassures her baby by running her trunk over its body or by placing it near the calf's mouth. When Vijayakumaran tabulated the various activities of a calf and its mother, he noticed that much of their contact was seemingly irrelevant. In some eighty per cent of cases there was no clear, immediate function that could be attributed to the exchanges between the calf and its mother.

Madhav had a simple explanation for this: the contact was a calf's way of letting its mother know that it was in fine health and a mother's way of confirming that this was indeed true. Human analogies immediately spring to one's mind. A listless child is signalling that it is in need of medical attention. Similarly, an elephant calf that is not fidgety enough may be indicating to its mother that she should slow down her pace of movement, provide it with shade and rest, or pour water over its body.

When the calf is a month old, it can pull up small herbs from the ground but, although it tries to, it is unable to uproot grass clumps. It is able to collect soil with its trunk and throws this under its body. By now it sometimes leaves its mother for short periods. It goes up to other members of the herd, often juveniles, not losing the opportunity to grasp their tails or to climb over them when they are lying down.

At between two and three months of age, the calf is totally at ease in water. It may even rush ahead of the rest of the group into a pond. While bathing the calf immerses itself completely underwater, sucks in water and blows it out of its trunk, and even clambers onto other elephants. The calf still stays close to the other members of the herd, quickly disappearing between their legs at the slightest hint of any danger.

By six months, various other elements of behaviour appear. The calf can manœuvre its trunk sufficiently to blow out water on to its back and sides. It can pluck tender grass or green leaves from shrubs and eat them. Curious about any intruders, such as cattle, it will now go forward a few steps, making a low rumbling sound and spreading its ears, a hint of the full-blown threat display which will develop in later years. However, for the moment, if the opponent retaliates, it will quickly retreat to the safety of the herd.

Before its first birthday it is able to feed to a limited extent on the leaves of most plants. It can pluck the leaves of bamboo, even holding a branch down with its foot, while feeding. Using its front foot to scrap the ground, it collects soil with its trunk for throwing over its body. It may even uproot small clumps of grass, beating them against its legs before eating them. Nevertheless, it depends on its mother for much of its nourishment. When a herd is slowly moving though the jungle foraging, the calf may wander away towards other older juveniles in order to play. Standing 120 centimetres (4 feet) tall, an increase of a foot from its height at birth, the one year old fits exactly beneath the belly of its mother. This is a useful guide to identifying calves below one year of age in the field. Its weight has increased from about 120 kilograms at birth to about 330 kilograms at one year.

During the second year of its life the juvenile is on its way to becoming nutritionally independent. Its ability to pull, twist, and tear plant parts increases substantially. It becomes adept at co-ordinating its trunk and front feet in order to remove soil from grass clumps. It is increasingly playful with its peers and elders in the herd. Butting, pushing, chasing, wrestling with the trunk, pulling another's tail, rushing forward threateningly, the juvenile is an endearing little rogue.

The significance of play in the normal development of behaviour in an animal has been realized only in recent years. Play experiences accelerate the development of the brain and nervous system, which in turn control various behaviours. In higher social mammals the role of learning in the development of behaviour is well known. Cognitive and motor skills, used in interacting with other individuals and with the environment, are sharpened. Play helps in the recognition of kin and the formation of social bonds which will come in useful in later life. In short, play prepares a young animal with the experience and skills that might one day be vital for its very survival when confronted with the unexpected.

A two year old elephant stands about 137 centimetres tall and weighs about 500 kilograms. In a male elephant, the tusks just stick out from below the lip line. The budding tusks can be seen up to six months earlier, but only if the trunk is lifted up, as when feeding. This is again a useful clue when aging elephants in the field.

Analysing the large amount of data I had on elephants born in captivity, I found that there is no difference between male and female calves as to their average height at birth or in their growth rates during the first two years of life. The pattern may, of course, be somewhat different in wild calves. In any case, in captivity the juvenile males clearly begin to outgrow the females from the third year onwards.

The juvenile males begin to explore the world on their own much earlier than do the young females. The young male also seems more intolerant of real or imaginary enemies. My observations one evening in April 1982 illustrate this point.

Meenakshi and Appu are drinking from a small pool in the Araikadavu. A flock of common mynahs also compete for the moisture. Appu rushes at the mynahs with low growls and chases them away.

The young males also interact among themselves more intensely than do the young females. I do not have quantified data to prove this, but it appears as though the young males organize mini-conferences while the rest of the herd rest or feed. On these occasions, two or three juvenile males get into a huddle a short distance away from the others and begin a session of play.

On the morning of 15 August 1982, I was observing Kali's joint family of nine elephants at the Araikadavu. The elephants were having a difficult time obtaining water, as only stagnant pools now graced the Araikadavu. The animals appeared to be in surprisingly poor shape for the peak of the wet season. This was rather disturbing. If the elephants did not have sufficient energy reserves now, how would they fare in the coming months?

The herd was around a bend in the stream, so Setty and I crept up close to them behind bamboo clumps. The warm smell of elephant mixed with that of wet soil wafted back to us as we watched them try to extract some moisture from the dry stream bed. My notes were as follows.

There is now no flowing water in the Araikadavu. The elephants are facing away from me. They are digging holes in the sandy bed. One large cow uses both a forward and a backward kick to make the hole. Simultaneously it uses its trunk to suck up the muddy water and with a forward flick spray it over the ground. After doing this a few times it drinks from the hole. Once it also sprays the muddy fluid onto its small calf, which appears to be not more than a couple of weeks old. I wonder whether it will survive the drought.

The drought has not dampened the spirits of the young tuskers. Three young males (three years old) move about twenty metres away from the rest and begin to wrestle using their trunks. One male goes back but the other two persist in their play. Now the small calf comes up to them and sprawls between them in the sand.

After being unaware of my presence for half an hour, the large cow put up its trunk and got our scent. She made a low rumbling sound and all the other elephants ran up to her. The entire herd immediately turned and silently came up the path from where we were watching them. By now we had retreated. When they reached the spot where we had stood they stopped for a moment and then veered away into the bushes.

Play-fighting intensifies as the males grow older. From simple butting or wrestling using its trunk, the play changes to a test of their relative strengths in pushing with locked tusks or even in the clash of ivory. It is rare, however, for a sub-adult animal to be injured. Through play-fighting an animal learns its strengths and weaknesses relative to other males in the population. Later on in life this may help in determining a male's position in the social hierarchy. When the stage is set for a serious clash, the earlier experiences acquired during play-fighting could possibly help prevent the fight from becoming fatal; a male would realize when to retreat from a more dominant opponent.

As the youngsters grow, they have tremendous scope for learning behaviour from elders in the herd. At birth an elephant calf's brain weighs only 35 per cent of what it will ultimately weigh during adulthood. The lessons learnt during growth are quickly assimilated—which plants can be eaten; when to migrate to the valley lush with bamboo; what to do when threatened by a predator; how to behave when pursued by an ardent bull. The importance of what is learnt by experience and how this interacts with the elephant's genetic make-up can be understood from the variety of behavioural responses seen among elephants. Each elephant is different from every other elephant, not only by virtue of its distinctive genes, but also because it has undergone unique experiences in life.

As more members are added to the family, as the adolescent males depart, as the elephants grow old and die, the family takes on a new look. Once a grandmother dies it is time for her daughters to go their own ways with their own respective families, though they still meet and socialize.

Potentially, a cow elephant can live up to eighty years of age or so. In the wild this age may be only very rarely attained because an elephant would normally die of starvation much earlier on, once all its teeth are worn out.

An elephant develops six sets of molar teeth on either side of their lower and upper jaws during its lifetime. The teeth do not all appear at the same time but do so progressively as the animal ages and the previous teeth are worn out. At any given time there are usually no more than two sets of teeth in use. The teeth appearing later in life are larger, are made up of more lamellae and last longer.

A calf is born with its first molars, called Molars I and II. Molar I is shed quite early on, between the age of one and two years. Molar II lasts until it is five or six years old. By this time Molar III is already in use and lasts until it is eleven or thirteen. Molar IV appears by the time it is nine and is worn out by the time it is twenty-five. Molar V erupts at thirteen years of age and lasts until it is anywhere between forty and fifty years old. Molar VI is the last one to appear, at the age of thirty to thirty-five, and lasts into old age. For the Asian elephant in the wild the last set of teeth seems to last until seventy years of age, or rarely, even longer.

By this age the old elephant seeks the relative security of a river or pond where it can feed on succulent plants and be ensured of adequate water. This tendency for elephants to die near water has no doubt given rise to the myth of elephant graveyards.

Going through my records of over a thousand elephants which were born in captivity or captured in southern India since the late nineteenth century, I found that a cow named Peri holds the record for longevity. She was captured in North Malabar on 11 April 1889, when she was at least 20 years old, and died on 9 December 1948 at the age of 79 years. In more recent years the captive cow Tara, who died on 28 April 1989 at 75 years, came close to breaking this record. One of Tara's long-standing companions in the camp at Mudumalai, the cow Godavari, also only just failed to break Peri's record.

Tara was captured on 15 April 1935 at Mudumalai and spent most of her life there. She was one of the most gentle of all elephants. Perhaps, as she spent the nights inside the jungle, her freedom hobbled, she sometimes met and socialized with her mother and sisters, or even introduced one of her dozen children to them. I wonder whether she ever yearned to be free like them.

In May 1982 M. A. Partha Sarathy came with a film crew to shoot a film on elephants for Indian television. They had only a few days to spare in my study area. By that time Meenakshi's clan had dispersed from the Araikadavu valley and it was difficult to get good sightings of the herds. So I took the team up to Kyatedevaragudi where Champaca's clan would still be coming to the pond. Even if no herds came, I knew that Biligiri would not disappoint them. He was a visitor almost round the year.

After driving around the jungles we took up position near the pond. I kept a sharp lookout while the crew relaxed, relating to them stories of all my wonderful sightings here to keep up their interest. After a couple of hours and no elephants, the crew was getting a bit impatient. Just as the cameraman began suggesting that we should perhaps pack up and move elsewhere, I noticed a flash of white moving among the trees. Biligiri climbed down the bund into the water, as I dramatically urged the crew to swing into action. Actually, there was no need for hurry as Biligiri was usually very relaxed.

Two months later Madhav [Professor Madhav Gadgil] visited me for a few days and we went around inspecting the damage to crops in the villages and trying to locate elephants. This time several herds appeared at Kyatedevaragudi. The herds remained in the now lush jungle until the end of August, when all of a sudden they made a bee-line south towards Punjur. As during the previous year the ripening *ragi* crop attracted the elephants' attention. This year, however, much of the crop had withered due to the poor rains and the elephants did not have the glorious feast they had had in 1981; though the patterns of raiding were similar to those of 1981, the monetary value of damaged crops was far less.

A solution had to be found to the problem of crop depredation. In November, the Asian Elephant Specialist Group arranged for a visit by Robert Piesse, an expert on electric fencing from Australia. I took him around my study villages to show the extent and circumstances of elephant incursion into cultivation. He explained to me the design of the high voltage electric fence that could 'knock the shit out of an elephant' coming into contact with the wire, yet not harm the animal in any way. He was confident that a combination of the fence and beeper that gave a high frequency sound would be sufficient.

In December 1982 an international workshop on elephant management was held at Jaldapara Sanctuary in West Bengal state of eastern India. The workshop was very creatively organized with

'live' demonstrations of elephant capture, care, training, and control. There was even a simulated *kheddah* complete with a drive into
a stockade. The workshop was attended by researchers and field
managers from all over the world. This was a wonderful opportunity
for me to exchange notes with so many other elephant people.

Cynthia Moss, who had been working for over a decade on
African elephants, was there too and gave a graphic presentation of
her Amboseli experiences. She described the intense greeting
ceremonies elephants of the same family indulge in when they meet
after even a temporary separation. She also outlined how elephant
society is organized—into families, bond groups, and clans—the
last level being obvious from the dry-season aggregation of
elephants. I was particularly thrilled to receive this last bit of
information; my own observations over the past two years having
been vindicated.

I returned to Hasanur to find that the elephants faced a grim year
ahead. In 1982 only about half the normal quantity of rain had
fallen over the study area. The elephants had so far managed... but
how would they cope with the dry spell that now loomed?

Extracted from Elephant Days and Nights, Ten Years With the Indian
Elephant *(Delhi: Oxford University Press, 1994).*

ZAFAR FUTEHALLY

Let Nature Take Its Course

Zafar Futehally is a businessman by profession and an active ornithologist and conservationist. From the 1950s onwards, he contributed regularly to newspaper articles on wildlife. The habits of mynas, the beak-structure of the skimmer, an account of a sanctuary he visited: these are a sample of the topics he covered in The Times of India *and* The Indian Express. *He also edits a bird-watchers newsletter that often proves how natural history, like astronomy is as open to the 'amateur' as 'the professional'. Futehally was also a senior office-bearer of both the Bombay Natural History Society and the World Wildlife Fund. His piece on the Anamalai preserve in Tamil Nadu included here reflects his concern about the natural flora being replaced by teak monoculture plantations.*

A visit to any sanctuary or National Park in India enables one to reflect on the difference between the healthy quality of the vegetation, and soil within a preserve area with that of the degraded over-exploited environment outside. In fact, one of the motivating factors for the establishment of natural reserves at the international level has been the felt need for having such areas as bench-marks to enable a comparison between the productivity and related aspects of natural as compared to exploited environments.

It must be said, however, that very few of our sanctuaries have a natural aspect. Many have been exploited extensively in the past by the Forest Department, and continue to be exploited even today. The complex of natural vegetation has been altered drastically, and hence one of the purposes for which National Park and sanctuaries are created, which is to preserve the original environment and to enable us to understand the workings of natural ecosystems, is not fulfilled under these circumstances.

For example, in the Anamalai Sanctuary, the lower reaches of the mountains have been planted with Eucalyptus, a native of Australia which should have no place in an Indian Sanctuary. In fact, because of the high demands of this tree and its inordinate consumption of ground water, and because of the inhospitable environment it provides for our wildlife, its monoculture is now being discouraged on ecological grounds, though because of its quick growth it is much favoured by wood based industries. The Sanctuary was so designated in 1973, but this has not reduced timber exploitation. The Forest Department officials are proud that the Sanctuary yielded a revenue of almost Rs 60 lakhs per year, and they are of the opinion that it is possible to continue with this exploitation, and at the same time to fulfil the objectives for which the National Park movement has been initiated.

The Anamalai Sanctuary is the largest one in Tamilnadu, and has an area of over 900 sq kms. Rising from the foothills where the elevation is just 350 metres above sea level, it ascends to a height of 2,400 metres, and encompasses within its range seven former reserved forests which consist of such extreme examples as the thorn forests of the plains and the temperate forests of the high mountains. The difference of temperatures and humidity between the base and the high elevation indicate the diversity of the flora and fauna of this reserve. In the foothills the night temperature rarely descends below 18 degrees C while in the higher reaches temperatures of below freezing point are not uncommon.

The Parambikulam-Aliyur project of Kerala adjoins this Sanctuary of Tamilnadu, and the two States have co-operated extremely well toward maintaining this extensive area in the Anamalai in as natural a condition as possible commensurate with the timber extraction which is allowed to go on.

Environmentalists would have liked to see this whole range covered with natural evergreen species of trees of the type which still exists in the famous Karian Shola near Topslip, where the rest houses are located. But these natural Sholas which have very high value but no price are being replaced by monocultures of teak and other trees whose worth can be measured in terms of money. It was here that recently a log of rose-wood was sold for Rs 2 lakhs to a

Japanese firm, and one cubic metre of the same species fetched the record price of Rs 47,000. Impressive though these figures are, it might be remembered that the total revenue from forests in Tamilnadu is only 1.1 per cent of the total revenue of the State so that if this revenue was forgone, and the foresters followed the Prime Minister's advice not to exploit the forest to the last rupee, but to consider its ecological functions, the State of Tamilnadu would perhaps be happier on the whole.

Incidentally, the range secured the name of Topslip because in the early years of the century teak logs were pushed over the edge and allowed to slip down to the valley from where they were transported to the shipyards of Bombay. This procedure must have damaged vegetation very seriously, and in fact careful removal of timber from within a forest has to be done in a very scientific manner, otherwise the destruction of the neighbouring vegetation causes a greater loss than the gain from the amount of timber recovered by selective felling. Even today, when selective felling is undertaken in evergreen forests only four or five trees are removed per acre, and because of the considerations listed above it has been suggested by conservationists that this policy should be discontinued.

Though monocultures are monotonous, and have their drawbacks, the spectacle of an endless teak forest is nevertheless an impressive sight, and the broad leaves of these trees break the force of the heavy rain in the Western Ghat region, and minimize soil erosion. The other dominant trees of this Sanctuary are Tarminalias, Albizzias and bamboo, and these together with a large number of others forming the understory intermingle to prove an excellent jungle home for wild animals.

During my 24-hour stay in the sanctuary recently, I saw a wide variety of wildlife, and what was rather satisfying was that the animals did not panic at our approach which was an indication that poaching had been contained, and that they were confident that the visitors had nothing more deadly than cameras in their hands. Apparently some months ago a high ranking police officer was caught poaching by the Forest Department staff and a deterrent fine was imposed on him. This incident had received much publicity in the press.

The Topslip region is very good bison country, and we were able to see a herd of these magnificent animals which from time to time suffer so severely from rinderpest transmitted by domestic cattle. The inoculation of domestic cattle which is now being very effectively done by the Tamilnadu Government (particularly in areas in and around sanctuaries) should be a great boon to the bison population of South India. While out at night peering into the darkness, depending on spotlights to pick up the forms of wildlife, I saw three wild dogs on the road. Wild dogs are not essentially nocturnal hunters but obviously they relish a meal at night. The large population of blacknaped hare and sambar and chital which were around must keep these dogs well provided. As is the case in Bandipur, these animals make it a practice to come and sleep near the rest houses. Perhaps nearness to humanity gives them a little more protection from predators than being right out in the forest. This behaviour of chital in the Anamalai and Bandipur is an interesting subject for study by a wildlife biologist. Wild dogs are still considered *persona non grata* in many sanctuaries for their method of feeding on deer and antelope while the victims are still alive, arouses our deepest sympathies for the prey. But this is nature's way of keeping the herbivores in top condition by the elimination of the week and infirm. I do not know whether the wild dogs had anything to do with it, but the herd of chital which I saw were in excellent shape and consisted of several impressive males in hard horn.

The loud hooting of both the common and the Nilgiri langurs indicated that these animals were given adequate protection by the Forest staff. Because of its allegedly medicinal properties, the flesh of the Nilgiri langur has been greatly fancied by tribals and others. Their loud hoo-ha, hoo-ha, hoo once reverberated over large sections of the Western Ghats, but now they are confined to very small areas.

During the morning's walk, when I was out looking for birds I was able to see a beautiful specimen of the Malabar squirrel (Ratufa bicolor). With limbs outstretched, these arboreal dwellers can leap twenty feet from one branch to another and hardly ever need to come to the ground. 'Apparently, they share with monkeys the habit of scolding, barking and raising a general alarm.' But the one we saw exuded friendliness, allowed us to stare at it for quite a while, and gave us a fine demonstration of its aerobatic qualities.

Originally published in The Indian Express, *24 October 1976.*

ZAI WHITAKER

The Riddled Ridley

The Snake Park at Guindy has long been a major landmark in the city of Chennai. Since 1971 visitors have come to look at cobras and kraits, to learn about the beauty and significance of reptiles and amphibians. Zai Whitaker had not only married Rom, who founded the park, but also become an active partner in the myriad activities that mushroomed around it. By the end of the 1970s, they were breeding crocodiles, publishing a journal and helping focus on a neglected group of animals—turtles. The story is told in her book, Snakeman, Story of an Indian Naturalist.

Only our innate obsession with land-living animals blinds us to the great phenomenon of the sea turtle breeding grounds along the coast and the dangers that they face. The Gahirmata beach in Orissa is one of only four such breeding grounds in the world of the Olive Ridley turtle. It is as much of a natural treasure as the water-bird colony at Bharatpur or the forests of Bandipur.

'Typical female, cannot make up her mind,' said Rom as we tugged at our coats ineffectively against the cold January wind. This particular lady had kept us waiting a good forty minutes and seemed to be in no hurry to get through with her nesting duties. She had, with reptilian solemnity, dug three trial nest holes already and was now heading ponderously to a fourth site to the north. We flopped down on the sand and decided to forgive her since she was an endangered species.

We had been lucky that night. There had been times when we'd walked ten or fifteen kilometres to arrive at every turtle nest too late: to find the V track of its flippers emerging from and returning to the sea distorted by those of the commercial egg collector. Inspite of the fact that all sea turtle species found in India are on Schedule I of the Wildlife Protection Act, poachers continue to plunder their nests. A pointed wooden stick or iron rod is plunged around the apex of the turtle's tracks to locate eggs; the rest is easy and the clutch is transferred to a bag and hauled off to be sold at the market. Along the Madras coast, poachers are generally not fishermen but *cheri* villagers from inland, who with their simple weapons collect over two lakh eggs each season from the Madras coast alone. To the fisherman the sea turtle is a god and a fast disappearing one. 'If we don't welcome this sea goddess she will stop visiting us', said one old fisherman as he performed a brief *puja* on a ridley hurrying back down the sloped beach to the sea.

This night we'd walked on to the beach in front of our house 40 kilometres south of Madras city and instantly saw that unmistakable black shape heaving its 40 kgs up the steep tidal embankment. Our torch was quickly turned off to avoid disturbing her. Sea turtles, who come ashore only to nest, will at this stage seek the safety of the sea at the slightest disturbance. Once nesting begins it is another story: we have tried—in the interest of science of course—yodelling, sitting on her back, using bright floodlights and much more, but these human follies were appropriately ignored.

The hard to please lady has at last found a suitable spot where the sand, humidity and temperature predict a good building site. The digging begins. The two hind flippers alternately scoop out and fling away the sand, sometimes in our earnest faces, to a depth of 35 centimetres. This is a laborious process for an aquatic animal and is accompanied by grunts and whistles and frequent pauses for rest. Finally there is a prolonged interval of several minutes. Then the cloaca, suspended over the nest cavity, is extended and the first ping-pong ball sized egg falls in gently. It is followed by hundred and twenty others, coming singly or in twos or threes in quick succession. The laying process takes about half an hour and ends on a somewhat incredible note: the female ridley carefully wipes her cloaca with sand, apparently to camouflage her return to the sea from predators such as jackals and dogs, which use their noses to find nests. The hind flippers then begin working again going like bicycle pedals to cover the nest cavity with sand. Dr Archie Carr, comparing the ridley's nesting habits with those of other sea turtles, writes that 'the ridleys seemed more like over-wrought creatures searching for something lost than like turtles about the business of procreation.' The nest is now even with the beach.

But the most dramatic movements are yet to come. Having filled her nest hole, the mother sea turtle packs the sand in by thumping her massive shell from side to side. Tucking her head in, she throws her weight about to good effect. The beach has listened to this deep boom for over 100 million years and we have been impressed by it over a hundred times. Alarmed by results of our first surveys of the olive ridley on the Madras coast, when we found that 90 per cent of all eggs were being eaten by humans, dogs and jackals in that order, the Madras Snake Park began a conservation programme for this troubled turtle. Volunteers walked the stretch of beach between Madras and Mahabalipuram at night, often in uneasy competition with poachers and returned doubled over under the weight of one or more clutches of eggs (each clutch averaged 100 eggs and weighed about 3 kgs). These were then planted in fenced foster nests in a friend's garden for the 50 to 60 day incubation period. Around the time hatching was expected to begin, generally in early March, we could visit the hatchery every morning to transfer the miniature *idli* sized hatchlings to the sea. Often we did not come in time and Jean and Janine Delouche had to spend their morning taking a thousand turtles to the sea. Incredibly, we remain good friends.

Recent research in the United States and elsewhere has revealed a startling feature of sea turtle biology: that the sex of the turtle is determined in the egg, by temperature! Thus an unsophisticated conservation programme does not preclude the possibility of doing more harm than good, by producing an all male population if temperatures are kept too high.

Inspite of the sore feet and persistent images of hot coffee and bed, those turtle walks were our most enjoyable evening entertainment. We sometimes found ourselves at two in the morning, curled up in a fishing boat on a bundle of nets, out of the persistent wind. The bright moonlit nights were magical and on dark nights our feet sent up sprays of phosphorous as we walked along the edge of the waves. Even on nights when we saw not a single turtle or nest we were compensated by the sea. We became specialists in throwing stranded marine creatures back into the ocean: sea snakes, sting rays, jelly fish. One night we almost stepped on three sea snakes feebly thrashing around in the sand, gravity bound and on the verge of suffocation. We very kindly put them in a bucket of sea water and took them home. Inspite of Rom's 'precautions' they escaped in the bathroom during the night and one almost disappeared into the loo in the ensuing struggle to re-bucket them.

Another night we had a team from German television who wanted to film ridleys nesting. The first thing that happened was that we ran into two egg poachers busily collecting their booty as the turtle was laying. One of the crew, a fiery sea turtle enthusiast, pulled out his little pen knife and flourishing it, announced in German that they—the poachers—should be prosecuted. The egg collectors, taken aback and nicely topped with *arrack,* prepared for their answer with their sharp probing sticks. We were only able to prevent violence by a bit of treachery and explained to them in Tamil that the foreigner was slightly mad. Later the jeep carrying the filming equipment which had thus far held its own in the sand got firmly stuck and would not be persuaded to budge. The tide was coming in with a greedy energy and by the time the wheels shot forward they were almost submerged.

During the years that we 'did' sea turtles, close to a hundred adult females were tagged with special metal tags on the right front flipper and some 20,000 hatchlings were released into the sea. While these miniatures were scurrying toward the ocean we were able to stand guard and discourage the ghost crabs, sea birds and dogs that would feast on a naturally hatched nest. It was an insight into how precarious the sea turtle's existence really is, with egg and hatchling predators ranging from crabs and sea birds to jackals and pigs. Once in the ocean many others join the fray; the estimate that only one in a thousand hatchlings becomes a breeding adult is therefore credible. Thus in terms of actual preservation of the species we accomplished very little, contributing perhaps 20 or 30 breeders to the world population. But because of this work much interest was generated in sea turtles and the data collected on them was a first for Indian shores.

The hatching and release programme has been continued by the Central Marine Fisheries Research Institute at Covelong near the Crocodile Bank and another one begun by the Tamil Nadu branch of the World Wildlife Fund. Other than egg collection and release of hatchlings, significant protection can be given by simply erasing tracks and transplanting nests before the poachers get them. Most important would be protection of the nesting beaches by the wildlife authorities during the nesting season. In our area the fishermen, with their religious feelings for sea turtles, should be easy to enlist to the cause.

The ridleys, one of the five species of sea turtles which nest on Indian beaches, is the most widely distributed in the world and suffers heavy exploitation for its eggs and meat. Also, hundreds of breeding females drown in the gauntlet of shrimp trawlers that scrape the coastal waters clean. Special nets which allow turtles to escape have been devised by the United States Fish and Wildlife Service. In India large numbers are caught each year, often while obliviously mating just offshore. Recent photographs from Digha beach in West Bengal show a section of the shore covered with over 500 upturned ridleys awaiting transportation to markets in Calcutta. The front flippers are usually tied or wired together but a turtle on its back is a fairly safe captive. A few years ago before the enforcement of the Wildlife Act, I watched a number of ridleys, green and hawksbill turtles being butchered at Tuticorin market and the carnage is hard to describe. The turtle's lower shell or plastron was split and pried off its body and the meat hacked off while it struggled in desperation. Death comes late always and for endless minutes the eyes blink and the mouth opens and shuts in the gruesome mass of flesh.

Fresh turtle blood was being drunk as an elixir at one rupee a glass and old men and women gulp it down, blood at the corners of their mouths like so many draculas. One of the merchants boasted about his illegal trade which included the export of the highly prized hawksbill shell to Japan. Once the Forest Department jumped down, these activities went underground and now you might have to get your cup of blood at 4 in the morning on the beach instead of at the market. (Recently, the 'Sea Turtle Blood Drinkers Association' of Tuticorin, petitioned the government of Tamil Nadu to lift the ban on sea turtle capture and slaughter in the interests of its purported—but baseless-cure for asthma and other diseases!)

Aside from an obvious need to change slaughter techniques, it is imperative that we study turtle biology and population dynamics with a view to using the resource carefully. Sea turtles remain one of nature's mysteries. They migrate thousands of kilometres from feeding to nesting shores. How do they find their way? The University of Florida and other institutions have been tagging turtles for over two decades in an effort to learn about their natural history. In India even the surface of this subject has not been scratched. In fact it was only a few years ago that the ridley *arribada*—mass nesting—was reported at Gahirmatha beach in Orissa. During this two or three year cyclical nesting invasion by ridleys, over 300,000 females are said to come up on several offshore sandy islands in such densities that they sometimes dig up each others' eggs in an attempt to find a nesting place. These figures make people think the ridleys cannot after all be in much danger, producing several million eggs in Orissa alone on each *arribada*. But we must bear in mind that the carelessly exploited Atlantic ridley in Mexico dwindled from over 40,000 in the 50s to under 1,000 by 1980.

The best thing that happened to sea turtles in India was Satish Bhaskar. Satish has been studying sea turtles and surveying their nesting beaches for the past six years, initially for Madras Snake Park and now under sponsorship of the World Wildlife Fund. He has walked practically the entire coast of the country including the Great Nicobar and Minicoy and has been bitten by dogs, attacked by *goondas* and investigated by a young crocodile (which tried to enter his mosquito net) in his quest to map the status of these marine jumbos. He discovered nesting sites of the gigantic 2 metre long leatherback turtle in the Andaman islands. But there, as on the mainland, sustained and uncontrolled exploitation is taking a heavy toll. It seems now that wherever sea turtles nest their meat is widely sold including that of the hawksbill which is seasonally poisonous.

Will sea turtles become only legends over the next decade? As I write this we are told by the watchman that poachers passed our house in the early morning with over a thousand eggs; and news comes from Satish that a good portion of the Kerala coast is now inaccessible to turtles because of embankments built to contain erosion. In our protein starved country turtle eggs and meat are an important resource and you can't tell hungry man to pass up free food. However, it is not so much local consumption that is eroding our turtle resources but a commercial network that reaches gigantic proportions in the north. If sea turtles are to survive, the present free for all must be replaced by a wise management plan geared toward total protection at present. But unless the right people are convinced of the importance of these marine reptiles their future is uncertain.

Originally published in The India Magazine, *June 1982.*

SHEKHAR DATTATRI AND ROM WHITAKER

Cobra

The Indian cobra has a range that covers much of the sub-continent. It is feared and worshipped, persecuted and protected and often evokes strong passions in favour or against it. Dattatri is a young film-maker and a reptile buff with well-known wildlife documentaries like 'The Unknown Jungle—Nagarahole' to his credit. Rom Whitaker, India's reptile person par excellence is by any accounts, a most unusual man, an American by birth, an Indian by choice, one who is at home with the Irulas, the tribe that excels at snake-catching in southern India.

For the tenth time in two hours the small head cautiously poked out of the tiny slit in the parchment-like eggshell. Scarcely daring to breathe, we waited, our cameras ready and our patience stretched almost beyond endurance. Suddenly, an egg on the far side of the box moved, and a 30 cm. spectacled cobra (*Naja n. naja*) hatchling slid out giving us no time at all to focus a camera on it. Meanwhile, the hatchling on which we had trained our cameras—and our hopes—probed the air with its sensitive forked-tongue and, deciding that it wasn't time to emerge, retreated back into the security of its egg. When it did come out an hour later, we had put away our equipment in sheer exasperation. Our long experience with reptiles had taught us to take such frustration with resignation. Yet, the baby cobra's reluctance seemed entirely justifiable. For the first—and last—time in his life it was leaving the calm, protective atmosphere of the enveloping eggshell to begin life in a brightly illuminated and perilous world.

Unable to resist the temptation, I picked up one of the beady-eyed, frisky little snakes gently but cautiously. Indignant at being handled, the volatile little serpent spread its small, prefect hood in protest and let out a sharp hiss. The sudden display was so startling that I let go post-haste. This was the baby cobra's defence strategy against potential enemies and predators, and it worked admirably.

The month of April in South India is an unfavourable period for cobras. The weather is scorching, there is little water to be found and even food is difficult to procure. It is at this time, however, that the *nalla pambu* (Tamil: *nalla*—good; *pambu*—snake) sets about the business of procreation. The deposition of eggs during the hottest part of the year is actually a successful adaptation because environmental conditions at the time ensure the high and stable temperatures necessary to incubate the eggs. This is the one time of the year the normally solitary cobras come together. The love life of cobras, as indeed that of most snakes, is not very well-documented and despite the countless hours spent in the field we have had few glimpses into their secretive lives. By piecing together field data and observations on captive populations, however, a fairly accurate picture emerges.

Our astute snake-catching tribal friends, the Irulas, whom we frequently accompany on field trips, have often discovered several male cobras holed up with a single female in a termite mound or rat hole. This suggests that the pheromones from a receptive female possibly attract inquisitive males. Disputes among males over possession of a female are common as is borne out by scabs and battle-scars on the bodies of several males examined by us. Whether or not they envenomate each other during these brief fighting bouts is not clear, but in all probability this is so for we have never come across instances of cobras killing each other. Clearly, a social dominance is soon established among the knot of males, making a fight-unto-death unnecessary.

Mating in snakes is a slow and deliberate affair lasting anywhere between 30 minutes to six hours or more depending upon the species. This is usually preceded by a courtship ritual during which the male induces the female to lift her tail to effect copulation. The male has a spinose, striated, or otherwise configured hemipene of which only one is used at a time. The structure of the hemipene is usually species specific, an adaptation which prevents interbreeding among even closely related species. A female may mate more than once and with more than one male during her period of receptivity. Courtship among cobras is a fairly prolonged affair and may go on for a whole day. It is an interesting and complex ritual with both sexes exhibiting hooding, head-bobbing and tongue-flicking as part of their repertoire. Intrigued by the long (by ophidian standards) period of courtship, researchers who have conducted careful studies on the subject have come up with an interesting explanation. They found that female cobras could not be raped. Male cobras could effect entry only when the female *voluntarily* opened her anal orifice and lifted her tail in readiness.

A month to forty-five days after mating, the pregnant female cobra seeks the security of a well-protected rodent burrow, (probably making a meal of its rightful occupants in the process) to lay her 15–20 leathery, white eggs. Although this is the normal number, clutches of up to 30 eggs are not uncommon (clutch size in many reptiles is positively correlated to the size of the female; i.e. a large female produces more eggs than a small one). However, extraordinarily large clutches of over 40 eggs are invariably the result of more than one female nesting together. This happens, we suspect, when there is a shortage of optimal nesting sites and inadvertently confers an advantage in that two (or more) females are better able to guard a nest.

This brings us to a most interesting aspect of cobra life history— nest-guarding. Snakes are not noted for parental care and usually the mother's connection with her eggs terminates once they are laid. Cobras, however, are among the few snakes that not only stay with their eggs throughout the incubation period, but actively defend them. During the sixty days it takes for the eggs to hatch, the female (and occasionally the male) stays with them, lying coiled on top, seldom venturing out and rarely, if at all, seeking sustenance. The highly emaciated condition of numerous nest-guarding females we have observed seems to lend support to this conjecture. How vigorously a mother cobra will defend her eggs depends largely on her individual disposition. Our experience tells us that unless she is too emaciated by self-enforced starvation, a female with eggs will aggressively fight intruders. Shy and complacent, cobras normally bluff their way out of threatening situations. Not so nest-guarding females. From the time of oviposition onwards there is a marked change in the female's disposition, characterized by an unusually nervy and aggressive temperament and a tendency to bite at the slightest provocation, even when she is separated from her eggs.

When disturbed, the female rushes forward with open hood, threatening to strike at the intruder, hissing forcefully all the while. Should this strategy fail, she then turns her head the other way to exhibit the bold patterns on her hood. To ignore this explicit warning means grave trouble. Cobra venom can kill fast.

We incubated several hundred cobra eggs under near-natural conditions in the laboratory (mean temp. 31°C; humidity 85 per cent) and invariably, they hatched in exactly 60 days. 'Hatched' here refers to the appearance of the first egg-tooth slit on the egg. Actual emergence can take anywhere between a few hours to three days. This delayed emergence is adaptive as it gives the hatchlings time to acclimatize to changing environmental conditions. The 25–30 cm. hatchlings (their size is correlated to egg size) liberate themselves from their 4.5—5.0 cm. long cleidoic eggs through the slits made by the egg-tooth and disperse in all directions. After 3–5 days in hiding the baby cobras slough their skin for the first time—an act that will, throughout their lives, serve as a cue to search for food. Having assimilated the small quantity of yolk left in their bodies at the time of hatching, the little ones now seek solid food—mice, frogs, skinks and, with surprising frequency, other small snakes.

The inclusion of snakes in their diet is surprising, because adult cobras are not given to regular ophiophagy (ophio: snake/phagy: eating). Cannibalism, however, though prevalent among the hatchlings, is not common. The emergence of the hatchling trips a biological switch in the mother cobra's head with the result that she now loses all her maternal instincts and goes off in search of a well-earned meal.

Many non-poisonous snakes, taking advantage of their musculature, kill their prey by constriction. Some others are endowed with adaptations such as extra long maxillary teeth which enable them to grasp their prey firmly. Cobras come into the world even better equipped. Contained in the broad head is a highly efficient death-dealing apparatus—a pair of short fixed fangs in the anterior portion of the upper jaw. Characteristic of members of the family *Elapidae* the fangs are supplemented with two small sacs of virulent neuro-toxic venom which not only helps to paralyze and subsequently kill the prey animal, but speeds up the digestive process as well.

The hatching of the eggs in August and September coincides with the peak of the south-west monsoon in South India, a most favourable period for both the mother cobra and her offspring whose immediate requirements are food and cover, in that order. The luxuriant crops in the field (favourite cobra habitat) provide cover while the resident rodent population—which increases with the sudden abundance of food in the form of the cultivated crop—constitutes the chief source of food for cobras. The significance of this snake/rodent/, predator/prey relationship is phenomenal in a country like India where around 40 per cent of the total crop produced is devoured by the prolific rodents. The number of cobras found in a crop-field far exceed that of a forest patch of equal area for the simple reason that fields harbour an unnatural concentration of rodents!

To gain an insight into the feeding habits of cobras we examined a random sample of 34 scats (excreted by cobras caught near paddy fields around Madras). 80.6 per cent of the samples contained remnants (fur) of one or more of the five species of rodents found locally. In terms of sheer versatility snakes surpass all other biological rodent controllers. Being opportunistic feeders, their diet is, of course, more varied than this. Toads, frogs, birds, lizards and less frequently other snakes are readily eaten to satiate their hunger. While on a field trip some years ago we had an opportunity to watch a four-and-a-half-foot cobra swallow a common monitor lizard (*Varanus bengalensis*) slightly more than half its length. Judging by the contortions and twists of the snake's jaws, it was not an easy meal.

COBRA WORSHIP

The cobra—perhaps more than any other creature—epitomizes Hindu India. For centuries these magnificent snakes have been venerated and worshipped, often on par with such powerful deities as Shiva and Ganesha with whom they are usually portrayed. In Tamil Nadu and Kerala devout Hindus will consecrate a termite mound in which a cobra is known or rumoured to reside. Offerings of milk, fruit and flowers are made in front of the mound in obeisance to the 'holy' snake. The most dramatic form of snake worship however, takes place every August during the snake festival of *Nag Panchami* in the village of Battis Shirala in Maharashtra. On that sacred day every neighbouring farmer worth his salt turns up at the village centre with an earthen pot containing a freshly caught cobra from the surrounding fields. Soon it is released along with several others on a cart and scores of angry frightened cobras are paraded along the streets for the village populace to admire and worship. It is a scene to make even the most seasoned herpetologist shudder. Of course, each year the victim of a particularly severe bite may succumb, but the news is accepted by the others quite calmly and dismissed with a fatalistic shrug. Such is the spell cast by the snakes.

Unfortunately for the cobra, skin dealers have no scruples or religious sentiments. Although India gave up the lucrative snake skin export trade in 1976 and brought in strong legislation on paper to protect these highly beneficial pest controllers, the underground trade in reptile skins continues to flourish to this day. Raw cobra skins fetch a mere ten rupees a piece for the catcher engaged in the hazardous occupation. By the time they end up as shoes, hand-bags or belts in fashion-hungry Japan or Europe, their value has multiplied a hundredfold. Both the snakes and the catchers however, get a raw deal.

Back to our baby cobras. The clutch of eggs that were now hatching, had been collected for a television documentary on the natural history of the cobra. The chosen location lay on the outskirts of Madras—a vast, arid, shadeless plain with low impenetrable thorn shrubs known locally as *Kaara chedi*. The monotony of this scorching desert is broken only by a few stately palmyrahs and several concrete-hard termite mounds. This seemingly inhospitable terrain however, conceals an amazing wealth of animal life. Chockalingam, an Irula tribal and our long time friend and guide, with forty years of snake hunting behind him, was best qualified to lead the way. The discovery, after two hours of patient searching, of a freshly sloughed cobra skin signalled a systematic search of the area culminating in the finding of a rat-hole bearing tell-tale signs of snake movement. Chockalingam now began the painstaking and skillful job of opening up the winding burrow. This unceremonious intrusion soon had its desired effect, sending us scampering backwards. There was a faint hiss and a blur of brown as five feet of furious female cobra shot out, hood spread wide and eyes glaring menacingly. It was with considerable difficulty that the experienced Irula finally bagged the vehemently protesting snake. Its emaciated condition and unusually aggressive disposition gave us reason to hope for eggs. Further investigation of the burrow revealed 17 soft eggs half-buried in the fine cool mud of the nest cavity. Carefully, almost reverently, we collected the precious treasure and transferred it to a plastic container with an inch of sterile sand at the bottom. Back at the Madras Snake Park where we work, the eggs were measured and marked. All the while we had to take extreme care while handling the eggs as any agitation or displacement during incubation could be fatal to the developing embryos.

Opening the egg box for a routine inspection one morning we were delighted to find slits on most of the eggs. The first baby cobra came out into the world at 10.00 a.m. and the rest emerged in quick succession. After they had been filmed, admired and delightedly handled, we coaxed them into a cloth bag and were soon driving towards the now rain-soaked and verdant plain. An hour later, at the very spot we had collected the eggs, we bid farewell to the frisky young cobras. They wasted no time and were soon out of sight under the protective thorn shrubs. The paddy fields with their perennial supply of food were only a few 'crawls' away and there was a hint of more rain to come. The juvenile cobras had many hazards to face before they attained adulthood three to four years later, when they would themselves begin the cycle of reproduction. At the vulnerable juvenile stage mongooses, monitor lizards and birds of prey had to be evaded and, later in life, professional skin hunters. The outlook does not seem very bright but the cobra is a resilient reptile. As long as the monsoons prevail and the fields flourish, this shy and spectacular symbol of India will silently survive and, we earnestly hope, remain forever respected and revered by man.

Originally published in Sanctuary Asia, *3(4), October 1983.*

VALMIK THAPAR

The Tigress, Her Cubs and the Father

Valmik Thapar's book, Tigers, The Secret Life, *overturned one of the most widely held beliefs of former tiger-hunters and wildlife experts alike. Tigers, it emerged, did have a family life and were not the loners everyone imagined them to be. The male tigers did not pass their cubs as ships in the night. These discoveries were made by Thapar in the small but amazingly wildlife-rich reserve of Ranthambore in Rajasthan. Here, under protection and safe from snare and rifle, tigers dropped their nocturnal cloak and offered new insights into how they related to one another. A film maker and author, photographer and conservationist, Thapar has now written or co-authored five books that tell us about tiger country. But nowhere does the 47-year-old writer's account uncover as many secrets as in his telling of the tale of the tiger cubs—and their father.*

The valley of Semli is in the heart of the forest. It is rarely visited by tourists and remains relatively undisturbed. At one corner of the valley is an underground spring that creates a small stream and flows into a ravine, thick with grass, trees and water. Since this is a vital source of water, the area attracts chital and sambar deer, the occasional chinkara or Indian gazelle and troops of langur monkeys that feed on the many fruit trees in the vicinity. It is also a good area for sloth bears that are drawn to the fruit. Strangely enough it was in the valley of Semli that two of our most exciting encounters took place. The first was in 1979 when we spent most of a night with a leopard and her two cubs.

The leopard had killed a spotted deer or chital but before the family could eat, a hyena appeared and.fought off the leopard, annexing the carcass. The leopard tried to retrieve it, but after a fight was forced up a tree to watch the hyena below, gorging himself on the deer. Because of the inaccessibility of the thick forest, such encounters are rare and have seldom been recorded. On another occasion we witnessed our first kill when a tiger sprang out of the grass and fell upon an unsuspecting chital. These experiences live within us even today.

This area has steep sharp cliffs, and narrow gorges, creating belts of excellent leopard country. Natural caves abound and though leopard sightings in Ranthambhore are very rare, especially since the increase in tiger sightings, it is here that the leopards live.

The valley of Semli leads to the ravine of Bakaula on one side and on the other lie the undulating hills of Lakarda. Laxmi was the resident tigress of Lakarda and Semli and her home range stretched across ten square kilometres. The resident male of the area was the Bakaula male, his range encompassing 22 square kilometres. Several tigresses live within the range of one male tiger and besides Laxmi, the Bakaula female and another tigress had their smaller home ranges in this area. Tigers prefer to lead solitary lives and within the home range of a male tiger there is little interaction between the females. They stick meticulously to their areas. This is made possible most effectively through scent marking. A tiger raises its tail and shoots out a fluid which is a mixture of urine and a secretion from the anal glands. Another tiger reacts to the smell by hanging its tongue out and wrinkling up its nose. This gesture is referred to as 'flehmen'. The smell can last for a few days to a few weeks. It is an excellent indication to tigers of how recently another has passed by and whether the area is occupied or not. This therefore discourages interaction or, in the case of two dominant males, may encourage possible conflict. A tigress in oestrus will attract a male tiger by the scent which pinpoints her position: she will wander throughout her home range calling and marking with great frequency. Specific trees and bushes that demarcate a tiger's range are spray marked regularly. Even claw marks on the bark of a tree act as territorial signals. The tiger is normally a silent animal, but vocalizations are also a form of communication between males or between a male and a female, and are vital between a tigress and her cubs.

Many thoughts of tigers and their behaviour filled my mind as I roamed the Semli Valley, hoping to catch a glimpse of the cubs.

I was convinced that Laxmi must have mated with the resident Bakaula male. Fateh's record of Noon and Kublai mating is fascinating. In 88 minutes he watched the tigers copulate eight times. The insertion is only for fifteen to twenty seconds, the process noisy and aggressive. Violent aggression can end the sexual act. The tigress snarls viciously, twists around and slaps the male away from her. Earlier she will have encouraged him by provocative movements, nuzzling, rubbing flanks; the time between copulation is spent in much love play, licking and nuzzling. Tigresses that do not conceive can come into oestrus again thirty to ninety days later. The gestation period is from 95 to 115 days and the bulge of the tigress's belly is only clearly visible in the last few days of her pregnancy. At this point she disappears from sight, and from our previous experience, sometimes remains unseen with her brood for ten to twelve months.

Early one morning, I was driving through the Semli Valley, wondering if Laxmi would show herself again. Dawn is a special time, the play of light, wafting mist, the cool fragrant air, all clothing the forest with an unmatched perfection. Suddenly I noticed the forest track was covered with fresh pug-marks. I examined them. A large tigress with her tapering pad, followed by a mass of tiny pug marks, her brood, had walked ahead of us some minutes ago. They must be around. Could they be just ahead of me? It would be unusual for Laxmi to walk such young cubs down an open track. Usually this does not happen till the cubs are four to five months old. I inched the jeep forward, my eyes scanning both sides of the track for a glimpse of the family.

A few hundred metres ahead I stop the jeep. It is time to wait for sounds of alarm. In the distance two sambar hinds move gingerly away, tails half raised. A chital looks sharply towards the forest. It is motionless. My eyes are unable to pick out anything. The shrill alarm of a peacock breaks the silence. Another peacock picks up the call. After a few seconds the alarm call of the chital pierces my ears. Frenzied and frequent calling now surrounds me. Quietly I watch the forest. It seems as if the tigers are walking towards the vehicle track. Suddenly shades of tan and black emerge from the dull yellow of the forest. Laxmi appears with three tiny cubs. One of the cubs jumps across the road. It looks about two and a half to three months old. I can hardly believe my eyes. It is my first glimpse ever of cubs this size. Laxmi settles down on the track for a few minutes. Her cubs look at me furtively from the cover of a bush. She soon rises and paces leisurely into the forest, followed by three scampering cubs. They move towards a network of ravines and disappear from sight. For me it is a dream come true. I rush back to base, heart pounding with excitement. In near hysteria I tell Fateh what I have seen. We sit down to plan strategies for the following weeks.

Observing tigers involves tremendous patience and resources of sensitivity and concern in order not to disturb the animal unduly. These needs are heightened a hundred fold when observing a tigress with cubs. Firstly, the cubs are vulnerable when small and the tigress can be aggressive. One has therefore to keep a certain distance so as not to intrude into the tiger's privacy. This causes problems in photographing them. But in this unique situation photography was secondary. The difficulties had to be overcome slowly: our first strategy was to build a confidence between us and the tigers.

I wondered what the cubs must have experienced over the last two months. There are no records of any observation of cub birth in the wild. Most of the information comes from captivity. The tigress chooses a thick bush or cave, secure and inaccessible to intruders, to deliver her cubs. A litter can be born in an hour but can sometimes take as long as 24 hours. The process is exhausting for the tigress and she gets some nourishment from the placenta and embryonic sac which she eats.

A tigress can deliver up to seven cubs and the sex ratio is one to one at birth. Mortality is high and usually two to three cubs survive the first few days. Some cubs are born dead, others die soon after birth. They are born blind and completely helpless. The eyes open three to fourteen days later, but clear vision does not come for a few weeks. In the first days the tigress must assist her cubs to find her teats, to provide them with their vital nourishment. Odour must play a critical role in this link with the mother, especially before the eyes open. The cubs remain within the security of the den and the tigress is devoted to their needs and ready to defend them against any danger from predators or scavengers. Laxmi must have had to hunt to feed herself close to the den but the spot was chosen carefully and the presence of deer and antelope in the vicinity was assured because of the water hole.

These first days in the life of the cubs are nerve-racking for the tigress. She treats any intrusion into the area around her cubs with great suspicion. If she feels disturbed or insecure for some reason she is likely to change her den by carrying each cub, one at a time, in her mouth, holding them gently by the head with her canines and molars.

Sometimes a tigress can shift her den four or five times in the first month. She spends a lot of time keeping her cubs warm and licking them vigorously, to stimulate them to defecate or urinate and for better circulation. All this activity happens without the male who fathered the litter. She is alone in providing this care and protection. The male tiger leaves soon after mating and has always been believed to be a danger to the cubs, often killing them if he has the chance. The tigress is therefore forced to protect her cubs against the male tiger.

The cubs spend their first eight weeks in and around the den. Soon they become frisky, exploring the area of the den and playing with each other. They quickly establish a teat order and gradually, a hierarchy amongst themselves. The tigress instills a sense of order and discipline by the occasional snarl, cough or growl. After two months their regular diet of milk is supplemented by meat and the tigress carries and drags parts of what she has killed to the den.

The next morning I find Laxmi sitting in a grass patch ten to fifteen metres from the forest track. Her three cubs surround her. One nuzzles her face, another rests against her back, the third watches us curiously. Very tentatively it moves a little towards us before rushing back to the security of Laxmi. The cubs now turn their attention on each other, leaping into the air and knocking into each other. They then dash towards Laxmi. She licks one of them thoroughly, then lies on her side to suckle them. All three soon find the right teat and feed, stimulating the flow of milk with their tiny paws. For fifteen minutes I watch this remarkable spectacle. I have never seen such a display of love and warmth, such evidence of a strong bond between a tigress and her cubs.

In the next days we encountered the family regularly in Semli, getting closer and closer to them each time. Laxmi was unconcerned about our presence in the jeep. Fateh had joined me and our cameras clicked away. The cubs got bolder, and one of them, the most confident, even approached to within a metre of our jeep. A secret life that we had only speculated about was suddenly unfolding before our very eyes. It was at this point that we discovered the sexes of the cubs. Two females and one male.

One afternoon I found Laxmi just after she had killed a chital

stag. She dragged it quickly in leaps and bounds up the rise of a
hill and into thicker forest. Of the cubs there was ho sign. In ten
minutes she came out of the forest and walked a hundred metres
towards a network of ravines. I decided to follow, taking the jeep
off the track, cross-country. In minutes she had approached a small
ravine and began calling, a low 'aooo', several times, and disappeared behind a bend. I took the jeep up a hill to look down. It
was a gorge thirty metres long, ten metres wide, and surrounded
on two sides by a cliff and rock overhang some twenty metres high.
There were two caves in the cliff face and the three cubs came
rushing out of one of them. Dense cover carpeted the floor of the
gorge and a large pool of water reflected the light of the evening
sun. A perfect hideout. Amidst a lot of 'pooking' sounds and
nuzzling, the cubs followed Laxmi out of the ravine, miaouwing
plaintively, as if they knew they were being led to a feast. Laxmi
sat for a few minutes in a clearing to lick her cubs and soon they
all strode off to where the carcass had been left. I followed through
thick bush and rock, until I could go no further. Through my
binoculars I noticed that she had opened the rump of the spotted
deer and the cubs had already been at it. Visibility was very poor,
but it was clear that the cubs were used to meat even before the
age of three months. Adult tigers begin eating from the choicest
portion of the carcass, the rump, moving slowly towards the neck.
Some tigers remove the stomach and intestines before eating and
others don't. Cubs tend to attack whatever portion of the carcass
they get to first. This was a time when communication between
them increased through a series of low sounds, a cough, a moan,
a squeak. An incredible variety exists in the language of the tiger!

Over the next few weeks both Fateh and I spent many days with
the family in their delightful hideout, observing and documenting
facets of their lives, events we had never seen before. It was April
and the onset of summer. The cubs spent much of the time soaking
themselves in the cool water, waiting for Laxmi. A bit of playing,
some climbing and exploring, and a lot of sleeping was their daily
routine.

Laxmi would spend most of the day patiently searching for prey.
For many hour she would wait perfectly camouflaged near a water
hole in the hope of a quick spring on an unsuspecting deer. Several
times we saw her bring portions of her kill for the cubs to eat. For
the cubs this was a moment of joy: they bounded towards her,

greeting her with squeaky sounds, and much licking before devouring the carcass. The cubs were becoming more adventurous, exploring the small ravine which was their hide-out, nibbling at twigs and branches, chewing whatever came their way, prodding at stones and boulders, investigating any small movement, be it insect, bird or butterfly. New sounds like the sudden booming alarm call of the sambar which had previously frightened them would now be accepted. They would raise their heads at such alarms, and the raucous barking of a troop of langurs would keep them alert and motionless. Even the shrill call of the stork-billed kingfisher needed getting used to: it was a whole new world of sight and sound.

With the remnants of kills in their hideouts the cubs would watch circling king vultures and endless crows as they attempted to land, but the gorge was too narrow for their safety. The cubs would chase the crows off their kills. The occasional mongoose that slipped in would also retreat from the ravine. For the first time these young tigers were interacting with other life in the forest.

One day I found the jeep tracks covered with pugmarks, not only those of Laxmi and her cubs but also those of a large male. On closer examination I saw that it was the pug of the resident Bakaula male. The measurement of the diameter of the pad, and the fact that there was a twist to one of his toes, confirmed his identity. Pugmarks can be distinctive but when cubs of the same age walk on a track it is exceedingly difficult to distinguish them. Discerning details from pugmark is an art which requires instinct, experience and knowledge of the home range of a tiger.

I was worried and looked desperately for the family, but couldn't find them. What was the male tiger doing with them? Had he attacked them? My anxiety continued for two days till I found them all intact in their hide-out.

Some days later, on returning to base after several hours with Laxmi, I found a very excited Fateh who yelled, 'You won't believe it but I've found Nalghati with two cubs only a month older than Laxmi's.' I couldn't believe it. Another family! We could do a comparison of their lives.

Nalghati lived in the valley of Nalghati, a narrow stretch between two hill ranges that snaked across the edge of the fortress and carried on for some six kilometres. Nalghati valley is nearly fourteen kilometres from the valley of Semli. Here the deer and antelope are more dispersed. The area of Nalghati is the home range of the resident male Kublai. The Nalghati tigress focuses her activity in this valley and the adjoining area of the lakes is the home range of the tigress Noon. Kublai is the resident of both areas. I tried initially to divide my time between both families but it became too hectic, and in the end I left Fateh to concentrate on the Nalghati family while I remained with Laxmi.

The first time that I saw the Nalghati family was at the end of April. Mother and cubs were resting late in the evening near a water hole. The cubs were a little rounder than Laxmi's, about a month older. At six that evening the cubs got up and nuzzled their mother in an attempt to wake her. One of them moved to find a teat. The other watched us and moved to a tree, quickly clambering up a low overhanging branch on which he settled comfortably. Young tiger cubs enjoy climbing and playing on the branches of trees, though as they grow older and heavier they become unable to clamber up them. In the area of Semli several branches bear the signs of tiger activity, but this was the first time I had seen a cub up a tree.

The Nalghati tigress soon rose and moved to the tree on which her cub was resting. It was dusk. She lifted her tail to mark the tree and her cub patted her head with his paws. This was the male cub. The other was a female and less confident in our presence. The cub clambered down and they soon moved into thicker forest.

Fateh had examined the area of Nalghati carefully. It was, after all, the place where we had first had glimpses of Padmini and her family in 1977. The Nalghati tigress seemed to have used a large, thick green bush with a sort of cave-like entrance as her den. Nearby was a small pool of water and all around high grass. Quite secure but nothing like Laxmi's impregnable hideout.

At this time both families were quite mobile. Laxmi had started walking her cubs around three square kilometres of the Semli valley, and, watching them on these early walks, it was fascinating to see the cubs scampering about with abandon as if experiencing a totally new and free world. The Nalghati tigress was moving her cubs through a stretch of two and a half square kilometres. It started from one corner of the fortress and ran up to a deep gorge, most of the area being on either side of a vehicle track. As the cubs grew, so would the area with which they had to familiarize themselves.

One evening I found Fateh in an agitated state. He had encountered Kublai, the resident male of Nalghati, in the vicinity of the family hideout. We had both now seen signs of the presence of the resident male around the families' areas. What could this interaction be about? All past records of sportsman/naturalists and recent studies by zoologists indicated that the tigress reared her young by herself and that the male tiger was a threat to her offspring. There are in fact numerous records of male tigers killing and devouring cubs. I found only two sportsmen who differed in this view some hundred years ago; they went so far as to state that the male tiger is not addicted to infanticide and has in fact been observed in the company of cubs of all ages. Widely differing views without evidence, and no photographs of a male tiger with cubs in natural situations.

Fateh and I decided to concentrate our energies on this development. Could we discover more about the reason for the presence of the resident males around the families? What was the role they were playing? We had two months before the onslaught of the rains in early July. The Semli cubs were nearly four months old, the Nalghati cubs nearly five months. We had only two months left in which to record the glimpses of their early life. After the rains the cubs would be ten to eleven months old and much larger. We were not even sure whether they would all survive the monsoon.

As temperatures cross 40°C in April or May, water holes start drying up and the deer and antelope congregate in large numbers around the limited water spots, moving little in the day or night. The tiger does much the same. His mobility is reduced and dependent on the availability of water, not only for drinking but also for predation. It is a 'pinch period' as the coats of the animals get patchy and rugged. The forest and everything under its canopy seems to shrivel, sweat and melt with the onslaught of the heat. Once in a severe drought a small herd of chital, in search of water for their parched mouths, jumped into a well too deep for them, and died. Such are the pressures of the summer. The blistering heat of the next two months would take its toll on us and the cameras and film. Our objective, to increase periods of observation, would not be easy.

On 29th April Fateh found the Nalghati tigress and Kublai sitting some twenty metres from each other under the shade of the flame of the forest tree. It was the first time that they had been observed together, but of the cubs there was no sign. Their absence was a

trifle worrying. The male and female spent much of their time
sleeping with little evidence of conflict. Sleeping or resting is typical
tiger activity on a hot day. Energy is carefully conserved.

Fateh returned the next morning to find a pair of king vultures
perched high up on a tree and scores of white backed vultures at
different points nearby. A pair of Egyptian vultures circled low over
a dense grove of bushes and shrubs. Above one of these thick bushes
several crows flew about in a frenzy. These were all certain
indications of the presence of a carcass. Fateh decided to negotiate
the difficult terrain in his jeep and soon found Kublai resting under
the shade of a tree. Kublai is a medium sized male weighing some
200–225 kg. He is probably three metres in length from tip of the
nose to tip of the tail. Records of the length of tigers have been
known to exceed 3.5 metres and nearly 275 kg in weight. The tigress
is at least 30 cm shorter and 45 kgs lighter but these are estimates:
our tigers have not been measured or weighed!

After much scanning with binoculars, Fateh glimpsed the Nalghati
tigress deep inside a bush, guarding the carcass of a sambar hind.
It was difficult to see, but it looked as if she had eaten a small portion
of the rump. Again, there was no sign of the cubs. I joined Fateh
and we spent the day under the branches of a tree, watching what
turned out to be one of the most exciting encounters with tigers
we had ever seen.

Early in the afternoon, the tigress spent half an hour feeding on
the carcass. The heat was intense, nearly 45°C. A hundred metres
away there was a small water hole surrounded by large boulders. We
decided to position ourselves around it. The tigers had to come to
the water at some point.

At four in the afternoon Kublai lazily ambles towards the pool
and slides into the water, hind legs first, soaking himself completely,
leaving just his head visible. Tigers don't like water splashing in their
eyes and most of them enter water backwards.

About twenty minutes later Nalghati follows and they both laze
around in the water. Minutes later both my heart and Fateh's must
have missed a beat. The male cub walks quite nonchalantly towards
the pool, not a flicker of surprise or fear on his face, circles the two
adults and enters the water near where Kublai is stretched out. Soon,
following her brother, the female cub walks to the pool, entering
the water to sit on her mother's paw. Nalghati licks her face. Fateh
and I cannot believe our eyes—the tranquillity of the scene is

extraordinary. One big happy family: Nalghati, Kublai and two five-month-old cubs all in close proximity, soaking themselves in this rather small pool of water. They lap the water at regular intervals. In half an hour the male cub rises, quickly nuzzles Kublai and leaves the pool. The female cub follows him and they play, leaping at each other, slowly drifting towards a tree, clambering up the branches to play a game of hide and seek amidst the foliage. The two adult tigers watch. Soon Nalghati leaves the water and disappears into the forest. The cubs continue to play with each other under the protective eye of Kublai. At dusk, Kublai heaves himself out of the water and moves towards the cubs. The cubs rush up to him. He licks one of them.

When we leave, Kublai is sitting a metre or so from the two cubs. We have witnessed what must be one of the most closely kept secrets of a tiger's life. It is the first photographic record of a resident male associating with a tigress and her cubs in his range.

The next morning Fateh decided to go towards Semli, acting purely on instinct. I went to Nalghati but was unable to find the tigers. They must have been around since the crows and vultures were still perched on the trees. When tigers are away from their kill, vultures and crows leave their perches in the trees, dropping to the ground to consume the remnants. If they are near the carcass, tigers have been known to kill the vultures as they land, with a smack of their powerful paws. So the birds waited patiently on the trees. The dense forest cover hid the tigers. I returned to base early and Fateh rolled up an hour later, beaming. I knew immediately that something exciting had happened.

It is 1st May, 1986. Just at the edge of Semli, in the gorge of Bakaula, Fateh finds the Bakaula male and Laxmi. They are sitting on the vehicle track facing each other. On both sides of the track are thick groves of jamun, cool, lush and green. There are pools of water of various sizes nearby. Laxmi rises briefly the nuzzles the Bakaula male before moving a little way ahead to lie down on her side. A stork-billed kingfisher calls near the water. A pair of Boneli's eagles circle above a cliff.

This tranquil scene is disturbed by the distant sound of a rolling pebble. Both tigers become alert, Laxmi moves stealthily towards the sound. The Bakaula male sits up expectantly. A sambar deer shrieks in alarm. Laxmi has disturbed it. Tail raised vertically, the sambar carefully walks down an incline. Laxmi is too far away to attack. The sambar's path is taking it unknowingly towards the Bakaula male, who crouches, muscles tense. The sambar approaches the vehicle track. The male tiger takes off like a bullet. Six bounds and it leaps on to the back of the sambar, bringing it crashing down. Quickly it transfers its grip to the throat. At the same instant a group of noisy tourists arrive, stunned at seeing a male tiger choking a sambar to death bang in the middle of the vehicle track. But the male is disturbed and walks off behind a bush. The sambar is not quite dead. It twitches with small spasms of life. Laxmi arrives.

Comfortable in the presence of jeeps, she grips the throat of the sambar for a couple of minutes, ensures that there is no life left in the deer and starts the tedious process of dragging the 180 kg carcass away, a few metres at a time, into thick cover. The Bakaula male watches her carefully. The carcass is now some fifteen metres inside the jamun grove at the edge of a small clearing. The tiger moves towards it. So does Fateh. An amusing scene confronts him. The male tiger, with his forepaws on the sambar's rump, has a firm grip on one of the hind legs. Laxmi has a firm grip on the throat. The carcass is stretched between the two tigers. A mock tug of war ensues as each tries to pull the carcass a little towards them. Both tigers emit low-pitched growls, interspersed with herculean tugs at the carcass. Then, with a sudden burst of energy and strength, Laxmi yanks the carcass some four metres away with the Bakaula male astride its rump: a remarkable feat, as sambar and tiger together must weigh about 450 kg. But it exhausts her and she lets go of the throat. The male quickly pulls the carcass out of sight.

Laxmi strides off. Fateh follows. She enters a dry stream bed that leads to her den. She starts to call and is greeted by birdlike squeaks from her cubs. The complex and elaborate language of the tiger resonates through the atmosphere. In minutes Laxmi returns with the cubs running around her in circles. One of them runs between her legs and tries to leap over her back. The other two are frisky and jump up the trunks of trees before slowly moving to where the carcass lies. The cubs have already learnt the art of sniffing and they follow the drag marks of the carcass. They seem quite relaxed, as if this wasn't the first occasion that they were going to share a feast with the Bakaula male. The male cub suddenly sniffs the spray mark of a tiger on a bush and wrinkles up his nose in the gesture of flehmen. Soon they all disappear out of sight to where the Bakaula male and the carcass lie. Within the last two days we have twice seen a remarkable facet of the family life of tigers: the resident male in the role of father.

After a quick breakfast Fateh and I rushed back to spend the day at Bakaula. At two in the afternoon the Bakaula male emerged and soaked himself in a pool of water. An hour and a half later he moved off and Laxmi emerged with her cubs to cool off at the water's edge. All of them looked well fed, their bellies bulging. From our past encounters we knew that there was a strict regimen in the feeding process. Most of the time mother ensures that each cub eats separately on a carcass. This avoids the conflict that can arise over food. When one cub has had enough he normally moves off to socialize with his mother or to drink. Then the next cub comes to feed.

At four o'clock Laxmi moved away from the water to rest in a small clearing. He cubs did not give her a moment's respite, jumping on her to find her teats. They succeeded, but within minutes Laxmi shrugged them off, rose and settled down again. The cubs continued to pester her and Laxmi snarled and rose again. This sequence was repeated several times. The cubs were into their fifth month and suckling them was now an irritation: their sharp teeth bothered their mother. For two days Laxmi, the Bakaula male and the cubs remained around the jamun groves, cooling themselves in the water, the cubs playing around between feeds. They all slept a lot. The cubs delighted in jumping on Laxmi's tail and she flicked it around in anticipation as if she were performing a rope trick.

May and June are the months when the heat is most intense and many water holes dry up. Tigers remain close to water, moving from one water hole to another. So do all the deer and antelope. Till early June Kublai and the Bakaula male were found in frequent contact with the families in their range. Every few days their pugmarks were found together and there was evidence to suggest that both resident males were interacting with the families, particularly over food. The tigresses and cubs would join their respective resident males on a kill, or the male would invite himself to their kills. In between, the resident males would go off to patrol their ranges. There was no question, then, of the male tiger practising infanticide. We did not know what happened in the first two months of the cubs' life, but we now had evidence that in the course of the next few months the male took an active part in providing food for the cubs and their mother, and therefore had a vital role to play in raising the family. The tigress does most of the hunting, as she spends all her time with the cubs. The resident males patrol their home ranges, but when they are with the tigress and cubs, they can hunt or assist in a hunt. Of course they still need to eat themselves, but they are conscious of the demands of the cubs.

But this contradicts reports from all over India of male tigers killing and devouring their cubs. Why did this happen? Was Ranthambhore different in some way? We had posed ourselves a series of questions for which we would one day have to find some answers.

I was convinced that as far as both these families were concerned, the resident male had fathered the litter and we had seen him in the role of father to the family.

At the end of May I was back in Delhi for a few weeks when I got a cable from Fateh; it read, 'Come immediately. Noon has given birth to two cubs.' I was ecstatic. Noon was my favourite tigress and the resident of my favourite part of Ranthambhore, the lake area. This is a system of three lakes with the imposing fortress of Ranthambhore stretched around it. What had happened in the park? Three tigresses, all with cubs, when for years we had not even come close to a family! Noon's area immediately adjoined that of the Nalghati family and this meant it would be especially interesting in terms of territorial behaviour and overlaps. Kublai was also the resident male of the lake area. In Kublai's home range there were now two tigresses with cubs.

I returned to Ranthambhore on 5th June. Fateh met me at the station and explained what had happened. Three days earlier, after an uneventful morning drive, Fateh had been in the middle of breakfast when Badhyaya, the forest tracker, rushed up and said, 'Sir, there are some little cat like babies in a thick bush, five hundred metres away, the road workers have stumbled upon them.' Fateh jumped up, splashing coffee all over himself. In twenty years of tiger pursuit he had never seen newly born cubs. But they might be leopards. Camera in hand, he rushed off on foot with Badhyaya. He could not take the jeep into the bush. This put him in a dangerous situation. If you catch her unawares, a tigress with cubs will charge, especially human beings on foot. Jeeps at least they are used to. This was Noon's area and she could be quite aggressive. In five years of watching, we had never seen her with cubs, even though Fateh had recorded her mating twice.

Fateh's tension mounted as they walked into a dense ravine at the edge of the metal road that winds itself from Jogi Mahal to Sawai

Madhopur. The fortress of Ranthambhore loomed overhead. A group of road workers stood in a nervous cluster pointing downwards. Fateh asked them to leave the spot and go home. Fateh and Badhyaya entered the ravine, slowly, step by step. Fateh is not easily frightened by things around him, but he did confess to me that this was the most nerve-racking moment of his life, not knowing when a tigress or leopardess might come charging out at him. But, since the cubs had been seen by the road workers, Fateh assumed that the mother was away hunting.

Paradise flycatchers flew around this evergreen area. The ravine has a perpetual supply of water and connects through an old dam to Padam Talao, the first in the series of lakes. A small stream flows through a rocky bed. The setting is very picturesque.

A couple of golden orioles flitted around a mango tree. Fateh could hear his heart pounding. They had carefully advanced thirty metres towards a thick green bush surrounded by bamboo. Badhyaya pointed excitedly but it was dark around the bush and their eyes could only adjust gradually. The tigress was still not around, but she might return at any time. Creeping forward, Fateh peered into the bush. A slight movement caught his eye. A tiny, striped head peered out and snarled: a tiger cub, as confident and aggressive as his mother. Two black-and-tan striped balls were cuddled up together, about fifteen days old, their eyes just open. Fateh quickly took some pictures of the cubs through the foliage and bamboo. A record was essential. In the distance a peacock called in alarm. The tigress might return any time and Fateh and Badhyaya retreated. Fateh still had to confirm the tigress's identity. Reaching the metal road, he quickly issued instructions to close the area to human intruders, and took a vantage point above the ravine.

A few hours later he saw Noon moving in the ravine. The identity was confirmed. Though the ravine was a perfect den for the tiny cubs, it was too close to the metal road which is the main highway to town. To close it to traffic for more than a few hours was impossible. During the next two days an endless steam of pilgrims started winding their way to the Ganesha temple, on top of the fort, to be blessed by the Gods. Roaring viciously, Noon mock charged three times. Some of the pilgrims fled. A worrying situation. The location of the den was dangerous not only for the cubs but also for people passing by.

That night Fateh was fast asleep on his roof under the open sky. In the heat of the summer this is the only way to remain cool. At

4.45 in the morning the peace and still of the night was suddenly shattered by the alarm call of a sambar and the shrill barking of a troop of langur monkeys. Fateh, jolted from sleep, tumbled out of bed and looked down. A predator was on the move. The first rays of morning light crept across the horizon. On the vehicle track below Noon was striding along, carrying one of her tiny cubs in her mouth. Another first in Fateh's life, but alas there was no light for a photograph. Noon crossed some ruins and clambered up over an old wall, disappearing into one of the most inaccessible areas below the ramparts of the fort, a hundred metres from Fateh's room. She soon returned, crossed the track and fifteen minutes later came striding back with the second cub in her mouth. Fateh heaved a sigh of relief. The cubs were now in one of the safest places within Noon's range.

Now we had three tiger families to document: an enormous task. From then until early July, we saw Noon several times but we never glimpsed her cubs.

The Semli cubs were in their seventh month, the Nalghati cubs in their eighth. They had been weaned completely off their mothers' milk, and were growing rapidly on their continuous and regular diet of meat. Both mothers were forced to hunt every day or every other day, depending on the size of animal killed. An adult sambar can last for three or four days, a chital one or two days, a wild boar a few hours, and so on.

Laxmi with her brood of three was forever on the prowl. The cubs' appetites had grown and they attacked ferociously and devoured whatever was presented to them. Their interactions and play had become rougher as they charged each other, tumbling and twisting in an effort to slap one another. This would finally help them in learning to hunt and defend themselves. The Nalghati tigress's male cub was the dominant one and always ate first, while his submissive sister waited her turn. He was also the more confident in our presence. In Laxmi's litter the male was the dominant one, eating first at a kill, and the female was the most curious of the lot, as far as we were concerned, approaching to within a metre or so of the jeep without any sign of fear. All the cubs still enjoyed being suckled by their mother, though I was not sure how much nourishment that provided. It seemed to be more a method of reinforcing the close bonds within the family. Both resident males were still in the vicinity.

The cubs were now learning the art of hunting. Laxmi's cubs spent much of their time stalking peafowl in the area. Bunched low, they would inch their way towards these birds, before breaking into a charge. The peafowl fled but the cubs were learning. They even chased the small red spur fowl and sometimes stalked the grey partridge. I have seen them chasing mice, hare and even squirrels. The cubs were alert to what was going on around their den. The mouth of the den led on to an open ground where chital and sambar grazed. Cloaked by the cover of leaves they alertly watched the deer or a troop of monkeys jumping from branch to branch. From this den they could peer all around and spot the occasional chinkara on an incline; birds, lizards and frogs, insects, butterflies and a variety of smaller and larger mammals were all observed and investigated from the secure cover of their hideout.

At dusk on 5th July we left Kublai in the company of the Nalghati family. The next morning dark clouds loomed. The rains were coming. Soon the vehicle tracks would be obliterated and our work would have to stop. Moving off, we suddenly encountered Kublai and Noon sitting together a short distance from where her cubs must have been. Kublai had walked about six kilometres through the night and was now consorting with the second family in his range. Again I was convinced he had fathered this litter as well. He was moving from one family to another, patrolling his range. I spent some time theorizing about the male tiger, his role as father and why infanticide occurs, when it does.

My conclusion, which Fateh laughs at, as it is not based on evidence, is this. A resident male can father several litters in his range. He performs the role of father to all of them, sharing his food and sometimes feasting on theirs. A problem only arises when the resident male is usurped from his range by a new male in a territorial encounter. These encounters can be violent; tigers can limp off from them with serious injuries or are sometimes killed. When a resident male is usurped, a new tiger will be eager to mate and procreate quickly with the females in his area. This is when the cubs suffer. Similar observations have been made with troops of monkeys when male bands seize control of a troop and the new male kills the infants so as to get the harem back into oestrus. Sometimes this also occurs within lion prides. It must happen with tigers too. Of course we need many more hours of observation and concrete evidence to prove it.

Young males leave the mother when they are between twenty and 24 months old. They tend to move to the fringes of an area where they will hunt, eat and develop their size, strength and abilities. It takes a year, and sometimes two, of evasive, elusive behaviour before they mature to match the powers of the resident males.

In Ranthambhore young and sub-adult males exist within the home range of the resident male, in the park and on the fringes. Scent marks keep them away from any direct confrontation. If they happen to encounter each other, conflict is usually resolved. I have once seen an accidental encounter between two males late at night, one slightly larger than the other. They rushed at each other with the most blood chilling roars. Nose to nose they snarled ferociously, but in seconds the younger male dropped to the ground and rolled over on his back in a gesture of submission. The conflict was over and the resident male walked silently away. I think a serious problem only arises when two equally strong males compete with each other, in an assertion of a territorial right, and neither is ready to submit. In some of these encounters a tiger can be killed and even eaten by the victor. I have never found a male tiger killed by another male, but I know that a tigress once killed an adult male to protect her cubs. The male might have been an aggressive transient. His carcass had been opened and a chunk of his rump eaten. There have been several cases of adult male tigers killing and eating small male cubs in other parts of India.

It would all have to wait till the rains were over. Torrential downpours struck the park. It rained all day without stopping. We rushed into town before the roads got completely flooded. The monsoon had arrived. The parched earth would now fill with water. The regeneration of life would start. The large herds of deer would break up, and move in twos and fours to the upper plateaus in search of fresh grass. The tiger would follow, leaving valleys which would soon brim with water. The coats of the deer would change yet again.

We would have to wait three months to resume our work. I wondered what the fate of the three families would be. Fortunately, what we might miss in the lives of the Semli and Nalghati litters, we would be able to document with Noon's cubs. We would have the opportunity to record every month in the life of a cub as it moved towards adulthood.

Excerpted from Tigers, The Secret Life *(London: Elm Tree Books, 1989).*

S. THEODORE BASKARAN

Chennai's Patch of Green

*The Guindy park in Chennai is the last remnant of coastal forest
and scrub with a distinctive community of wild plant and animal
life. It holds one of the world's only wild herds of blackbuck in
an urban setting besides a variety of birds and reptiles. Theodore
Baskaran, a senior officer in the Post and Telegraph Department
has watched wildlife in Guindy for decades. Baskaran himself is
a truly Renaissance figure, being a regular columnist on the
natural history of India in general, south India in particular, and
having written two monographs on Tamil cinema. As he suggests,
Guindy is a very special place in a growing metropolis; it is no
coincidence that many wildlife biologists cut their teeth in this
little gem of a forest that still holds out against a sprawling city.*

'O let them be left, wildness and wet;
Long alive the weeds and the wilderness yet.'

G. M. HOPKINS

There is the beach, a river, an estuary, scrub jungles, lakes and
hills—all within city limits. Very few metropolitan cities in the
world are as blessed as Chennai in having such divergent geographi-
cal features.

But, the beach has been vandalized, the river defiled beyond
recognition, the hills being blasted for gravel to produce concrete
and the lakes reclaimed by a land-hungry population. However, a
remnant patch of original coastal scrub jungle has survived, and in
time given State protection.

The city's Guindy National Park gives us an idea of how the

landscape was centuries ago, when the area was blanketed in wilderness.

This area, once the private property of a certain Gilbert Ricketts, was bought by the Madras Government in 1917, along with his residence, the Guindy lodge. This was made the home of the Viceroy of the erstwhile Madras Presidency and after Independence, rechristened the Raj Bhavan. The Governor, A. K. John, suggested that the estate be preserved as a sanctuary and Jawaharlal Nehru supported it. It was then declared a deer park in 1959. However, over the decades, portions got allotted for various reasons and it shrank in size considerably. The threat of the park disappearing was real and at that time, there were not many in the city concerned about the impending loss.

In 1973, one afternoon, Indira Gandhi, who was in Chennai, paid an unscheduled visit to the Snake Park. A pioneer conservationist, Siddhardha C. Buch, interceded for the deer park while taking her around, and pointed out the threats. Convinced, Indira Gandhi asked him if he could have a plan sent to her office in three days time. It was sent, in the form of a long telegram. The area was soon declared a national park and further utilization stopped.

The park is now home to mammals like the Black buck, the Spotted deer (introduced), the jackal, the Black-napped hare, the Palm civet, the lesser civet cat and the mongoose. In all wildlife sanctuaries, primarily meant for mammals, glittering bird-life flourishes and often goes unnoticed. This is true of Guindy too.

Though the park is mainly for the chital and the Black buck, closer observation reveals a variety of birds. While the Adyar Estuary, not far away, attracts millions of waders during the migratory season, the Guindy Park is home to a variety of birds. Some species visit the park during the migratory season or stop there for a while en route.

Early morning is the best time to visit the park. The splendour unfolded on one visit. A shower the previous night made it ideal. The dawn chorus of grey partridges, a call that closely resembles the screeching noise made by the unoiled pulley of a *kavalai* used by farmers to irrigate fields, provides the background music.

If you stand still, you might watch the partridges materialize out of the brown earth of the mud track and scurry into the bushes. As the sun comes up, the sharp and loud call of the tailor bird, a ridiculously small bird for the volume of its call, punctures the morning silence. Soon the lora, a tiny bird of green and yellow, joins in with its very fluid whistle.

Bulbuls, including the white browed variety, are common here. To encounter one of those common dining parties on a morning after rain, one has to tramp around the shrubbery.

Flycatchers of many varieties will be there in the party. The green bee-eater has all the colours of the rainbow in its plumage. We saw a few young ones also. They apparently nest here.

The Magpie Robin soon announces its presence with a liquid whistle. The Indian Robin, a miniature replica of the former, hops around the bushes, silently.

Small minivets fly from tree-top to tree-top. Frugivorous birds gather in great numbers in the banyan and neem trees, when the fruits are ripe.

On the northern side of the park, there are a number of palmyra trees. On quite a few, only the stump is left. The top of the stumps is invariably occupied by nesting mynas. The birds are busy feeding the young ones in the morning. The holes in the trunks have been claimed by rose-ringed parakeets. They are a noisy lot and keep chattering incessantly.

A golden-backed woodpecker announces its arrival by a shrill, derisive laughter-like call, swings up and perches bolt upright on the trunk. After glancing sideways, it begins to deliver hard, speculative taps on the trunk to locate worms and grubs. The drama on the palmyra stump goes on, with endless variation.

Another resident that gains importance because of its rarity is the green-billed malkoha, a cuckoo that builds its own nest. The body is like the common *koel* but the white-tipped tail is longer. The beak is green and there is a bare patch of blue around the eyes. We do not know much about this bird and the park is a good place to observe and study it. One could see the other cuckoo, crow-pheasant also.

The most attractive visitor however, is the paradise-flycatcher. The body is like that of a bulbul's, with a black crest, but the male, silvery white in colour has a foot-long tail of two or three feathers. When it flies, the tail goes wavy adding to the unearthly beauty about this bird.

There are two lakes inside the park. The little grebe arrives by the end of August and the wagtails by September. While the other wagtails generally prefer to be near water, the forest wagtail frequents scrub jungle.

This bird swings its tail sideways in graceful sweeps, unlike the others of the group that shake their tails up and down. We saw only one forest wagtail, perched on a low branch and sweeping its tail compulsively, like a ballerina during a stage-wait.

Birds cannot be confined to a particular area. It is tougher to protect birds than animals. Many are given to migration. While roosting, they gather in great numbers at certain vulnerable spots. Even a catapult in the hands of the unscrupulous can mean the end of a bird as large as a rock-pigeon. The only way out is to make people conscious of the bird-life around them and involve them in the joys of watching it.

The park has a sizable cross-section of the birds of Tamil Nadu and it is certainly an ideal locale to get introduced to them. It has been a school for conservationists.

It was here that quite a few wildlife enthusiasts and conservationists honed their interest, began their life-long involvement with wildlife and now contribute to the cause of conservation in our country. Straightaway, I can think of R. Sukumar, the elephant expert, Shantharam, the ornithologist and Shekhar Dattatri, the wildlife filmmaker.

Originally published in The Hindu, *5 October, 1997.*

Abbreviations

BNHS	Bombay Natural History Society
DFO	Divisional Forest Officer
IBWL	Indian Board for Wildlife, formed in 1952, the key advisory body to the Indian federal government on wildlife-related matters
IUCN	International Union for the Conservation of Nature. Founded in 1948, collects scientific information on conservation.
WWF	World Wide Fund for Nature, originally known as the World Wildlife Fund, a major international fund-raising and lobbying conservation group.

Glossary

Amildar	Revenue official
arribada	Spanish term for arrival, refers to mass nesting of turtles on beaches, e.g. in Gahirmatha
arrack	Country liquor
baith	Literally, to sit
banya	Trader, moneylender, member of a mercantile caste
bandobast	Arrangements, refers here to organization of camping and beats to hunt or watch wildlife
Barasingh, Barasingha	Literally a stag with 12 tines; used for swamp deer of central and north India; also refers sometimes to the Kashmir stag
babool	Acacia
battue	A large shoot, a continental European term
bauleah	Pond or marsh
beat	Patch of forest beaten in a shoot; also, the actual beating in a shoot
ber, byr	*Zizyphus jujuba,* tree which grows in north and west India; the fruit is eaten by many animals
bhagar	Pond or marsh
bhang	Hashish
bheel	Pond or lake in eastern India; not to be confused with Bhils, a tribal people

Bhil or Bheel	A tribe in western and central India
Bij Parad	Annual ritual hunt of the Murias, a tribe in central India
budgerow	Boat-house in Bengal, used by hunters in the Ganges delta
bund	Dam, embankment
chana	Parched gram
charpoy	Bed, often made of rope and wooden frame
chars, churs, chaurs	Wet grassland
chela	Understudy; used for younger male in twosome of wild buffalo or elephant; also for a jackal that follows a tiger
chinkara, chikara	Indian gazelle
chita	Cheetah, or hunting leopard, now extinct in India
chital, cheetal, cheetul	Spotted deer, a species with a wide distribution in India
chota shikari	Junior hunter
chowkidar	Watchman, guard at a post (*chowki*)
chuprassy	Peon
cooly	Labourer
Coronda	Karonda, a fruit tree
dak	Post
darbar, durbar	Court; also used for a court official
Dawk Bungalow	Rest-house
degchi, degchie	Large utensil for cooking
deodar	Himalayan Cedar
dhoolie	A type of palanquin
Dollond	Eyeglasses
Doorgah Poojah	Annual festival of goddess Durga
filwan	The one who takes care of elephants, *née mahout*

gaddi	Seat of power; alternately, elephant pad
ghats, ghauts	River wharf or crossing; also for hills or range of mountains (e.g. Western Ghats)
Gonds	Tribe of central India
goondas	Musclemen, scoundrels
goral	A goat-antelope of the foothills of Himalayas
goru (guru)	Teacher, mentor
Gujars	Pastoralists of the Himalayan foothills
gur	Unrefined sugar, jaggery
hangul	Kashmir stag, sub-species of red deer found in the Valley
Harpat	Kashmiri name for Himalayan black bear
hankh, hanka, honk	Beat, hunt
hookah	Pipe traditionally used to smoke tobacco
howdah	Platform with seats for riding on elephant back
hulkaras	Beaters in a shoot
jemadar	Supervising officer
jheel, jhil	Small pond, or lake in north India
Kavalai	Tamil word for a device used to lift water for irrigation
kedah, keddah, khedda	Stockade; driving elephants into a stockade; traditional catching technique
khabar, khubr	Literally news, used to refer to information on presence of game
khanat	Medieval water system, often underground
khillut	Gift or reward from a superior or ruler
khud	Literally, a hole, a depression in the ground
kill	Remains of an animal killed by a wild carnivore

khansamah	Cook, house-keeper
koonki	Tame elephant trained for elephant-catching
Korkus	Tribe of central India
kota, kotah	Stone tower
kraal	Elephant training stockade in southern India
kukri	A curved knife
Kuruba, Karumba	Tribe in hill ranges of southern India
kutchery	Court
lathi	Staff or bambo stave
lebru	A small bullock cart
machan	Raised platform, usually on a tree to shoot or film from
madapolam	Fine white fabric or goods made from it, originally made at Madapollam in south India
mahout	Elephant trainer, often a hereditary post, highly skilled in the care and husbandry of elephants
mahseer	Freshwater fish much sought after by anglers
makhna, muckna	Male Asian elephant without tusks
maidan	Grassland, open patch or clearing
margs	paths, footpaths
mela shikar	Noosing of wild elephants from the backs of tame elephants, method mostly used in Assam
Mhowa	*Bassia latifolia;* its flowers and fruits are popular with wild animals and people alike
moonshee, munshi	Account-keeper
Mughs	Pirates off Bengal coast, often slave-raiders

mukkam	Place of encampment, especially for travellers
Murias	Tribe of Bastar, central India
musth	Psychological disturbance in male elephant, marked by discharge of fluid from temporal glands, time of sexually aggressive behaviour
nala, nullah	Dry stream-bed
natchni, nautchni	Dancing girl
ness	Settlement of buffalo-herding pastoral people in Gir Forest, Gujarat, usually fenced in with thorns
pagi, puggee	Tracker, from 'pag' or 'pug' meaning track or footprint
pan	betel leaf
phand	noose used to catch elephants in Assam
phandi	Professional elephant-nooser, mainly in north-east India
poojari	Priest
ragi-flour	Sorghum, millet
rukh	In Kashmir, the game reserve of the Dogra rulers; in central India, government-owned grasslands
ryots	peasants
sahiblog	White men, masters, white-collar officers
sakhni	Female elephant with tusks, rare in Asian elephants
Sal	*Shorea robusta*, major timber tree in north India
salaam	Salute
sambhar, sambar, sambur	Largest Indian deer
Santhal	Tribe in eastern India
serow	Himalayan goat antelope
shaitan	Devil

shamiana	Canvas or cloth tent
shikar	Hunt; used for a particular expedition ('out on shikar'); also for ritual or ceremonial hunts ('the Viceroy's shikar'); or for catching ('elephant shikar')
shikari, shikkaree, shikarie	Hunter; professional village-based hunters; in Gir Forest, Gujarat, for game-watchers who no longer kill animals
shola	Thickly wooded valley in south Indian hills, patch of evergreen tropical forest
sola topee	Hat worn by the British to protect from strong sunlight
soondry	*Heritiera minor*, a tree which grows in the Ganges–Brahmaputra delta
sowari	Horse rider
syce	Groom
swaraj	Self-rule
tamasha	Literally, fun; a kind of theatrical display
tat	Short for *tattoo*, an Indian native pony
Tehsildar	Local official, in-charge of a *tehsil*
Terai, Tarai	Moist flat lands south of the Himalayan foothills, wet savannah in north India
thakur	A term of respect, Lord, master, especially applied to Rajput nobles
Todas	A mainly pastoral tribe in the Nilgiris
Toria, toras	Rocky outcrops on central Indian plains
tote	Home, cottage
urna	Wild
Yuvraj	Crown prince
Zamindar	Rent-receiver in eastern India or a large land-owner, extending control over a *zamindari*

Bibliography

Ali, Sálim, *The Fall of a Sparrow*, Delhi: Oxford University Press, 1985.

Anderson, K., *Nine Man-Eaters and One Rogue*, London: Allen & Unwin, 1955.

———— *Man-Eaters and Jungle Killers*, London: Allen & Unwin, 1957.

———— *The Black Panther of Sivanipalli and Other Adventures of the Indian Jungles*, London: Allen & Unwin, 1959.

Baldwin, J. H., *Large and Small Game of Bengal and the North West Provinces of India*, London: Henry S. King, 1876.

Baskaran, S. Theodore, 'Chennai's Patch of Green', *The Hindu*, 5 October, 1997.

The Dance of the Saras: Essays of a Wandering Naturalist, Delhi: Oxford University Press, 1999.

Best, J. W., *Forest Life in India*, London: John Murray, 1935.

Braddon, E., *Thirty Years of Shikar*, London: William Blackwood, 1895.

Champion, F. W., *With a Camera in Tigerland*, London: Chatto and Windus, 1927.

———— *The Jungle in Sunlight and Shadow*, London: Chatto and Windus, 1934.

Corbett, Jim, *Man-Eaters of Kumaon*, London: Oxford University Press, 1944.

———— *The Man-Eating Leopard of Rudraprayag*, London: Oxford University Press, 1947.

———— *The Temple Tiger and More Man-Eaters of Kumaon*, London: Oxford University Press, 1954.

Dattatri, S. and R. Whitaker, 'Cobra', *Sanctuary Asia*, October 1983.

Daver, S. R., 'A Novel Method of Destroying Man-Eaters and Cattle-Lifters Without Firearms', *Journal of the Bombay Natural History Society*, vol. 49, 1951, pp 54–66.

Davidar, E. R. C., *Cheetal Walk, Living in the Wilderness*, Delhi: Oxford University Press, 1997.

Dharmakumarsinh, R. S., *Birds of Saurashtra, India*, published by the author, Bombay, 1951.

———— 'Following the Lion's Trail: The Lion-trackers of Mytiala', *The India Magazine*, March 1986, pp 166–72.

———— 'Gulam Hussain Baazdaar, The Falconer', *The India Magazine*, June 1983, pp 40–9.

————— *Reminiscences of Indian Wildlife*, Delhi: Oxford University Press, 1998.

Divyabhanusinh, *The End of a Trail, The Cheetah in India*, Delhi: Banyan Books, 1995, reprinted at Delhi: Oxford University Press, 1999.

Dunbar Brander, A. A., *Wild Animals in Central India*, London: Edward Arnold, 1923, 1931.

Fletcher, F. W. F., *Sport in the Nilgiris and in Wynad*, London: MacMillan, 1911.

Forsyth, James, T*he Highlands of Central India, Notes on Their Forests, and Wild Tribes, Natural History and Sports*, London: Chapman and Hall, 1879.

Fry, C. B., *Life Worth Living, Some Phases of an Englishman*, London: The Pavillion Library, 1939, 1986.

Gee, E. P., *The Wildlife of India*, London: Collins, 1964.

Hamilton, Douglas, *Records of Sport in Southern India*, London: R. H. Porter, London, 1892.

Hardinge, Lord, *On Hill and Plain*, London: John Murray, 1933.

Johnsingh, A. J. T., 'Dhole: Dog of the Indian Jungle', *Sanctuary Asia*, 1984.

Johnsingh, A. J. T., and G. S. Rawat, 'On Jim Corbett's Trail', *Blackbuck, Journal of the Madras Naturalists Society*, vol. 10, no. 2, 1994.

Khacher, Lavkumar, 'A Fine Effort—The Lions of Gir', WWF—Indian Quarterly, 2nd Quarter, 1979.

Kirkpatrick, K. M., 'Aboriginal Methods Employed in Killing and Capturing Game', *Journal of the Bombay Natural History Society*, vol. 52, 1954, pp. 285–90.

Krishnan, M., *Jungle and Backyard*, Delhi: National Book Trust, 1961.

————— *Nights and Days, My Book of India's Wildlife*, Delhi: Vikas, 1985.

————— 'Fights to the Death', *The Statesman*, 11 December 1983.

————— 'Our Wildlife: A Great Legacy Dissipated', *Illustrated Weekly of India*, 24 August 1980.

————— 'Did-he-do-it?', *The Statesman*, 11 July 1983.

Manfredi, P., ed., *In Danger*, Delhi: Ranthambore Foundation, 1997.

Mervin Smith, A., *Sport and Adventure in the Indian Jungle*, London: Hurst and Blackett, 1904.

Mundy, G. C., *Pen and Pencil Sketches in India, Journal, A Tour in India*, London: John Murray, 1858.

Noronha, R. P., *Animal and Other Animals*, Delhi: Sanchar, 1992.

Pollock, F. T., and W. S. Thom, *Wild Sports of Burma and Assam*, London: Hurst and Blackett, 1900.

Rice, William, *Tiger Shooting in India; Being an Account of Experiences of Hunting Expeditions on Foot in Rajpootana, During the Hot Seasons from 1850 to 1854*, London: Smith, Elder and Company, 1854.

Roussellet, Louis, *India and its Native Princes. Travels in Central India and the Presidencies of Bombay and Bengal*, London, 1882.

Sanderson, G. P., *Thirteen Years Among the Wild Beasts of India: Their Haunts and Habits from Personal Observations; With an Account of the Modes of Capturing and Taming Elephants*, London: W. H. Allen & Company, 1878.

Simson, F. B., *Letters on Sport in Eastern Bengal*, London: R. H. Porter, 1886.

Singh, Arjan, *The Legend of the Man-Eater*, Delhi: Ravi Dayal, 1993.

Singh, Kesri, *Hints on Tiger-Shooting (Tigers by Tiger)*, Mumbai: Jaico, 1969.

Sukumar, Raman, *Elephant Days and Nights, Ten Years with the Indian Elephant*, Delhi: Oxford University Press, 1994.

Suydam Cutting, *The Fire Ox and Other Years*, London: Collins, 1947.

Thapar, Valmik, *Tigers, The Secret Life*, London: Elm Tree Books, 1989. Reprinted as *The Secret Life Of Tigers*, Delhi: Oxford University Press, 1998.

————— *Land of the Tiger*, London: BBC Books, 1998.

Thompson, Edward, *Letter from India*, London: Faber and Faber, 1943.

Ward, G. C. and Diane Raines Ward, *Tiger Wallahs*, New York: Harper Collins, 1993, reprinted as *Tiger-wallahs: Saving the Greatest of the Great Cats*, Delhi: Oxford University Press, 2000.

Whitaker, Zai, 'The Riddled Ridley', *The India Magazine*, June 1982.

Wilson, Guy Fleetwood, *Letters to Nobody, 1908–13*, London: John Murray, 1923.

Copyright Statement